Economic Analysis in Historical Perspective

Internationally written and refereed, *Butterworths Advanced Economics Texts* seek to inform students and professional economists by providing clarity and rigour in economic analysis.

General Editor

Bruce Herrick
Department of Economics,
Washington and Lee University, USA

Consulting Editors

John Enos
Magdalen College,
University of Oxford, UK

Michael Roemer
Harvard Institute for International Development,
Harvard University, USA

Gerald Helleiner
Department of Political Economy,
University of Toronto, Canada

Pan Yotopoulos
Food Research Institute,
Stanford University, USA

Published titles

Cases in Economic Development by Michael Roemer and Joseph J. Stern
Comparative Economic Development by David K. Whynes

**THE UNIVERSITY
OF BIRMINGHAM**

INFORMATION SERVICES

THE US must be returned promptly if
OTHER another borrower
DATE BELOW

Butterworths Advanced Economics Texts

Economic Analysis in Historical Perspective

Edited by
J. Creedy
Professor of Economics, Durham University

D.P. O'Brien
Professor of Economics, Durham University

Butterworths

London Boston Durban Singapore Sydney Toronto Wellington

First published 1984

© Butterworths & Co. (Publishers) Ltd 1984

British Library Cataloguing in Publication Data

Economic analysis in historical perspective.—
   (Butterworths advanced economics texts)
   1. Economics—History
   I. Creedy, J.   II. O'Brien, D.P.
   330'.09   HB75

   ISBN 0–408–11430–4

Library of Congress Cataloging in Publication Data
Main entry under title:

Economic analysis in historical perspective.

   (Butterworths advanced economics texts)
   Bibliography: p.
   Includes index.
   1. Economics—History.   I. Creedy, John, 1949–
II. O'Brien, D. P. (Denis Patrick), 1939–
III. Series.
HB75.E3   1984   330'.09   83-20906
ISBN 0–408–11430–4

Typeset by Scribe Design Ltd, Gillingham, Kent
Printed and bound in England by The Camelot Press Ltd, Southampton

Acknowledgements

We should like to thank Julie Bushby and Kathryn Cowton, who shared the considerable amount of typing and retyping required during the preparation of this book. We are also grateful to those colleagues who read earlier drafts of some of the chapters.

J. Creedy
D. P. O'Brien

Contributors

J. Creedy is Professor of Economics at Durham University. His main research interests are concerned with public policy, labour economics and the history of economic thought. He is the author of *State Pensions in Britain* (1982), editor of *The Economics of Unemployment in Britain* (1981), and co-editor (with B. Thomas) of *The Economics of Labour* (1982), and author (with others) of *Economics: An Integrated Approach* (1984).

D. P. O'Brien is Professor of Economics at Durham University. His research interests include the history of economic thought and competition policy. His publications include (with D. Swann) *Information Agreements, Competition and Efficiency* (1968), *J.R. McCulloch: A Study in Classical Economics* (1970), *The Correspondence of Lord Overstone* (1971), (with D. Swann *et al.*) *Competition in British Industry* (1974), (with D. Swann *et al.*) *Case Studies: Competition in British Industry* (1974), *J.R. McCulloch: Treatise on Taxation* (1975), *The Classical Economists* (1975), (with W.S. Howe, D.M. Wright and R.J. O'Brien) *Competition Policy Profitability and Growth* (1979), (co-editor with J.R. Presley) *Pioneers of Modern Economics in Britain* (1981) and (with A.C. Darnell) *Authorship Puzzles in the History of Economics* (1982).

R. F. Ekelund is Professor of Economics at Auburn University. His research interests include the history of economic analysis, welfare economics and the economics of regulation. He is co-author (with R.F. Hébert) of *A History of Economic Thought and Method* (1975), and co-editor (with E.G. Furubotn and W.P. Gramm) of *The Evolution of Modern Demand Theory* (1972).

R. F. Hébert is Professor of Economics at Auburn University. His main research interests are in the history of economic thought. He is co-author (with R.F. Ekelund) of *A History of Economic Theory and*

Method (1975) and (with A.N. Link) of *The Entrepreneur: Mainstream Views and Radical Critiques* (1982).

A. S. Skinner is Professor of Political Economy at Glasgow University. His research interests include eighteenth-century political economy and the theory of the firm. He is the author of *A System of Social Science: Papers Relating to Adam Smith* (1979), editor of *Sir James Steuart's Principles of Political Economy* (1966), and co-editor (with R.H. Campbell and W.B. Todd) of *The Wealth of Nations* (1976).

M. C. MacLennan is Senior Lecturer in Political Economy at Glasgow University. His research interests include industrial and regional policies in the European Community. He is co-author (with G. Denton and M. Forsyth) of *Economic Planning and Policies in Britain, France and Germany*, and (with K.J. Allen) of *Regional Problems and Policies in Italy and France*.

A. C. Darnell is Lecturer in Economics at Durham University. His research interests include econometrics and the history of economic thought. He is co-author (with D.P. O'Brien) of *Authorship Puzzles in the History of Economics* (1982).

J. S. Chipman is Professor of Economics at the University of Minnesota. His research interests include international economics, welfare economics, demand theory and the history of economic thought. His publications include *The Theory of Intersectoral Money Flows and Income Formation* (1951), and he is co-editor (with L. Hurwicz, M.K. Richter and H.F. Sonnenschein) of *Preferences, Utility and Demand* (1971) and (with C.P. Kindleberger) of *Flexible Exchange Rates and the Balance of Payments* (1980).

Contents

List of Figures

Chapter One

Introduction

J. Creedy and D.P. O'Brien

The purpose of this book is to place a number of major subject areas of economic analysis in historical perspective. Conventional work on the history of economic analysis is arranged around particular authors, schools of thought or so-called revolutions in economic thinking. In modern journal articles or monographs it is seldom possible for authors to place the discussion in historical perspective; indeed, it is not always possible to place work in the context of contemporary literature. However, each chapter in this book attempts the much more difficult task of tracing the evolution of the main current ideas about a specified subject, and considers the ways in which important questions were raised in the past and the factors which influenced methods of analysis and the nature of assumptions used.

The best-known general books in the history of economic analysis, such as those by Schumpeter (1954) and Hutchison (1953), or the rather different text by Blaug (1964), have concentrated on the twin subjects of value and distribution. The following chapters therefore deal with areas which have not received such detailed treatments. These areas are, in order of appearance, Monetary Economics, Welfare Economics, Public Finance, Oligopoly and the Theory of the Firm, Economic Statistics and the Balance of Payments.

Economics has in recent years been undergoing something of a 'crisis of confidence', and in this kind of atmosphere it is not surprising that there is greater interest in the work and results of earlier generations. But the study of the evolution of ideas does not only provide an 'antidote to despondency', it often indicates just how painfully slow the progress in economic understanding has been. The need to study earlier work and preoccupations has been stated quite bluntly by Schumpeter (1954):

Modern problems, methods, and results cannot be fully understood without some knowledge of how economists have come to reason as they do (p.6).

It is useful to add to this important point the argument that this kind of work can often provide a stimulus to further research in fruitful directions. As Schumpeter again persuasively argued,

> A man's mind must be indeed sluggish if, standing back from the work of his time and beholding the wide mountain ranges of past thought, he does not experience a widening of his own horizon (p. 5).

In any attempt to place current ideas in historical perspective it is also worth while keeping in mind the point clearly made by Black (1976) in discussing changing attitudes, during 200 years, towards the work of Adam Smith. He suggested that

> just as the size and shape of objects appears to change in visual perspective as the position of the observer changes, so in historical perspective the significance of an event or an idea changes as it is seen from different points of time (p. 42).

The authors of each of the following chapters have had to deal not only with this problem of changing perspectives but with the severe constraints imposed by the economics of book publishing. Each author has been faced with enormous problems of selection and emphasis, and it is almost certain that a different set of authors would choose different formulae for arranging and selecting material. While an attempt has been made to use a consistent style of presentation, the editors have not attempted to impose their own preferences or judgements on the individual contributors.

Furthermore, the book does not examine general issues such as the question of whether economics has developed according to its own 'internal logic', or the debate between 'relativists' and 'absolutists', or wider methodological questions. These issues are perhaps best examined by a single author, or by joint authors working very closely, but it is hoped that this book may nevertheless provide some useful materials for such studies. It will, however, have succeeded if it manages to 'widen the horizons' of the reader, and to stimulate the study of earlier valuable literature.

References

BLACK, R.D.C. (1976). Smith's Contribution in Historical Perspective. In *The Market and the State* (ed. by T. Wilson and A.S. Skinner), pp. 42–63. Oxford, The Clarendon Press

BLAUG, M. (1964). *Economic Theory in Retrospect*. London, Heinemann Educational Books

HUTCHISON, T.W. (1953). *A Review of Economic Doctrines 1870–1929*. Oxford, Oxford University Press.

SCHUMPETER, J.A. (1954). *History of Economic Analysis*, London, George Allen and Unwin

Chapter Two

Monetary Economics

D.P. O'Brien

2.1 Introduction

In this chapter an attempt is made to place the body of modern monetary discussion, with which students are familiar, in historical perspective. The problems of attempting an exercise of this sort are particularly acute in the field of monetary writing, where there is an enormous and prolix literature covering several centuries of effort. Indeed, it is probably true that monetary theory was the first branch of economics to reach sophisticated levels of analysis and that its analytical concepts have the longest history. Considerable compression has thus been necessary; and in the process a number of writers who are important in post-1945 monetary theory have perforce been neglected, both because their contribution can be embodied in the summary of the modern position which is given in each section of this chapter and because particular contributions which may be important in relation to the literature produced within a short span of time tend to seem rather less important when viewed against the historical perspective of the long evolution of monetary theory.

The very nature of money has been an issue throughout much of the development of monetary theory, and this is considered first. Next comes the discussion of theories of the demand for money, distinguishing between those approaches which emphasize velocity and those which emphasize the demand for balances. In considering approaches to the supply of money it is easy to find both independent supply and demand-determined supply in the literature over a long period, and this leads to different approaches to monetary control both in the great nineteenth-century debates and in the twentieth-century literature. Some of the differences over monetary control relate to different approaches to the rate of interest, and section 2.5 discusses the history of interest theory. However, the major source of division concerning monetary control is, inevitably, the transmission mechanisms, and these are discussed in section 2.6.

The overall picture which emerges is of a monetary theory which steadily *evolved* rather than being subject to *revolutions*. The changes of direction which monetary theory has taken have been changes of focus, of ranking of the objectives of monetary policy, rather than of analysis and concepts, both of which have developed to their present state over very long periods.

2.2 The concept of money

2.2.1 MONEY DEFINITIONS AND THEIR RATIONALE

Money is typically defined by specifying functions which have to be performed. First, and most importantly, there is the medium of exchange function. Then there are the roles of money as a store of value, unit of account and standard for deferred payments. These qualities are seen as reducing transactions costs and as transmitting and summarizing information.

To fulfil these functions, whatever is used as money must have a number of characteristics. Those typically emphasized as necessary are general (even universal) acceptability, homogeneity, divisibility and portability. But there is by no means universal agreement on the categories of assets which possess these qualities to a satisfactory degree; and such disagreement has existed throughout the history of monetary theory. Nowadays the narrowest definition of money is of currency plus sight deposits in commercial banks. To these, some of the most influential modern monetary writers, especially Friedman (1969), add time deposits in commercial banks.

The question of whether interest-bearing deposits are money has given rise to some considerable controversy in modern times. Pesek and Saving (1967) take the view that demand deposits, held for the flow of amenities they yield, are money, while time deposits, held solely for interest, are not[1].

On the other hand, a number of writers have followed the important and influential work of Gurley and Shaw (1960) in emphasizing the importance of deposits in Non-Bank Financial Intermediaries. In Britain, the Radcliffe Report (1959) went so far as to substitute for the quantity of money the broad (and undefined) concept of general liquidity. Although the Radcliffe Report is often regarded as 'Keynesian' it is in fact more extreme than Keynes himself on a number of issues, including the very idea that the concept of money is irrelevant. In fact, the quantity of money is not really defined in the Report; para. 388 refers to 'notes plus bank deposits', but the latter are unspecified, and it would seem from the rather cavalier reference to 'some notion of the "supply of money"' that the concept was considered obsolete[2]. Monetary policy, it was felt, should aim at liquidity rather than the supply of money.

It is perhaps the vagueness of these views, and of the associated policy recommendations (which are difficult to disentangle), which make it clear to the reader that there is something more than semantics involved here. Nevertheless the view that concern over the definition of money is misplaced is, and always has been, easy to find in the literature (for example, Friedman, 1969). However, as will become clear in considering the historical background, the matter is not so simple. There is in particular a desire to distinguish those assets of which it is true that an excess supply affects all prices and not just the assets' own prices (Yeager, 1968; Morgan, 1969). This provides a clue to what is surely the overriding issue, and the one to which niceties of welfare economics[3] come second, the question of monetary control[4].

But the welfare aspects of the money definition also have a long history. Thus the welfare advantages arising from the replacement of non-interest-bearing commodity money by non-interest-bearing credit money as enumerated by Johnson (1969, p. 34)—basically the resource use freed by the replacement of commodity money—are also spelt out by Adam Smith (1776, pp. 310–314).

However, the historic discussions frequently started by emphasizing the *functions* of money and the necessary characteristics if something was to be able to perform those functions. Thus Smith's discussion, which stressed the role of money in supporting division of labour and specialization through providing a means of conducting transactions without barter, emphasized divisibility and durability as necessary qualities, enabling money to act as a standard of value, medium of exchange and store of value (1776, pp. 26–33) following the tradition extending back to Pufendorf. In the nineteenth century a similar discussion may be found in J.S. Mill (1848, pp. 483–488). George Warde Norman, an important member of the Currency School, said that money was a sign of value, standard of value, measure of value, in universal demand and formed the medium of exchange[5]

The qualities required of money to fulfil this role were those possessed by gold; divisibility, durability, universality of demand and constancy.

This approach was carried forward by the successors of the classical economists. Thus Wicksell (1906, trans. 1935, pp. 6–24) referred to money as a measure and store of value and medium of exchange, while Marshall (1923, pp. 12–20) defined the functions of money as acting as a medium of exchange, store of value and standard for deferred payments.

The functional approach was carried over by Keynes, who referred to the functions of discharging debt and acting as a unit of account, and by Mises, who stressed the importance of money as a medium of exchange supporting division of labour while following Menger in adding to this the role of money in facilitating credit transactions and acting as a store of value[6].

There has, just as in the modern literature, always been a tendency to dismiss the question of the definition of money as semantic[7]. But underlying the apparent insignificance of the dispute has been the deep-seated issue of monetary control. This explains why the definition of money was most frequently disputed during the era of the monetary control debate in the 1840s and 1850s. This is why it was necessary to identify the functions of money and the means of payment which had the required qualities to perform these functions. In so doing it became possible to identify the strategic area of control.

2.2.2 MONEY AND CREDIT

The control rationale comes out particularly clearly in Norman's work. Overstone, too, insisted that deposits must be distinguished from currency because a decrease of deposits would not correct an adverse exchange rate. They did not deny that the behaviour of deposits could affect monetary stability but they held that deposits were ultimately merely a means of economizing on real money. It was the latter that it was important to control directly[8].

On the other hand, the leading figure in the Banking School, Thomas Tooke (1838–1857, V, pp. 505–506) argued that bank notes should not be distinguished from other forms of paper credit and that there was no invariable connection between notes and the credit superstructure. James Pennington (1829), who, although he belonged to neither Currency nor Banking camp, had certain sympathies with Tooke's position, argued that there were limits to monetary control because deposits were money and they could be multiplied without a change in the currency base. Thus the question of control, underlying the definition of money, brings us to the vexed question of bank deposits. It may surprise the modern reader to learn that in the eighteenth and nineteenth centuries most writers excluded bank deposits from the category of money. Thus Cantillon (1755, pp. 143, 301–305) saw bank deposits (and even bank notes) not as money but as factors affecting velocity of circulation[9] (Holtrop, 1929, p. 507). The Currency School resisted strongly the suggestion that deposits were money[10]. Later, Marshall excluded cheques from the money supply because of limited acceptability, and Wicksell distinguished between metallic money and deposits[11].

A particular argument used against the inclusion of bank deposits in the money supply was that they lacked the power to close finally a transaction. But this 'final closing' argument was rejected by J.S. Mill, who argued that even Bank of England notes ultimately depended upon the solvency of the Bank; the argument, if pushed to its logical conclusion, limited money to metal. Tooke rejected the argument as fiction; notes were only used for a small balance after clearing[12].

This opposition to the 'final closing' argument was not, however, because the Banking School wished to 'monetize' bank deposits. Rather, writers like Tooke and Fullarton held that bank notes and deposits were both forms of credit—thus following Henry Thornton (1802). They held that gold and silver and inconvertible legal tender notes were the only true money, but that this was irrelevant since credit instruments exercised monetary effects which were not controlled through control of proper money. Tooke rejected the argument of Norman that notes could be distinguished from deposits on the grounds that if notes were withdrawn their place would have to be supplied by coin; this was true, in Tooke's view, only of small-denomination notes. In attempting to make convertible notes into a special category the Currency School were, he argued, confusing legal tender *inconvertible* notes, on the Continental pattern, with convertible notes. Only the former were money[13].

The Currency School accorded a unique place to convertible notes because they believed that, as bank reserves, these notes controlled an inverted credit pyramid. Such an idea was rejected by those who refused to distinguish between notes and other forms of credit, especially Fullarton and J.S. Mill. These writers stress the independent importance of bank credit. It was perhaps natural that writers like Mill, Fullarton and Tooke, who regarded bank notes as a form of credit, should stress the effects of other forms of credit[14].

This attitude carried over to Marshall (1926, p. 140), who, despite including notes in his definition of money, followed Mill in insisting on the importance of credit as exercising a purchasing power similar to that of money. The line of thought continues through to the Radcliffe Report; and Cramp (1960, p. 595) has pointed to a close parallel between the Radcliffe concept of liquidity and Mill's concept of purchasing power.

This is not surprising, since the Banking School extended their concept of credit widely to include bills of exchange. Following the calculations of William Leatham (1840), Tooke (1844) stressed the importance of bills of exchange in performing the functions of money. The emphasis on the importance of bills of exchange derives from Thornton (1802, p. 81), in whose work the Banking School's roots arguably lie; but Thornton had seen bills of exchange not as money but as part of a superstructure of paper credit resting on a monetary base. The Banking School were unconvinced that the credit rested on such a base and was thus limited by it. The Currency School, on the other hand, believed that 'economizing expedients' like bills of exchange could not, except in the very short run, affect the price level independently of the supply of currency; Norman, in particular, emphasized that they were imperfectly acceptable (because some knowledge of the drawer and acceptor was required) and that the credit generated in this way would have to be made good in currency.

2.2.3 DEPOSITS AS MONEY

As already indicated, the Currency School had a narrow definition of money, excluding deposits, and denied any independent influence to deposits, while the Banking School had an even narrower definition of money, like the Radcliffe Report, but regarded money as not unique in its effect on demand. There is, however, a third strand in the nineteenth-century writings in which deposits were included *as part of the money supply*. The leading writer here is undoubtedly James Pennington, who, although he ultimately became a supporter of the Currency School had, for a long time, some sympathy with positions adopted by Tooke. In a letter of 1829 to Tooke he argued that bank deposits and *country* bank notes were identical, and that the money of the metropolis was largely in the form of bank deposits. Writing to Tooke again in 1838 Pennington again equated money with deposits and treated a reduction in bankers' deposits at the Bank of England as equivalent to a reduction of notes. Longfield, too, seems to have taken the view that the only real distinction between currency and deposits was in their velocity of circulation[15].

It was ultimately this view which, not without difficulties, triumphed in the twentieth century. Thus Pigou (1917, pp. 39–41) defined money as legal tender money plus bank deposits subject to cheque; and he was followed, with some hesitation, by Keynes. Although Keynes (1923, p. 141) considered bank credit the main determinant of the price level, he was for long reluctant to call bank deposits money. In his *Treatise* (1930) he distinguished bank deposits as 'bank money' from money proper, citing Knapp's theory of statist money. Bank deposits were 'not money proper but an acknowledgement of debt' (Vol. I, p. 8). But having thus limited money Keynes was forced to decide that what he called 'current money' was predominantly bank deposits, including, be it noted, unused overdraft facilities (Vol. I, pp. 27–29, 37). All this, however, related to deposits subject to cheque; time deposits were 'scarcely money' (Vol. I, p. 38) and they did not constitute a constant proportion of total deposits, so that it was seriously misleading to treat bank deposits as identical with cash.

Keynes's treatment seems to have been influenced by Hawtrey and by Mises (1912), whose work, originally appearing in German, distinguished between commodity money, fiat money and credit money (trans. 1934, p. 61) as Keynes was later to do (1930, Vol. I, p. 6).

2.3 The demand for money

In the modern monetary literature it is now customary to distinguish between a 'classical' model and a 'Keynesian' model. The former is characterized by a stable velocity function, with demand for balances dependent upon transactions, the length of payment periods and expenditure patterns. The latter model is characterized by emphasis upon the transactions, precautionary and speculative motives for holding money, leading to a portfolio approach and to a fusion of the motives for holding money into a multiplicative form associated with Baumol's (1952) square-root rule, later developed by Brunner and Meltzer (1967)[16].

The most influential modern treatment of the demand for money undoubtedly springs from the work of Friedman (1969), who has advanced the quantity theory of money as a theory of the demand for money. Friedman's use of wealth as an argument in the demand for money function has been seen by some commentators as the most important development, although the only genuinely novel element is the significance attached to the ratio of non-human to human wealth. Perhaps the most critical elements in this approach are the idea that the elasticity of the money demand function with respect to the price level is unity, and that the function itself is stable.

The latter hypothesis has been tested through extensive econometric work, employing models fitted with various lags to allow for adjustment of money holdings to target levels. Such studies have been linked with opposition to the view, associated with Keynes, that the interest elasticity of demand for money is extremely high, and the related view, found noticeably in the Radcliffe Report, that there is no upper limit to velocity of circulation.

It is thus helpful, if seeking to understand the way in which analysis of the demand for money has developed, to examine the rise of the concept of velocity of circulation before moving on to analyse the nature of money demand; and it will emerge that this approach has been adopted by a number of major writers.

2.3.1 VELOCITY OF CIRCULATION

The concept of velocity dates from at least as early as the seventeenth century and, at that date, the two approaches—velocity and demand for money—seem to have differed only in the degree of emphasis attached to one or other way of looking at the problem. The seventeenth-century emphasis was upon business balances—a significant point, as will become clear. There are important seventeenth-century discussions of velocity by Petty and Locke, the latter emphasizing the cash balance aspect of velocity, while in the early eighteenth century we find velocity treated by Potter and Cantillon[17]. In the nineteenth-century literature it is mentioned at an early stage by Ricardo, followed by James Mill[18]; but the most detailed early nineteenth-century treatment is by Henry Thornton (1802, pp. 96–97), who analysed factors affecting the demand for money as the determinant of velocity. Others who discussed velocity included J.S. Mill and Attwood, the latter distinguishing between income and transactions velocity of circulation[19].

Velocity is discussed by Marshall and by Wicksell[20], both of whom, excluding bank deposits and bills of exchange from the money supply, treated them as means of increasing velocity, which they believed to show a secular upward drift through the development of credit and communications. Indeed Wicksell pointed out that the gains from economizing on cash balances acted as an incentive to devise means for doing so.

The author whose emphasis on velocity is most well known is undoubtedly Irving Fisher. Fisher made statistical studies of velocity, which he said was determined by individual habits of thrift and payment, by systems of transactions (including the degree of synchronization of payments and receipts) and by general causes such as population density and transport rapidity. The important point which Fisher wished to emphasize was that velocity was dependent on 'technical conditions' and was not functionally related to the money supply, though it might move in a pro-cyclical way[21].

Keynes, although he attacked the velocity concept, used it extensively[22]. The most extreme dismissal of the concept is to be found in the Radcliffe Report, which seems to have envisaged a *short-run* response to monetary tightness, involving raising of velocity through learning by financial institutions, a view which Artis has traced to earlier work by Minsky. Even so, it is hard to understand why velocity should not approach some limit asymptotically[23].

With the possible exception of Fisher, it is doubtful, however, whether any of the writers whose discussions of velocity have been mentioned regarded velocity as some exogenous constant. They were all clear that velocity could change; what distinguishes the various approaches is the degree to which they thought velocity stable in the *short run*, for even in the case of Fisher it is clear that he envisaged the possibility of secular changes. However, in order to understand the degree of short-run instability anticipated it is necessary to look at the analysis of the demand for balances.

2.3.2 THE DEMAND FOR BALANCES

The analysis of the demand for balances starts with emphasis by Petty upon transactions demand, leading, at an early stage in the work of Adam Smith, to a distinction between the personal and the business motives for holding balances[24]. However, the precautionary motive for holding balances also makes an early appearance; it was Thornton who laid considerable emphasis upon this and, in turn, influenced Marshall. Thornton's analysis is particularly striking, because he has the demand for balances varying with the state of business confidence, and as responsive both to the rate of interest and to what has become known in the modern literature as 'brokerage', that is, the cost of realizing assets to obtain balances. But perhaps the most striking thing is that all this clearly implies that velocity is *not* fixed in the short run[25].

These ideas continued to appear throughout nineteenth-century treatments of the demand for money. Thus in Senior's *Lectures on the Value of Money* there is a clear discussion of the cash balance demand as a function of income per head and the degree of progress beyond barter[26]. Both Joplin and Tooke separate the personal and business motives for holding money; and this was continued by Bagehot and Giffen[27]. The idea of precautionary balances which were affected, in the short run, by the degree of confidence in business activity is found in a number of writers, including J.S. Mill and Tooke[28].

The marginal revolution gave these insights a particular twist by emphasizing the marginal utility of holding cash balances, and the balancing of this marginal utility against the marginal disutility of the interest foregone. Walras abandoned a Fisher-type equation approach in favour of a cash balance one, consistently with his emphasis upon the fundamental role of marginal utility[29]. Wicksell emphasized the transactions and precautionary motives, distinguishing between personal and business holdings, with the latter being related to turnover and, long before Baumol, derived a square-root rule, although from rather different reasoning[30].

But Marshall was, of the marginalist writers, perhaps the most influential of all in relation to the analysis of the demand for money. Deriving his cash balance approach explicitly from such predecessors as Petty, Locke and Cantillon, and his concept of velocity from the Bullion Report, with its emphasis on demand for balances varying with the state of confidence, Marshall argued that the demand for such balances depended primarily upon income and wealth. There was also a precautionary motive for holding balances, and since this precautionary motive included sums held to avoid missing investment opportunities, it extended to a speculative motive as well. Marshall naturally adopted the view that the marginal utility of cash balances was equated with the marginal cost of holding balances, particularly interest foregone; but taking his discussion as a whole the factors which received most emphasis were, first, the role of income and wealth in determining the demand for balances; second, the *long-run* changes in the demand for balances deriving from economic growth and the development of economic institutions; and third, *short-run* changes in the demand for balances caused by variations in confidence and in the price level[31].

Marshall's monetary work was followed by that of other English economists. Pigou provided a detailed formal approach to the demand for balances, emphasizing the marginalist maximization principles and expressing the idea in the now-familiar form of the 'Cambridge equation', while Lavington emphasized the transactions and pre-cautionary motives for balances and the marginal utility approach to their size[32].

Perhaps the most important and original of Marshall's English successors was Hawtrey. He naturally presented the transactions and precautionary motives for holding balances but also, by retaining the older tradition of a clear distinction between personal and business saving, continued to attach importance to the investment motive for holding balances. It is interesting to note that he applied this motive to personal saving. Thus Hawtrey presented the demand for money, as early as 1919, in terms of transactions, precautionary and invest-ment motives, on the lines which Marshall had sketched out but in considerably more detail. For Hawtrey's analysis of what he called the 'unspent margin' provides the bridge between the cash balance approach and the later development of the consumption function. The size of the 'unspent margin' was a function of income and of wealth for individuals, with wealth defined as *expected* wealth governed '(in the main)' by ruling prices. The business 'unspent margin' was deter-mined, as with Wicksell, by turnover[33].

It is from this background that Keynes's analysis of the demand for money developed. Keynes used an algebraic form similar to that earlier put forward by Pigou while basing the analysis upon the utility optimization approach and stressing that demand for balances was not necessarily stable. In fact, the feature which perhaps most distinguished his *Tract* is the extent to which he seemed anxious to emphasize the instability of the demand for money[34].

In his *Treatise* he disowned the equation of the *Tract* but continued to use what was basically a very similar approach, with marginal utility determination of the demand for balances and considerable emphasis upon the instability of the demand for money because of unstable business demand. Indeed, the distinguishing feature of the *Treatise*, the most interesting of Keynes's works from a monetary point of view, is its emphasis upon the predominant role of business deposits, and the various motives—production, speculation, finan-cial—for holding these. This, of course, was not entirely new; nor were the other elements of the analysis, including the discussion of the transactions and precautionary motives which gave rise to income deposits and of the speculative motive which gave rise to savings deposits[35]. The distinguishing feature of the book is really the emphasis upon short-run instability[36].

The presentation in his *General Theory* of the now-familiar transac-tions, precautionary and speculative motives was then not particular-ly novel[37], at least if these elements are taken in isolation. The same is true of the idea of shifts in 'liquidity preference' because of changing expectations[38].

The same inheritance was shared by D.H. Robertson. Robertson also proceeded from a marginal utility approach to the demand for balances and presented the transactions and precautionary motives, but he was less concerned to stress problems associated with instability and more interested in the effects of monetary expansion in producing forced saving, or, as he liked to call it, 'Automatic Lacking'[39].

2.3.3 ELASTICITY OF DEMAND FOR BALANCES

The idea that the elasticity of demand for balances with respect to changes in the price level was likely to be less than one (and might even be negative under certain circumstances) dates back to the early years of the nineteenth century, following the episode of the *Assignats* in the French Revolution. The elasticity of demand for balances with respect to the price level was a matter of concern to Say, Thornton, Senior and J.S. Mill[40]. There were two threads here. First, there might be the desire to part with a depreciating medium (loss-avoidance); second, there was a desire to exchange money for commodities in order to benefit from a rise in the price of the latter (profit-seeking). The same view is found later on in the work of Goschen and of Marshall. The effect of interest on the demand for balances was discussed by Fullarton and Giffen as well as by Jevons[41].

It is interesting that the responsiveness of the demand for balances to changes in the price level and the rate of interest was a matter of common concern before the formal promulgation of the elasticity concept in Marshall's work. However, from Marshall onwards there occurs both the formal invocation of the elasticity concept and an increasing tendency, stemming in particular from Pigou, to treat the elasticity of demand for balances as equal to one. However, in the case of Pigou it appears, from his reaction to criticism by Cannan, that although he considered the demand curve for balances to have an elasticity equal to one, he envisaged that demand curve as *shifting* in response to inflationary expectations[42]. Keynes, with the experience of the post-World War I inflations in Germany, Austria and Russia before him, was able to elaborate upon this. He agreed with Cannan (and Lehfeldt) that the elasticity of demand for balances was not equal to one, and argued that inflationary experience showed that inflation initially increased the demand for balances as people expected the price level to fall back, but that as soon as they learnt of their mistake they would economize on balances[43].

Thus it is apparent that the idea that the demand curve for balances was a rectangular hyperbola in form, which was put forward by a number of writers after 1890, was only advanced on the basis that other things were equal; and care was taken to emphasize that other things were unlikely to be equal, either in the short term—because of inflationary expectations—or in the long term—because of changing habits and forms of payment[44]. A nice example is provided by Wicksell (1906, in 1935, p. 142) who, having advanced the concept of a rectangular hyperbola, then shortly afterwards (p. 145) emphasizes the role of velocity changes.

2.4 The supply of money

In the modern literature on the supply of money there are two approaches which differ in the weight which they attach to limitations on the power of banks to create credit imposed by the need for reserves and to the distribution of the available stock of wealth between assets of varying liquidity, one of which is money, the quantity of which is then determined by asset preferences and relative prices[45]. The differences of emphasis lead to a position in which one group of writers can be regarded as treating the money supply as determined by supply factors whereas the other group can be regarded as treating the money supply as demand-determined.

A famous modern version of the bank deposit multiplier, which is the predominant approach amongst the first group of writers, is that of Friedman and Schwartz (1963). The direct nature of their multiplier is modified through drains of money abroad and into non-bank financial intermediaries. Its critics claim that both the reserve ratio (r) and public holdings of cash (c) vary; instability in these will, of course, cause the multiplier to vary. This does not, however, pose insuperable problems if the factors causing r and c to vary can be identified; and flexible multipliers have been developed which take account of variations in r in response to the risk-adjusted rate of return and in c in response to income, the price level and the interest on balances. The end-result has been to identify long-run stable multipliers but to suggest that the deposit multiplier is unstable in the short run.

The high-powered money base upon which the multiplier operates must be exogenous to the banking system; critics of the multiplier approach have emphasized that it may become endogenous, especially if the authorities are willing to trade freely between cash and Treasury Bills in order to stabilize the short-term rate of interest (Dennis, 1981).

The alternative approach to deposit multipliers may be referred to by the term 'portfolio theory'. It is associated in particular with the work of Tobin (1956, 1958, 1963, 1965) and also with the growing importance attached to deposits in non-bank financial intermediaries, following the work of Gurley and Shaw (1960) and of Clayton (1962). The portfolio approach, which has its roots in General Equilibrium theory, concentrates on two particular criticisms of the multiplier approach; first, that the multiplier approach treats cash and other assets as in two distinct compartments, instead of looking at the allocation of the assets of a bank as in a continuum-balancing risk against return; second, that multipliers conceal the economic decisions which underlie them (Goodhart, 1975, pp. 111–112).

The basic argument is that the money supply is endogenous: and the volumes of both deposits and of high-powered money are dependent upon portfolio decisions taken by the general public, the financial sector and the governmental sector.

Much of this criticism seems rather strained. While there may be good reasons for arguing that the money supply is demand-determined, the multiplier itself implies a simple portfolio approach with only two assets, cash and bonds, with the latter always preferred up to a prudential limit because of positive yield. However, an important, and associated, thread in this school of argument is that concentration upon bank deposits is misplaced. Banks, it is argued, are not different from other financial intermediaries except in the initial re-deposit ratio (see, for example, Tobin, 1963, p. 410). The roots of both these approaches go back a very long way indeed.

2.4.1 SUPPLY-DETERMINATION

It had been understood since the eighteenth century, by such writers as John Law, Bishop Berkeley and the American statesman Alexander Hamilton, that bank deposits were a multiple of cash held by the banks; and the inference had been correctly drawn that the banks must create deposits[46]. But the mechanics do not seem to have been clearly understood. In the 1820s the mechanism of deposit creation through lending and re-deposit was explained by James Pennington in a memorandum to Huskisson (Sayers, 1963). Pennington also allowed Tooke to publish two letters in which he explained the operation of the deposit multiplier, although denying that he had in mind a direct mechanical relationship (Pennington, 1829, 1837). Pennington was followed by Torrens (who, with his usual acuteness, seized the essential point very quickly and expounded it in his *Letter to Lord Melbourne* of 1837) and by Joplin (1844).

Such an idea was naturally of considerable value to the Currency School, who wished to emphasize monetary control through control of the high-powered money base in the form of convertible Bank notes. They were not prepared to insist upon the idea of a direct and mechanical multiplier; such an idea would have been contrary to their insistence upon variations in the demand for money with phases of the cycle. But they did view the upper superstructure of credit as resting upon the high-powered money base: and the most important part of this superstructure was bank deposits. It was thus that the Currency School, especially Overstone, long opposed the introduction of a

'Relaxing Power' into the Act of 1844; this, which would allow the issue of Bank of England notes beyond the strict limits of that Act, would involve loss of control of the high-powered money base and thus make the money supply demand-determined[47].

Thus the idea of multiple deposit creation on a reserve-asset base, and the associated idea of monetary control through that reserve-asset base, were well established in the nineteenth century; and Giffen's treatment of the role of bank reserves led Marshall to apply the standard mathematical technique to obtain the expression for a sum of a series which he then expounded, in apparent ignorance of the work of Pennington, Torrens and Joplin, before the Gold and Silver Commission in 1887[48]. Fisher in his *Purchasing Power* of 1911 expounded the deposit multiplier and made explicit allowance also for the cash holdings of individuals[49].

However, the concept of the deposit multiplier is widely associated with the names of Macleod, Phillips and Crick[50]. In fact, Macleod does not (like Joplin) explain the re-deposit and multiplier aspects. He simply assumes that extra deposits will be created. Chester Phillips, in a book published in 1921, explained the mechanics using the summation of a series and providing the (elementary) algebraic basis. He distinguished, as elementary textbooks now do, between reserve loss if a single bank tries to expand its loan and expansion by the banking system as a whole. Joplin had, however, dealt with the case of multiple banks, although leaving the question of reserve loss a little cloudy.

Phillips' analysis was extended by Lawrence (1928a,b). Although finding fault with some of the former's assumptions concerning the stability and uniformity of the process, he extended the idea to the point (1928b, p. 368) of arguing that banks could make multiple loans on the basis of borrowing from the central bank, thus making control through Bank Rate ineffective—in that penalty borrowing rates could be more than recouped through multiple loans—if all the banks expanded together.

Despite the attention which the work of Phillips and the others has received, it is doubtful whether it added very much to the body of theory already in existence concerning bank lending, although the work of Phillips and Lawrence is remarkable for its use of empirical material. The main line of the argument continued in England after Marshall and became a ruling orthodoxy.

Thus Hawtrey, in his *Currency and Credit* of 1919, viewed the banking system as working with fixed reserve ratios and with control of the level of lending through the high-powered money base. He conceded that reserve ratio control might be placed in difficulties because of lags in the system leading to unforeseen pressure on bank reserves; but the basic model which he had in mind was clearly that of multiple loans on a reserve-asset base[51].

All this is particularly important, because Keynes followed Hawtrey closely on matters of banking practice[52]. As early as 1911 Keynes
had been critical of Fisher, arguing that both the bank cash reserve
and the public cash holdings were not fixed (Keynes, 1911, p. 395).
But in his *Treatise* Keynes (1930) advanced a straightforward deposit
multiplier model (Vol. I, pp. 25, 26, 47). Indeed, it is interesting that
Keynes was unable satisfactorily to meet the argument of Lawrence
noted above concerning the inability of the central bank to control
lending; after a rather unconvincing attempt to suggest that reserve
losses by one bank alone would prevent multiple-deposit creation on
the basis of loans, even at a penal rate, from the central bank, Keynes
was forced to dismiss the Lawrence argument as 'purely academic'
(Vol. II, p. 223). This was hardly convincing; and modern writers
who stress the ability of banks to manufacture their own reserves
would be much more sympathetic to Lawrence.

A similar endorsement of the deposit multiplier is to be found in the
work of Hayek and of D.H. Robertson, although the latter cites
Phillips and Crick. It is interesting, however, that Lavington seems
less convinced of such a mechanical relationship[53].

But, as indicated earlier, there is a long line of writers who have
argued that the money supply, at least as defined in modern terms, is
demand-determined rather than dependent upon supply factors.

2.4.2 DEMAND-DETERMINATION

The origin of this school of thought is arguably in Adam Smith's
discussion of the Real Bills doctrine[54]. Smith's argument is that a
bank should not advance more than the amount of capital which a
merchant would otherwise have kept by him in cash. The bank would
thus never exceed the value of the gold and silver which would be
required if there were no paper money advanced by banks. The limit
would be observed when only real bills of exchange were discounted.
The authoritative modern descendant of this argument is to be found
in the Radcliffe Report, which seems to see the supply of money as
endogenous and to regard Central Bank control as working only
through the effect of alterations in interest rates on the 'liquidity' of
the private sector taken as a whole. In both cases there is the
implication that meeting the needs of trade, in a prudent manner, is
the correct path for banking to follow.

But Smith and the Radcliffe Report were talking about very
different monetary regimes; in particular, Smith was talking about a
paper currency convertible into gold and silver. However, his doctrine
was taken over by the Anti-Bullionists and applied to a doctrine of
*in*convertible paper. But the moderate Bullionists, especially Thornton, also emphasized the elasticity of supply of paper credit. Thomas
Tooke provides the link between the moderate Bullionists and the

Banking School in the 1840s; and Tooke, albeit under a regimen of convertibility, and making a sharp distinction between convertible and inconvertible notes, came to argue that the money supply, at least as defined in modern terms, was demand-determined. Causality ran from the price level to the money supply, and price fluctuations were due to real causes rather than to variations in the quantity of money. This did not mean that banking prudence was not required; it certainly was. But circulation depended upon transactions demand while deposits depended upon demand for means of making large payments. Any excess issue of notes would be returned to the banking system via the principle of 'Reflux', either through being deposited again with the bank or through being used to pay off securities or, should the paper become depreciated, through demanding coin. The circulation was dependent upon money income, in Tooke's view. In truth, Tooke tended, in his later years, as contemporaries and successors have pointed out, to explain prices by prices[55].

Tooke's most effective ally was Fullarton (1845)[56], who held that while the value of an inconvertible currency was determined by its amount, a convertible currency was demand-determined in amount with bills of exchange and deposits as 'a vast and inexhaustible *fund* of potential currency' (p. 44). There was always more credit available than was required (pp. 46–47). Thus over-issue of notes is excluded by the principle of Reflux, while there is an unlimited potential supply of credit available to meet all monetary needs. The emphasis upon a spectrum of liquidity and of substitutes for money as narrowly defined foreshadows both Radcliffe and the portfolio approach.

J.S. Mill (1848, pp. 511–541) relied rather heavily upon the approach of Tooke and Fullarton. Near-money was effective as real money, and the supply of this was not controlled by the supply of reserve assets.

2.5 Monetary control

The modern approach to monetary control is predominantly in terms of control of a large aggregate such as Sterling M_3 through Open Market Operations and Bank Rate. Such an approach has its roots in the 1930s, especially in the writings of Hawtrey and of Keynes, and in the Macmillan Committee of 1931, of which Keynes was a member. This was for much of the post-war period eclipsed by the sort of 'Keynesianism' associated with the 1950s; but it has revived under the influence of Friedman, and of other writers, who have assigned to money a definite causal role.

Criticism of such an approach has come from a number of sides. On the one hand there has been a school of thought which has held that such a large aggregate cannot be easily controlled directly and that control should instead centre upon the monetary base; that is, reserve assets[57]. In turn, a typical modern criticism of resort to base control is that, in order to reduce reserves, government must sell central government debt. Since it cannot rely on sales of marketable debt or tap issues, this reduces to controlling the supply of Treasury Bills. Operating in this end of the market has serious implications for the short-term rate of interest (Coghlan and Sykes, 1980, pp. 2, 4–5).

However, the main line of criticism of such an approach is that the money supply is, in fact, endogenous. Monetary control is rendered almost impossible by the Public Sector Borrowing Requirement (enormously increased since the mid-1960s) together with the continuous flow of National Debt maturities, flows across the exchanges, the difficulties of knowing what reaction there will be to Open Market Operations and uncertainty over the interest elasticity of aggregate demand (Goodhart, 1975, p. 152). Thus monetary control involves two serious problems; the impetus to monetary growth coming from the public sector deficit and the uncertain (and possibly unstable) response to attempts to control this growth (Goodhart, 1975, pp. 159–160). Pessimism is also to be found in the Radcliffe Report (p. 162). The general position taken in the Report was that the banks would have no difficulty in lending more if they could find suitable customers, that they could manufacture reserve assets as required, that the monetary authorities made this easy for them by trading freely between cash and Treasury Bills in order to protect the rate of interest on Treasury Bills and that the flow of debt maturities and the increasing development of financial institutions both made orthodox monetary control almost impossible[58]. The rate of interest worked through reducing the capital values of assets held by potential lenders, so that they became locked into a particular asset structure and reluctant to realize an asset, and sustain a capital loss, in order to provide funds for a borrower. This was coupled with the supposed 'psychological' effects of 'changes of gear' in interest rates[59].

This pessimism about orthodox monetary control should not surprise us, however, given that the Radcliffe Report represents a continuing strand of monetary thought in which these problems have always been present. A part of the same stream is the Yale School, in which 'monetary theory broadly conceived is simply the theory of portfolio management' (Johnson, 1970, p. 102)[60].

In England the Radcliffe view has led to an interesting development in the thesis (Coghlan, 1980) that changes in the money supply are demand-determined—but that the demand is for *bank credit* and that satisfying such demand can lead to an excess supply of money.

Perhaps the broad distinction which could be made between the different schools of thought about monetary control is between control-optimists and control-pessimists. It is interesting to see that the roots of this divide lie at least as far back as 1844.

2.5.1 MONETARY CONTROL AND THE BANK CHARTER

The Currency School (as represented by Overstone, Norman and Torrens) and the Banking School (as represented by Tooke, Fullarton and J.S. Mill) were agreed upon the need to have a convertible paper currency. Both parties believed that this would check monetary profligacy on the part of government; the Currency School also believed that, properly managed, a convertible paper currency would have an anticyclical effect[61].

Thus both parties were agreed that specie should play a central role in the money supply, its amount varying according to international flows of precious metals resulting from changes in relative international price levels leading to payments imbalances. But beyond that point there was a clear choice. The Currency School were essentially monetary base advocates. The note issue should be controlled directly in accordance with inflows and outflows of precious metals so that there was no room for the exercise of discretion by the Bank in adding to the high-powered money supply. Notes were at the base of the monetary system, and the credit superstructure rested upon them[62].

With a rigid and automatic system of monetary base control, monetary policy would act counter-cyclically. For as economic activity picked up and prices tended to rise, so the balance of payments would be moving into deficit and the Bank would be losing gold. Because it was losing gold it would be forced to contract the note issue; and this act of monetary contraction would, because the credit superstructure rested upon the note issue, check the boom before it got out of hand. Conversely, the downswing would induce monetary expansion automatically.

The Banking School were not optimistic about the effects of monetary control, and believed that rigid control of the monetary base would cause economic dislocation. Their position really arose from elements in Thornton's exposition during the Bullion debate. Thornton (1802), paying particular attention to the micro-economic effects of monetary policy, stressed the distress caused by monetary contraction and argued that, because it caused economic dislocation, it might well correct neither internal nor external monetary disequilibrium. There was, he believed, very little *short-run* connection between the note issue and prices, and in a famous passage he recommended monetary flexibility (p. 259), and caution in the use of monetary contraction.

Thornton was, like Tooke himself in that earlier controversy, a moderate Bullionist. Thus it was that Tooke, in the 1840s controversy, again favoured monetary discretion against an automatic monetary system, the philosophy of which was ultimately based upon the Ricardian definition of excess, i.e. that an amount of notes in circulation, when the country was losing gold abroad, was, *by definition*, in excess. Rather Tooke argued that 'overtrading' and 'overbanking' were unavoidable, and would not be checked by controlling the note issue or by separating the Bank of England into a Banking Department and an Issue Department. The latter would only split the Bank's resources between two departments; in order to protect the diminished reserve the Bank would then have to engage in frequent and severe movements in Bank Rate; and the end-result of this would be commercial dislocation rather than monetary control. The correct way forward lay in the exercise of monetary discretion by the Bank on the basis of an enlarged gold reserve[63]. Like Thornton, the members of the Banking School tended to stress the necessity of a lender of last resort; and it is undoubtedly true that events forced upon the Currency School a similar recognition. It became ultimately accepted by both sides that, in the event of a financial crisis, the rigid limits of the 1844 Bank Act on note issue would be relaxed, thus enabling the Bank of England to make exceptional advances to the money market[64].

2.5.2 MONETARY CONTROL AFTER 1870

Although the Currency School was victorious in the debates over the renewal of the Bank Charter, a majority of writers after 1870, it is probably true to say, followed the Banking School in emphasizing the need for monetary discretion. Tooke's plan for a large reserve was followed by a number of writers, including Giffen and Goschen, but Bagehot's influence seems to have been particularly strong. His stress upon the role of the Bank as lender of last resort, and as holder of one central reserve, enabled him to carry forward Tooke's plan. But though Bagehot was in favour of discretion, he was also optimistic about monetary policy; the vein of pessimism which surfaces repeatedly in the Banking School is much less evident in his work[65].

Bagehot influenced Marshall (1926, p. 111) who indeed took from him the plan for a large reserve—it is strange that Marshall makes no reference to Tooke in this connection. Like Bagehot, Marshall managed to combine an emphasis on the need for discretion with optimism about the power of monetary policy as exercised through Bank Rate and Open Market Operations. But there is a subtle change of emphasis with Marshall; rather more attention is paid in his work to questions of short-run internal equilibrium and rather less to questions of long-run external equilibrium than in the work of his predecessors. This led him to stress the need to meet business monetary requirements and to avoid rigidity in monetary arrangements[66].

This shift of emphasis was carried over to his successors, who themselves made one further and highly significant shift; from a concentration upon notes to a concentration upon deposits[67].

But, despite the changes of emphasis, it would not be untrue to say that Marshall handed on to his successors the Banking School legacy, combined with an increased optimism about the efficacy of monetary policy. Thus Lavington advocated the use of a large reserve to avoid fluctuations in the rate of interest, the cushioning of gold flows, and the exercise of monetary policy through Bank Rate and Open Market Operations, aiming at the targets of price, interest rate, and exchange stability[68].

Hawtrey also argued for the use of such indicators together with output, employment, the demand for credit, and the level of transactions. He, too, believed in the necessity of an 'elastic' supply of money, and was optimistic about monetary control. However, Hawtrey deserves special mention amongst Marshall's successors for emphasizing the difficulties of monetary control in the presence of a Public Sector Borrowing Requirement, a matter which, as we have seen, has caused much modern concern[69].

Keynes, in the *Tract* and the *Treatise*, also displayed this combination of emphasis on the need for banking discretion in the pursuit of short-run stabilization objectives with optimism about the power of monetary policy. In the *Tract* he argued that the currency supply and the reserve ratio should be varied to *offset* variations in the demand for cash; and he suggested that open market operations were effective in controlling bank deposits which determined the price level. However, the price level was not the only criterion of the need to exercise monetary policy; output, the demand for credit, the rate of interest, and employment are all mentioned[70].

In the *Treatise* Keynes sees the stability of the price level as the test of whether excessive Bank Credit is being created. If the price level rises, this indicates that investment is greater than saving, and the creation of bank credit should then be controlled through open market operations and Bank Rate. Keynes did not agree that reserves could be manufactured by the banks and, although he envisaged the introduction of control of reserve ratios, he was confident that the creation of credit by the banks could be controlled through the more normal weapons[71].

Not all of Marshall's successors, however, combined optimism and a belief in the need for monetary discretion. Robertson, who (like the Currency School) regarded monetary forces as things which could magnify or diminish a trade cycle but as subsidiary to real forces, was pessimistic about monetary control. He did not agree with Fisher that raising the rate of interest far enough would bring an upswing under control; and although he discussed central bank control through open market operations and the use of the rate of interest, he believed that credit rationing might well be necessary in the upswing, while monetary policy was weak in depression[72].

The writer whose position perhaps most completely anticipates modern pessimism about monetary policy was Lawrence. He criticized the endorsement of open market operations by Keynes and others. The central bank was not free in its dealings in securities, the supply of government securities depended on the public sector borrowing requirement, and the banks could manufacture reserves. Coupled with his detailed attention, like Phillips, to redeposit ratios, which made him sceptical about bank deposit multipliers, these views find considerable echo amongst the monetary pessimists of the present time[73].

Few writers combined optimism with a belief in automatic monetary policy. The chief writer who did so was Irving Fisher, who, in his proposal for a 'compensated dollar', put forward a mechanism of automatic adjustment in the currency unit to changes in the price level[74].

2.6 The rate of interest

In the modern literature the rate of interest is treated in terms of some kind of IS–LM model[75]. Essentially the position is taken that there is an equilibrium rate at which income is stable and the money market clears. Given the price level, the money supply, the demand for money and the willingness to part with it at different rates of interest, income and the rate of interest are simultaneously determined.

This is a superficially satisfactory model. In fact, however, it glosses over a lot of the questions which economists have considered in the course of the development of the theory of the rate of interest, representing a synthesis of *some* of the elements found in previous theories.

In particular, as will become apparent, earlier writers were concerned about the price level in relation to the rate of interest; and they also used the concept of the 'natural rate of interest', which may be interpreted as the going rate of profit upon marginal investment[76].

The Radcliffe Report dismissed many of the traditional arguments, associated with earlier work by writers like Hawtrey, Wicksell and Keynes, concerning the role of the rate of interest. It played down the interest control effect both in relation to stocks and in relation to fixed investment. Moreover, the Committee believed, like Tooke, that large fluctuations in the rate of interest could undermine the stability of banks—they were concerned about the effects of capital values[77].

The Radcliffe treatment of the rate of interest, unlike most of the modern literature, does have the merit both of showing awareness of the breadth of considerations relating to the rate and of attempting empirical investigation. Its conclusions may seem a little eccentric viewed from a perspective in the early 1980s, when governments are continually being told about the restrictions on economic activity resulting from high rates of interest; but it provides a convenient bridge between the modern literature and the comprehensive discussions of early years.

2.6.1 FOUNDATIONS OF INTEREST THEORY

The importance of the rate of interest was recognized in the seventeenth century. Locke believed changes in the rate to affect both trade and the value of money; and Sir Josiah Child of the East India Company argued strongly for a reduction in the rate from 6 per cent to 4 per cent, attributing superior Dutch performance in trade and growth to a low rate of interest in Holland[78].

In Mercantilist writings the rate of interest frequently appears as a purely monetary phenomenon. From the time of Hume, Massie and Smith there was insistence that the rate of interest was a real phenomenon, and it was equated with the marginal productivity of investment[79]. Both Thornton and Ricardo insisted that there was a real rate of interest, which could be identified as marginal profitability; and both writers, followed by many others, insisted that changes in the money supply produced only temporary variations in the market rate, which must ultimately equalize with the real rate. Thornton, and later Ricardo, pointed out that the distinction between the money and the real rate had important implications for Bank policy; there was no limit to the amount which the Bank could lend if the money rate were less than the real rate. Thornton was particularly clear on this. He also distinguished between the nominal and the deflated rate of interest, and expressed the view that nominal rates will adjust during persistent inflation to cover the loss of principal[80].

This analysis provided the foundation for the discussion in the era of the Bank Charter Act, the period in which the Bank of England began to use Bank Rate as a policy weapon[81]. Both Banking and Currency School writers treated the natural rate of interest as the net profit on capital after allowance for risk and trouble of employment. The market rate fluctuated around the natural rate, which was determined by the intersection of the demand for investible funds and the supply of such funds. Once an investment had been made, however, it ceased to affect the rate of interest directly. But the market rate of interest was, in the short term, a monetary phenomenon, and it was recognized, as it had been by Thornton and Ricardo, that changes in the money supply could temporarily affect the rate of interest[82]. The treatment of the subject by J.S. Mill is particularly noteworthy in the light of accusations by Keynes that previous writers had regarded the rate of interest as equating the demand for and supply of savings rather than the demand for and supply of money. Mill argued that the rate of interest would equalize the supply of and demand for *loans*, and that people's willingness to make loans from their available funds varied with activity. The demand for balances ('liquidity preference') varied with the cycle[83].

In dealing with the operation of Bank Rate, the influence of the Bank was treated as a short-term money-market influence. Nonetheless it was important. The Bank could give a danger signal by raising the Rate, thus inducing bankers to ration credit in order to strengthen their liquidity. Conversely, a very low rate of interest could generate an unsound state of credit and price rises, which would stimulate further demand for loans in anticipation of inflation.

2.6.2 MARSHALL AND HIS SUCCESSORS

Marshall was, of course, well read in the preceding Classical literature, especially in the work of J.S. Mill. He regarded the real rate of interest as being determined by the supply of 'free' or 'non-specific' capital (made up of savings and depreciation allowances) and demand for that capital for investment purposes. Demand was a function of available investment opportunities and of price expectations. Expectations had a vital role to play. The money rate of interest fluctuated around the real rate, and could be affected, in the short term, by changes in the supply of money. When these raised prices, the resulting profit opportunities increased the demand for loans; a high rate of interest was thus associated with high and rising prices[84]. In this connection Marshall acknowledged Fisher's important contribution. Fisher had argued in his *Appreciation and Interest* (1896) that, in the long term, the rate of interest rose to cover the loss of principal in inflation. Thus high and low prices were associated with high and low interest. The idea was not new; as indicated earlier, it was put forward by Thornton and J.S. Mill. But both Fisher's detailed and careful work in testing the hypothesis, and Marshall's emphasis on price variations in relation to the rate of interest, helped to maintain the long classical tradition and give it new momentum[85].

Pigou followed Marshall in the analysis of the real and money rate. Nevertheless he was critical of the idea that equilibrium could be attained by equating the *money* with the *real* rate of interest. He believed that the 'income velocity' of money could be affected by changes in expectations without credit changes—bank credit was not the only source of instability. Nevertheless he accepted that Bank Rate could control both credit and the short-run rate of interest, although the link with the bond rate was not secure[86].

Lavington paid attention to the role of the New Issues market. He argued that a high rate of interest discouraged placing of new issues[87]. Hawtrey believed that the New Issues market equated savings and investment not only by means of variations in the rate of interest but also through credit rationing. He believed that credit was unstable, and that the primary way of controlling it was through the rate of interest. This had an important psychological effect, as it altered future profit expectations. Hawtrey, who has been described as the foremost modern exponent of Bank Rate, saw Bank Rate as affecting output through decisions about stock levels; the effect on output produced effects on income, and variations in incomes affected both the price level and the money supply[88]. He was extremely critical of Keynes's analysis of Bank Rate. In his view, the short-run rate of interest had little effect on the bond rate because changes in the short rate were not expected to last. In turn, the bond rate had little effect upon fixed investment, to which, as will become clear, Keynes attached great importance[89].

Perhaps the most original treatment of the rate of interest, despite its traditional roots, was that put forward by D.H. Robertson. He proposed a version of Marshall's real and money rate, explicitly in *flow* terms. In analysing the real rate he identified the sources of funds as individual and corporate saving, depreciation, increases in bank lending and dishoarding. The demand for funds came from the desire to make investment in fixed and working capital, to replace capital, to obtain command over liquid balances and to make consumer expenditure. He included in his analysis the traditional 'schedule of the marginal product of loanable funds'; but since he emphasized that the productivity of investment was continually changing both as a result of exogenous forces (such as discoveries) and of endogenous forces (the cycle), the essentials of the analysis differ only from the Keynesian 'marginal efficiency of capital' in greater comprehensiveness and the use of a dynamic framework. This is particularly evident when it is appreciated that consumption (and thus saving) in one period was a function of disposable income in the previous period.

Robertson's analysis of the money rate was similarly derived from Marshall. He carried over the Marshallian association between high and rising prices and high and rising interest rates, and was concerned about the saving imposed upon the community by rising prices resulting from credit expansion by the banks[90].

In his *Tract* Keynes offered little analysis of the rate of interest; what he had to say was mainly concerned with rising interest rates during inflation, but without acknowledgement to important predecessors, especially Fisher. (In his *Treatise*, as Marget notes, Keynes made the explicit claim that this issue had been ignored by economists[91].)

In the *Treatise* Keynes adhered to Marshall's analysis of the real and money rates of interest. He based the analysis in this work on the concept of a natural rate of interest (following Wicksell). When the market rate equalled the natural rate, savings equalled investment; there were no supernormal profits and price stability prevailed. Keynes laid considerable emphasis on savings and investment analysis in this work. Economic equilibrium would prevail when the division of output between consumption and investment was the same as the division of income between consumption and saving. The role of Bank Rate was then critical in balancing the expansion of bank

credit to achieve equilibrium between savings and investment. In this
work Keynes believed particularly in the sensitivity of fixed investment to Bank Rate, and attempted to establish that long- and
short-run interest rates were closely linked[92].

However, Hawtrey was able to show conclusively that the link
between short- and long-run rates did not hold to anything like the
extent to which Keynes believed, and that he had used a very partial
data set[93].

But Keynes had by then shifted his analytical focus, dropping the
natural rate of interest and advancing in his *General Theory* a version of
Marshall's money rate of interest. He dismissed the concept of the
natural rate and asserted that such an idea was based upon a
full-employment economy. He now stressed *movements in* the investment demand schedule rather than its sensitivity to variations in the
rate of interest. In his analysis of the rate of interest he presented his
now-famous discussion of 'liquidity preference', dividing the demand
for money into transactions, precautionary and speculative motives.
(The transactions and precautionary motives for holding money were,
as indicated above, commonly recognized. The speculative motive
had been foreshadowed by Hawtrey's 'savings' motive and, above all,
by Marshall's 'bulls and bears' 1923, pp. 58–59.) The rate of interest
then depended on the interaction of the schedule of the 'marginal
efficiency of capital' with the availability of funds, which depended
upon decisions to save out of income and to part with savings and
make these available for investment[94]. It is here that the analysis of
liquidity preference is central.

2.6.3 AN INDEPENDENT TRADITION

So far, the discussion of the rate of interest has concentrated on the
line of succession from the classical inheritance through Marshall and
the English economists. There is, however, another line of succession
stemming directly from the work of Tooke and linking up with the
capital theory of the Austrian economist Böhm-Bawerk. This is to be
found in the work of Wicksell and his followers.

Wicksell borrowed from Tooke the observation that prices and the
rate of interest were positively correlated both with respect to level
and to changes. From Böhm-Bawerk's capital theory he took a formal
analysis of the natural rate of interest. In a work published in 1898 he
put forward a theory of a cumulative upward inflationary process
resulting from a money rate of interest below the natural rate, which
was apparently based upon these sources and written in ignorance of
the work of Thornton. If the money rate was below the natural rate
this would present profit opportunities. Entrepreneurs would demand
factor inputs and thus factor prices would rise. The rise in these prices
raised factor incomes and thus the demand for final products. This in

turn enabled the entrepreneur to cover his increased costs. Inflation-ary pressures were increased because a lowering of the rate of interest reduced carrying charges, and thus enabled the entrepreneur to pay a higher price for inputs even with the same output prices; and the upward movement of prices created inflationary expectations, shifting both demand and supply curves. Ultimately the upward process would be checked under anything other than a pure credit system, because the banks would have to raise the discount rate to check the drain on their reserves. But their rates were sticky, and they tended to follow movements in the natural rate after a lag, when the effect upon their reserves had become apparent: this explained the positive correlation between upward movements in prices and the rate of interest. However, to stop the process it was not sufficient to restore a lowered interest rate to its previous level, as the inflationary process widened profit margins; it was necessary to push the money rate into equality with the real rate. Once this happened, the inflationary process would peter out[95].

The natural rate is defined in barter terms, with explicit reference to the capital theory advanced by Böhm-Bawerk and Jevons[96]. This explains the ancestry of Wicksell's own approach; but it is not, of course, necessary to the introduction of the concept of a natural rate, and it is, indeed, not particularly easy to understand why, in terms of such limited models, the natural rate should fluctuate, as Wicksell anticipated it would.

The argument owed a considerable debt to Tooke, with his emphasis on the positive correlation between price and rate of interest movements. Nonetheless, Wicksell did not take his analytical appar-atus from Tooke; he was particularly critical of Tooke's argument that a reduction in the rate of interest lowered the price level by reducing cost of production, and showed that this line of argument could be used to imply instability in the balance of payments[97].

Wicksell's work was published in German and obtained a following in Austria, where Böhm-Bawerk's work was influential. In particular, he was followed by Mises, who used the argument to develop the idea of over-production of investment goods in the upward cumulative process, and by Hayek[98]. There was also, of course, a Swedish school stemming from Wicksell's work and discussion of the concept of the natural rate by writers like Davidson and Cassel. Thus the Swedish economist Myrdal, writing in 1933, noted that English economists did not seem to be more than superficially familiar with Wicksell's work, and wrote wryly of Keynes's 'unnecessary originality' in his *Treatise*[99].

2.7 Transmission mechanisms and the effects of money

Modern texts distinguish between a 'classical' and a 'Keynesian' model. In the former, money is demanded for transactions purposes only, velocity is stable, full employment is assumed, the money supply is exogenous, money is neutral, wages and prices are flexible and changes in the money supply produce an 'effect on prices *directly* through spending of excess balances. In the latter, money is demanded for transactions, precautionary and speculative motives, with the latter providing a floor to the rate of interest, velocity is unstable, there is quantity adjustment and unemployment, a demand-determined money supply, rigid wages and prices, and a supposedly 'Keynesian' transmission mechanism where changes in the money supply work *indirectly* through from the short end of the money market to the bond rate and the demand for investment goods.

Although useful for textbook purposes, this is extremely inaccurate as an historical record. It has been noted that Keynes's analysis of the demand for money was only a variant on what had gone before: that the transactions and precautionary motives were routinely discussed in previous writings and that the speculative motive, though not in the precise form that Keynes gave it, was also recognized. Stable velocity was certainly not a general assumption, and many writers, especially the Banking School, had envisaged a demand-determined money supply.

Moreover, money has hardly ever been regarded as neutral. The quantity theory has sixteenth-century roots; and by the eighteenth century it is possible to find writers who explain the effects of money supply changes at length[100]. In particular, David Hume (1752) emphasized that changes in the supply of money stimulated both output and employment through increasing the profit margin. His analysis passed to the classical economists; and it is discussed and (largely) endorsed by Henry Thornton, who saw changes in the money supply affecting employment, consumption and investment as well as producing inflation because of limited elasticity of aggregate supply. Discussions of the matter are also to be found in the work of Malthus, Torrens, McCulloch, Newmarch and Cairnes. Only Ricardo and James Mill firmly opposed the Hume analysis of the inflationary mechanism[101].

Thus Marshall inherited, both from the classical writers and from his contemporary Giffen, a well-established view that changes in the money supply were not neutral, except in the very long run, and that they produced changes in output and employment. In particular, deflation lowered profit levels and produced economic disorganization, although it had the benefit of increasing real wages and encouraging entrepreneurial search[102].

The influence of Marshall's analysis runs through twentieth-century monetary writing, at least in England. Keynes in his *Tract* (1923) regarded the quantity theory as 'fundamental', (1923, in 1971, p. 61) and in his *General Theory* (1936) we find a discussion of the price, income and employment effects of changes in the money supply with allowance for varying elasticities on lines similar to those of Thornton[103].

2.7.1 CLASSICAL TRANSMISSION

Analysis of transmission in the classical writings is complex, containing both the 'direct' and 'indirect' mechanisms of the modern textbooks. Hume, Cantillon and Ricardo emphasized the direct mechanism; but even in their work we find the indirect mechanism[104]. The leading member of the Currency School, Overstone, emphasized the indirect mechanism and held that there was no simple connection between the money supply and the price level, the effects of changes in the money supply depending upon whether they were pro- or anti-cyclical[105]. With members of the Banking School the emphasis upon the indirect mechanism is even greater. Fullarton is particularly interesting, because he articulated clearly the indirect mechanism. This was taken over by J.S. Mill, who passed it on to Marshall[106].

Thus the Marshallian emphasis upon the indirect mechanism is wholly classical. Apart from the writers already mentioned, the indirect mechanism is clearly present in Thornton's work. Marshall himself was immediately preceded by Sidgwick and by Giffen, both of whom presented the indirect mechanism[107].

Marshall advanced the following mechanism. Gold flowed in and collected in the banking system, bank reserves rose, the banks sought to lend more, the rate of interest was initially depressed, demand for both inputs and outputs rose as a result of credit extension, the price level rose and the demand for transactions balances increased. Increases in the price level and increases in the rate of interest were positively correlated; Marshall explained this by the stimulus to the demand for credit produced by the initial expansion and—under the influence of Fisher—the incorporation into the nominal rate of interest of allowance for inflation. The idea of a direct mechanism is for him a mere curiosity[108].

Marshall's analysis of the transmission mechanism was passed on to writers like Robertson and Keynes. The importance of the rate of interest was also stressed by Hawtrey[109].

Of course, it was not only Marshall who enjoyed this classical inheritance. In particular, Wicksell made the indirect mechanism the centrepiece of his analysis of an upward cumulative inflationary process. Amongst Wicksell's successors was Hayek, who blended this analysis with an Austrian theory of production, arguing that, as new money filters in, it affects the relative profitability of different stages of production, with producer's goods becoming initially more profitable. Then wages rise and the relative profitability of consumption goods is restored while the banks refuse further credit to the investment goods sector, which has thus to free resources. Unemployment results[110].

There was also an extensive American literature, of which Sprague's statistical investigation of the indirect mechanism is particularly noteworthy. (Friedman's work is in a long United States tradition of statistical studies in the quantity theory[111].) Also written under American influence was the work of Martin (1931), who has a detailed analysis of the circular flow involving both direct and indirect mechanisms[112]. Indeed, it is interesting to note that even the semantic classification of the literature into direct and indirect mechanisms dates from at least ten years before Keynes's *General Theory* (Angell, 1926, p. 120).

2.7.2 THE CREDIT CYCLE

Monetary writers coupled their concern with transmission mechanisms with the identification and analysis of a credit cycle. Amongst the classical writers are McCulloch, Overstone (whose concept of a cycle much influenced Marshall), Tooke, Fullarton and Bagehot. These writers, from McCulloch onwards, envisaged profit variability and the behaviour of investment as of key importance in the cycle; and this was emphasized also by Marshall's predecessor, Giffen[113].

Marshall himself attributed considerable harm to credit fluctuations. In the upswing the demand for manufactured output rose, the extension of credit increased, prices, profits and wages all rose and speculation was stimulated. At the peak of the boom lenders became cautious and a capital shortage developed with investments uncompleted. The unloading of stocks produced a collapse of prices, the failure of speculators and a cumulative downward slide into an economic trough in which there was an absence of confidence. A key role was given to variations in profitability caused by the lag of wages and interest behind price changes[114].

Though Robertson emphasized real forces in the cycle, Hawtrey clearly derived his monetary analysis of the cycle from Marshall. Amongst the novel contributions of Hawtrey was a systematic emphasis upon lags and limited knowledge. A transactions demand lag in the upswing, and an order-completion lag, involved belated demands for cash and for credit unanticipated by the banks, who continued to expand credit as long as their reserves were satisfactory. Ultimately they were forced to contract—too late and too severely, producing depression. They should look beyond reserves to general indicators, because the economy was not self-stabilizing[115].

In the United States Fisher selected the lag of the deflated rate of interest behind profits as the key factor in the credit cycle; but American monetary economics paid much more attention to empirical testing than British work, and Fisher's case was damaged by the investigations of Minnie England, who found that other cost lags were probably more important and that the deflated rate of interest did not catch up with the rate of profit until *after* the peak of the boom[116].

2.7.3 EXPECTATIONS

Within the credit cycle (and linked with changes in the demand for balances) there occurred changes in expectations which radically altered willingness to invest. Such factors had been emphasized by Thornton, McCulloch and Overstone as well as the inflationist Attwood, while J.S. Mill envisaged shifts in the investment demand schedule with expectations. This passed to Marshall, who envisaged cumulative movements of expectations within the cycle, seeing the chief cause of depression as a 'want of confidence' which particularly affected fixed capital investment. He made explicit acknowledgement to Overstone[117].

Thus it is hardly surprising that Pigou emphasized the psychological factors in the trade cycle and regarded money itself as only an aggravating force. He stressed the importance of profit expectations variability and showed how these were affected by price movements. Lavington envisaged investment varying with the levels of confidence, thus intensifying business cycles[118].

Hawtrey's treatment of expectations is particularly interesting. He laid emphasis upon expected profits and changes in these in relation to the rate of interest; and he showed the psychological importance of Bank Rate in inducing contraction through its effect on expectations[119].

Keynes's own analysis in the *General Theory* afforded a crucial role to expectations as affecting investment, in his presentation of the 'marginal efficiency of capital', but his flamboyant paragraphs about the trade cycle and the shifting marginal efficiency of capital only reflected, in analytical content, a very long tradition, but with a pessimistic turn common at that date[120].

2.7.4 EFFECTIVE DEMAND

The expectations element of the *General Theory* is thus hardly novel. Nor was its emphasis upon effective demand, as writers like Haberler and Robertson pointed out, despite Keynes's claims to the contrary[121]. In England, at least, the pioneering performance was that of Hawtrey, in whose work the immediate roots of the consumption function lie. He focused attention upon the flow of income and expenditure. The importance of credit creation is that it affects income, and thus expenditure, but income and expenditure do not directly keep pace with each other. There are thus changes in what Hawtrey called the 'unspent margin'. He advanced, as early as 1919, an algebraic model of the circular flow of income and expenditure, showing the way in which credit affected orders, income and outlay. Employment was dependent upon aggregate demand: and a reduction in employment further reduced aggregate demand. Monetary contraction brought about unemployment through its effect on consumer income and outlay[122].

Of course, Hawtrey was not alone. Robertson's essay of 1915, *Industrial Fluctuation*, was an important exercise in analysis of aggregate demand in real terms; and another striking example is provided by Durbin's *Problem of Credit Policy* (1935), written under the influence of Hayek. In the United States the work of Mitchell was outstanding; and he in turn influenced Martin (1931). These writers provided a detailed analysis of the circular flow of purchasing power which was in some respects more sophisticated than Keynes's 'psychological law'[123].

There were also populist writers, including J.A. Hobson and Foster and Catchings—acknowledged by Durbin and by Keynes in his *Treatise* but ignored in the *General Theory*[124].

2.7.5 RIGIDITIES

The importance attached by Marshall to rigid wages and business charges in aggravating the cycle was taken by him from Bagehot and Giffin; and there seems no doubt that he envisaged quantity and employment variations in depression. Both Robertson and Lavington laid some emphasis upon rigidities; but it was Hawtrey who dwelt particularly upon quantity variation, the impact of monetary policy being initially on output rather than prices. Pigou also stressed quantity adjustment with rigid wages and prices. This problem is also a main theme of Durbin's book[125]. Thus the emphasis on adjustments in output and employment in the *General Theory*, while it presents some contrast with Keynes's own *Treatise*, presents rather less strong contrast with the general tenor of previous writings.

2.7.6 SAVINGS AND INVESTMENT

It is largely true that, with the exception of discussions of forced saving by writers like Cantillon, McCulloch, Hume, Malthus and Horner[126], saving and investment were treated as single acts by the classical economists. It is among Marshall's successors that the treatment of savings and investment developed along modern lines out of his cash balance approach. Lavington took the view that while some people save and invest concurrently, others build up balances of savings till a favourable opportunity for investors occurs. This can cause fluctuations in employment which are not offset by the 'law of large numbers', because investors react together to common causes. This line of argument is also to be found in the work of Hawtrey. Indeed, as Davis has pointed out, Hawtrey had a model in which output changes brought savings and investment into equilibrium. Robertson also certainly deserves at least equal credit with other members of the Cambridge School for the development of savings and investment analysis, despite the weird terminology he employed. In the United States the analysis was developed both by orthodox economists like Mitchell and by 'heretics' like Foster and Catchings. In Sweden the distinction developed from the work of Wicksell, and in so doing it embodied, like the work of Robertson, dynamic elements[127].

'Investment' as treated both by the classical economists and by Marshall typically referred to fixed investment. This is hardly surprising, given the economic history of the Victorian age. The word 'speculation' from Tooke to Marshall typically refers to this, as well as to stocks, and we find writers like Fullarton, Jevons and Giffen all referring to fixed investment. Only Hawtrey placed the overwhelming emphasis on stocks—quite deliberately, because of the lack of influence of short-term interest rates on the bond market. Keynes, however, in his *Treatise* gave the impression that all previous writers, except Wicksell, had neglected fixed investment and dealt only with investment in stocks. He himself paid considerable attention to investment both in this work and in the *General Theory*, in which he built upon a formal concept which came, as he acknowledged, from Fisher—the Marginal Efficiency of Capital. This was a marriage of marginal productivity analysis with classical expectations defined in terms of the expectation of yield and the *current* supply price of the capital asset[128].

2.7.7 TARGETS AND INDICATORS

The predominant classical targets were price stability and the avoidance of commercial crises. Marshall also tended to couch his discussions of economic stability in terms of a mix of objectives, but with the emphasis on price stability, which was felt to be the key to stabilization generally. Thus Hawtrey, in listing the objectives of monetary policy as wage, price, profit, output and debtor/creditor relationships stabilization, was following this tradition. This does not alter the fact that he was interested both in unemployment—which by 1932 he considered the biggest single problem—and the course of real wages. But, as a pioneer of stabilization analysis, he rejected Fisher's prescription of pursuing stabilization measures solely with reference to the price level; in his view this would involve moving too late, and thus it was necessary to look to other indicators such as output, employment and the balance of payments. Similarly, Lavington suggested the use of exchange rates, international reserves and price variations as indicators[129].

It is from this background that Keynes's own thought comes. In the *Tract* he mentions stabilization of business and employment, but the whole thrust of the emphasis is upon *price* stabilization; and it is rather puzzling to find that Keynes sees a clear *choice* between external and internal price stability, as if price stability in an open economy were independent of exchange stability. In the *Tract* he follows Hawtrey in rejecting Fisher's stabilization proposal and in advocating a wide range of indicators[130]. In the *Treatise* the question of employment is a little more in evidence, but it is largely treated as a subordinate issue when discussing the speed of adjustment of prices and wages[131]. Pigou had, however, already begun the shift to placing the emphasis on employment. His *Industrial Fluctuations* paid far more attention to unemployment than Keynes's *Treatise* published three years later. It is in the *General Theory* that there is a dramatic change in Keynes's focus, with employment as virtually the only argument in the social welfare function, it being held that the economic system tends to stabilize at a level of less than full employment[132]. In his singlemindedness the Keynes of 1936 had almost only one predecessor, the inflationist Thomas Attwood, although his name may be coupled with Foster and Catchings, who drew from their analysis the moral that what was required was an ever-increasing money supply—the same moral as has been drawn in practice under policies inspired by the *General Theory*.

2.8 Conclusion

There is space for only a brief conclusion. This chapter should at least have made clear the very high degree of continuity which is to be found in monetary thought. It exhibits, in terms of concepts and techniques, a degree of continuity which can only be matched by international trade. But this necessarily raises awkward questions to economists reared upon the idea of a Keynesian Revolution.

It seems clear that Keynes's contributions were not primarily in novel analysis or concepts. His achievement was to succeed in persuading economists to place employment considerations at the forefront of their thinking. His victory was due not so much to analytical capacity as to flair, timing, literary punch and the sheer pressure of events. The personal magnetism of the man comes through his pages, and it is hard to resist either the charm or the panache of Keynes's economic writings, though it is hard to forgive his misleading comments on writers like Fisher and, in particular, Marshall. But such was his success that, when the monetarist counter-revolution occurred, the Keynesian change of focus had to be deflected by emphasis on the concept of the natural rate of unemployment, which Keynes himself had rejected.

It is in such changes of focus, rather than in the tools of analysis, or the concepts and interactions of variables, that the paradigm changes, Scientific Revolutions or switches to a progressive Scientific Research Programme have consisted. The tools in this field have remained basically the same: the questions altered.

Notes

1. For perceptive criticism of this, see Laidler (1969), Sprenkle (1969) and Friedman and Schwartz (1969).

2, Velocity itself apparently has no upper limit (Radcliffe, 1959, p. 133).

3. See Johnson (1969, pp. 30–31).

4. On this, see Yeager (1968, p. 53) and Laidler (1969, p. 515).

5. Norman (1841, pp. 12, 69). See also Overstone (1971, II, p. 714).

6. Keynes (1930, repr. 1971, p. 3); Mises (1912, trans. 1934 pp. 29–37).

7. E.g. Mises (1912, trans. 1934, p. 51) and Mill (1848, p. 539).

8. Overstone (1971, II, p. 715). See also Robbins (1958, pp. 113–115).

9. Cantillon (1755, pp. 143, 301–305) and Holtrop (1929, p., 507).

10. Norman (1841, pp. 32–35, 45–46, 52, 57, 73, 79–80, 92–93); Overstone (1857, p. 461; 1971, II, p. 714). See also Robbins (1958, p. 103) and the references in notes 47 and 62 below.

11. Marshall (1923, pp. 13, 15; 1926, p. 35); Wicksell (1906, trans. 1935, p. 27; 1898, trans. 1936, p. 68).

12. Overstone to Torrens (1971, II, p. 716); Robbins (1958, p. 106); Mill (1848, p. 539).

13. Fullarton (1845, pp. 33, 36, 41–47); Mill (1848, pp. 483, 495, 651–677); Tooke (1838–1857, III, pp. 121, 123–130, IV, pp. 154–165; 1844, pp. 20–23, 25, 33–37).

14. Fullarton (1845, p. 47); Mill (1848, pp. 539–541).

15. ˙Sayers (1963, pp. xxxiv–xxxvi); Pennington (1829, pp. 126–127; 1838, pp. 369, 377); Longfield (1840, repr. 1971, pp. 114–120).

16. For useful discussions see Laidler (1973) and the excellent text by Dennis (1981).

17. References will be found in Holtrop (1929) and Marget (1938–1942, I, p. 96). See, in particular, Petty, ed. Hull (1899, I, p. 112).

18. For Ricardo, see (1951–1973, III, p. 90); for J. Mill, see (1826 (Winch ed.), p. 278).

19. J.S. Mill (1848, pp. 494, 497–498); Attwood (1817, p. 27) quoted in Marget (1938–1942, I, p. 358n).

20. Marshall (1923; pp. 43, 45); Wicksell (1898 trans. 1936, p. 59) and 1906–1935, II, pp. 23, 65–68, 72.

21. Fisher (1911, pp. 79–89, 152, 154, 270, 305, 352, 360); (1933, p. 140).

22. For comment on this, see Marget (1938–1942, I, pp. 298–302).

23. Artis (1961, pp. 351–352, 359).

24. Petty, ed. Hull (1899, I, pp. 112–113, 310–311; II, p. 446); Smith (1776, ed. Cannan (1976 pagination), I, p. 342).

25. Thornton (1802, pp. 90, 92–94, 96–97, 194, 234, 359). For comment, see Hicks (1967, p. 175) and Holtrop (1929, pp. 515–516). On Thornton's influence on Marshall, see Eshag (1963, p. 13, n. 55).

26. Senior (1829–1840, p. 11). For comment, see Eshag (1963, pp. 14–15) (an important essay).

27. For Joplin and Tooke references, see Marget (1938–1942, I, pp. 320–324, 405–408). See also Bagehot (1873, p. 154) and Giffen (1877, pp. 34, 35, 147).

28. Mill (1844, pp. 70–72); Tooke (1838–1857, I, p. 156).

29. This is frequently forgotten despite two important articles by Marget (1931, 1935). See also Jaffé (1951).

30. Wicksell (1898, trans. 1936, pp. 39–42, 56, 59, 63–65; 1906, trans. 1935, pp. 23, 67, 71, 83–84); Baumol (1952).

31. Marshall (1923, pp. 43–48; 1926, pp. 36, 268–269).

32. Pigou (1917, pp. 40–42, 45–48, 50–54; 1927, p. 136); Lavington (1921, pp. 30–31).

33. Hawtrey (1919, 1928 ed., pp. 34–43, 46, 60; 1913, pp. 10–14, 23).

34. Keynes (1923, repr. 1971, pp. 37–38, 62–67).

35. Keynes equated income deposits with demand deposits and savings deposits with time deposits.

36. Keynes (1930, repr. 1971, I, pp. 31–37, 41–43, 211, 218–221, 224, 229; II, pp. 19, 29–30, 38–39, 73–75).
37. The same may not be true of the liquidity trap.
38. Keynes (1936, pp. 170, 172, 195–199, 207).
39. Robertson (1926, pp. 47–50; 1928, pp. 34–37; 1940, p. 66). On the question of whether real or money balances were involved, see Eshag (1963, pp. 21–22).
40. Thornton (1802, p. 243); Senior (1829–1830, pp. 79–81); Mill (1848, p. 526); Holtrop (1929, p. 519).
41. Goschen (1864, pp. 112–113); Marshall (1923, pp. 47, 152, 283); Fullarton (1845, pp. 71, 139–142); for Giffen, see Eshag (1963, p. 14, n. 55); Jevons (1875, p. 245).
42. Pigou (1917, pp. 43–44, 60; 1923, pp. 191, 196n). Marget (1938–1942, II, pp. 650–651, nn. 51, 53) notes that the relevant material was added to the 1923 reprint of the 1917 article.
43. Keynes (1923, repr. 1971, p. 40, 41, 42–43, 45–53). See also Marget (1938–1942, II, p. 645).
44. See Pigou (1917, pp. 42–43; 1923, p. 177); Mises (1912, trans. 1934, p. 145); Marshall (1923, pp. 45–47, 256, 282–284; 1926, pp. 39, 43, 44, 140, 176); Marget (1931), Marget (1938–1942, II, p. 648).
45. As Johnson (1970, p. 104) has pointed out, the concept of a *rigid* deposit multiplier is a 'straw man'; in fact, neither approach completely excludes the other.
46. References will be found in Macleod (1892–1893, I, p. 354).
47. See Overstone (1971, I, pp. 89, 104, 106–107, 113, 133); Norman (1841, pp. 42, 72–75, 80–81). However, fixed reserve ratios were slow to develop within the banking system. See Wadsworth (1968) and Hughes (1960).
48. Giffen (1877, pp. 30–32), Marshall (1926, p. 37).
49. Fisher (1911, ch. 3, especially pp. 46, 50, 52).
50. Macleod (1863, art. 'Credit'; 1892–1893, I, pp. 324–326), Phillips (1921, pp. 32–76); Crick (1927).
51. Hawtrey (1919, 1928 edn, pp. 27–28, 54–55, 225–227; 1932, pp. 153–154) and compare Keynes (1924, pp. 66–67).
52. See Eshag (1963, p. 136, n. 98).
53. Hayek (1933, pp. 153–173); Robertson (1928, p. 92); Lavington (1911, p. 59), (1921, pp. 43–44).
54. Smith (1776, I, p. 323, 1976 pagination).
55. Tooke (1838–1857, II, pp. 160–161, 165–166, 175–177, 183, 190–191, 343–344; III, pp. 223, 245, 276; IV, pp. 127, 185; V, pp. 344–345; 1844, pp. 38, 60, 62). There is some contrast with Tooke's (1826) more moderate position.
56. Fullarton (1845, pp. 63–64, 69, 83, 85–86, 101, 109, 194–195, 207).
57. For references, see Dennis (1981, chs 1, 2, 7).
58. See, in particular, Radcliffe (1959, pp. 48–49, 51, 59–62, 127, 158, 160–163, 167, 174).
59. Radcliffe (1959, pp. 133–134, 154–155). For perceptive criticism, see Morgan (1969, especially pp. 11, 21).
60. As Johnson (1970) has argued, the approach is 'long on elegant analysis of theoretical possibilities, but remarkably short on testable … propositions' (p. 105).
61. Discussions of the debate will be found in O'Brien (1971, I, pp. 70–144; and see I, p. 71, n. 1 for a list of classic discussions of it) and O'Brien (1975, pp. 153–159).
62. Notes predominated in reserves until 1873 (Wood, 1939, pp. 119–125).
63. Tooke (1838–1857, III, pp. 172–288; IV, pp. 166–197, 293–402; V, pp. 272–284, 309–315, 501–502, 551–593, 637–638; 1844, pp. 103–109); Fullarton (1845, pp. 130–169, 189–212).

64. See O'Brien (1971, pp. 128, 137). It was not Bagehot's *Lombard Street* but Tooke and the Banking School who established the last-resort role—Wood (1939, p. 165n).
65. Bagehot (1873, pp. 153–198, 303–309); Eshag (1963, p. 125).
66. (1923, p. 258; 1926, pp. 110–112, 163, 281, 322–324).
67. See Cannan (1924) for a belated and unsuccessful attempt to reverse this.
68. Lavington (1921, pp. 57–59, 150–152, 159, 163, 169–170).
69. Hawtrey (1919, 1928 edn, pp. 54–57, 132–140, 146, 227; 1923, pp. 39, 117, 132–133, 141–144, 146).
70. Keynes (1923, pp. 68–69, 141, 143–144, 148–149).
71. Keynes (1930, II, pp. 189–249).
72. Robertson (1915, pp. 218, 344–362; 1922, pp. 84, 93; 1926; 1928, p. 59, 166–169, 171–172, 177).
73. Lawrence (1928b, especially pp. 266–267, 273–276, 329–332).
74. Fisher (1933, pp. 138–140) and references therein.
75. For an excellent exposition see Dennis (1981).
76. Friedman's version of the model reintroduces the natural rate—Friedman (1970, 1971).
77. See Radcliffe (1959, pp. 131–153, 158–162, 175–178, 180–181). See also Artis (1961, pp. 348, 362–363).
78. Holtrop (1929, p. 506), Letwin (1963, pp. 5, 7, 10); O'Brien and Darnell (1982, ch. 3).
79. Smith (1776 (1976 pagination), p. 109); Hume (1752, p. 49); Rotwein (1955, pp. lxvii–lxxii).
80. Thornton (1802, pp. 254–258, 296–297, 336); Ricardo, ed. Sraffa (1951–1973, I, pp. 110, 296–298, 300, 363–364; III, pp. 88–90, 143, 150, 194n., 374–375; V, pp. 12n, 130, 346, 445).
81. From 1833 as the Usury Laws were relaxed.
82. Tooke (1838–1857, II, pp. 355–362; III, p. 155; V, pp. 556–557, 559; 1844, pp. 77–86; 1856, pp. 71–74, 76, 92); Overstone (1857, pp. 173, 253, 264, 581–585, 630).
83. Mill (1848, pp. 637–741, 645–647); Keynes (1936, pp. 166–167).
84. Marshall (1923, pp. 254–263, 288–289; 1926, pp. 41, 45, 49, 51, 127, 130–131, 270–272). See also Giffen (1877, pp. 107–115; 1887, pp. 38–39, 47–49), Jevons (1884, p. 95).
85. Fisher (1896, pp. 56, 60, 66–67, 76); Marshall (1926, p. 271); Mill (1848, p. 646); Thornton (1802, p. 336).
86. Pigou (1927, pp. 239–251, 256–257).
87. For Lavington's discussion of interest see his (1921, especially pp. 57–62, 163).
88. Hawtrey (1919, 1928 edn, pp. 132, 135–137, 413–414, 436; 1923, pp. 106–109; 1938, pp. 27, 37, 61–63, 175–177, 216, 246); Davis (1981, pp. 206, 214); Hicks (1969, p. 313).
89. Hawtrey (1938, pp. 170–171, 173, 185, 189–190, 198).
90. Robertson (1928, pp. 59–60, 164–165, 168–174; 1940, pp. 2–3, 7–8, 10–24, 83–92; 1963, p. 247). Presley; 1979, pp. 133, 148–149).
91. Keynes (1923, repr. 1971, pp. 20, 22–23); Marget (1938–1942, I, p. 196). See Keynes (1930, repr. 1971, II, pp. 177–186) for an interpretation in terms of his Fundamental Equations.
92. Keynes (1930, I, pp. 137, 139, 161–167, 172–173, 177, 180–181, 186–189, 197; II, pp. 85, 204, 315). See also Eshag (1963, p. 57).
93. Hawtrey (1938, pp. 146–207, especially pp. 185–189).
94. Keynes (1936, pp. 165–183, 242–244). It is unfortunate that Keynes should have claimed more novelty for his approach than was justified. See also Eshag (1963, pp. 64–65).
95. Wicksell (1898, trans. 1936, pp. 95–106, 111, 114, 118–119, 122–156). On the

question of stability see *ibid*. pp. 100–101 and Hicks (1939, pp. 205–209, 251–254).

96. Wicksell (1898, trans. 1936, pp. 122–156).
97. *Ibid*. pp. 98–99.
98. Mises (1912, trans. 1934, pp. 355–363); Hayek (1933, pp. 201, 210, 212–218). However, Hayek's interpretation of the natural rate is in terms of market clearing.
99. Myrdal (1933, trans. 1939, p. 9).
100. See Bodin (1568) and Christiernin (1761). The latter's contribution is particularly noteworthy.
101. Thornton (1802, pp. 195, 235–240); O'Brien (1970, pp. 155, 160–161); O'Brien (1975, pp. 163–165); Newmarch (1857, pp. 195–196); Cairnes (1873, pp. 53–76); Ricardo (1951–1973, IV, pp. 36–37; V, p, 524). (But even Ricardo did not regard money as neutral—IV, pp. 359–360.) J. Mill, ed. Winch (1826, p. 294); J.S. Mill (1848, pp. 542–555).
102. Marshall (1926, pp. 7–10, 34–35, 90, 97–98, 286–287); Giffen (1886, pp. 94–100). See also Eshag (1963, pp. 90–98).
103. Keynes (1936, pp. 295–297, 300–301). See also (1923, repr. 1971, pp. 1–30, 32, 65).
104. Hume (1752, pp. 38, 43–44, 57–58); Cantillon (1755, pp. 159–161, 163–165, 167, 177, 191, 213–215); Ricardo (1951–1973, I, p. 364; III, pp. 54–55, 91–93). See also Christiernin (1761, pp. 26, 104–105, 112–113).
105. (1857, pp. 120, 202–204, 253, 573–574).
106. Fullarton (1845, pp. 56–57, 62, 64–68, 101–102); Tooke (1838–1857, II, p. 344; IV, pp. 178–187; 1844, pp. 62–63). See also Tooke (1826, pp. 37, 42–48); Newmarch (1857, pp. 169, 189–190, 200–201, 233); J.S. Mill (1848, pp. 496–497, 642, 646–647).
107. Thornton (1802, pp. 195, 234–235, 241–242); Sidgwick (1887, p. 249). On Giffen (and Marshall's familiarity with his work), see Eshag (1963, pp. 17–18) and Angell (1926, p. 120).
108. (1926, pp. 38–45, 123, 140–142, 158, 257, 274).
109. Robertson (1915, pp. 213–215, 228); Keynes (1930, repr. 1971, I, pp. 202, 233–238, 244; II, p. 189; 1936, pp. 173, 196–201, 248, 298); Hawtrey (1919, 1928 edn, pp. 247–248; 1932, pp. 151–154, 287–288).
110. Wicksell (1898, trans. 1936, pp. 136–154; 1906, trans. 1935, pp. 162–163, 194); Hayek (1935, pp. 22, 76–98).
111. For references, see Angell (1926, pp. 127–131).
112. I am grateful to Dr J.R. Presley for this reference.
113. O'Brien (1970, pp. 156–159 and references); Overstone (1857, pp. 119–120, 167); Tooke (1826, p. 48); Fullarton (1845, pp. 58, 105); Bagehot (1873, pp. 142–143, 147); Giffen (1877, pp. 23–26, 62–63, 102–107, 115). See also Eshag (1963, pp. 77–89).
114. Marshall (1879, pp. 152–163; 1890, p. 594; 1923, pp. 75, 249–251, 261; 1926, pp. 7–9, 54, 129–131, 285–286).
115. Robertson (1915, pp. 215–223, 234–235); Hawtrey (1919, 1928 edn, pp. 9–51, 152–154). See also Keynes (1923, repr. 1971, pp. 67–68); Davis (1981, p. 210); Eshag (1963, pp. 102–103).
116. Fisher (1911, pp. 55–73); England (1912).
117. Thornton (1802, p. 195); O'Brien (1970, pp. 155–156; 1975, pp. 164–165); Overstone (1857, pp. 131. 167, 431–432); Mill (1848, p. 643); Marshall (1879, pp. 153–155; 1890, p. 711; 1923, pp. 18, 250, 257).
118. Pigou (1927, Part I, chs iii, iv, vii, xii, xiii, xvii); Lavington (1921, pp. 48, 71). See also Mitchell (1928, pp. 17–18 and Haberler (1937, pp. 134–135).
119. Hawtrey (1919, 1928 edn, pp. 153–154; 1932, p. 158); Davis (1981, p. 209); Hicks 1969, p. 313).

120. Keynes (1936, pp. 141–149, 197–198, 298). See also Martin (1931, ch. xii) on business pessimism.
121. Haberler (1937, p. 111); Robertson (1948, p. xvii; 1915, pp. 235–238). See also Marshall (1879, p. 154; 1890, pp. 710–712).
122. Hawtrey (1919, 1928 edn, pp. 11, 30–40, 45, 52, 59, 132–155; 1932, pp. 146–151, 321); Angell (1926, pp. 182–184); Davis (1981, p. 209).
123. Mitchell (1928, pp. 37–40, 100–105, 117, 130–131, 136–137, 139, 146–149, 151–154); Keynes (1936, p. 96).
124. See Foster and Catchings (1924, ch. xvii and 1928, sec. vii); Keynes (1930, repr. 1971, I, p. 160; II, p. 21n); Durbin (1935, p. 29). The similarity of Keynes's treatment of saving to that of Foster and Catchings was noted by Haberler (1937). For Hobson, see Nemmers (1956). For the origins of the Keynesian multiplier, which can be traced back to Bagehot, see Wright (1956), Eshag (1963, p. 95), Hegeland (1954) and Dorfman (1970). For a dissenting view, see Shackle (1967, pp. 186–202).
125. Marshall (1923, pp. 18–19; 1925, p. 191), Eshag (1963, pp. 81, 95, 102–103); Hawtrey (1919, 1928 edn, pp. 151, 154, 453; 1932, p. 321); Davis (1981, p. 216); Pigou (1927, Part I, chs xviii, xix).
126. Hayek (1932); O'Brien (1970, pp. 159–160).
127. Lavington (1921, p. 70), Hawtrey (1919, 1928 edn, pp. 46–47, 51); Davis (1981, p. 217); Presley (1979, Part II); Mitchell (1928, pp. 37–40).
128. Eshag (1963, pp. 104–105); Keynes (1936, pp. 136–144, 220–221, 306–309, 313–322, 375–376); Fullarton (1845, p. 104); Tooke (1826, pp. 42–43); Giffen (1887, p. 101); Jevons (1884, pp. 28–29); Marshall (1879, p. 153; 1890, pp. 710–711; 1923, pp. 249–251, 261; 1926, pp. 51–52, 127, 157–158, 168–169, 250, 285); Hawtrey (1919, 1928 edn, pp. 9, 13, 133–134, 138, 150–151; 1932, p. 188); Davis (1981, p. 209); Keynes (1930, repr. 1971, I, p. 177).
129. Marshall (1923, pp. 260–261; 1926, pp. 285–288); Hawtrey (1919, 1928 edn, p. 435; 1932, pp. 315, 320); Lavington (1921, p. 159).
130. Keynes (1923, repr. 1971, ch. 1 and pp. 68, 149, 118–119, 125–126, 138, 147, 149).
131. Keynes (1931, repr. 1971, pp. 242, 245–246).
132. Keynes (1936, pp. 250–254, 280–281).
133. On Attwood, see O'Brien (1975, p. 165). Myrdal correctly forsaw the likely outcome of pursuing the single objective of employment maximization (1933, trans. 1939, pp. 195–196).

References

ANGELL, J.W. (1926). *The Theory of International Prices*. Cambridge, Mass., Harvard University Press
ARTIS, M.J. (1961). Liquidity and the Attack on Quantity Theory. *Bulletin of the Oxford University Institute of Statistics* **23**, 343–366
BAGEHOT, W. (1873). *Lombard Street*. Repr. (ed. by H. Withers). London, Murray, 1931
BAUMOL, W.J. (1952). The Transactions Demand for Cash: An Inventory Theoretic Approach. *Quarterly Journal of Economics* **66**, 545–556
BODIN, J. (1568). *La Réponse de Jean Bodin à M. de Malestroit*. Repr. (ed. by H. Hauser). Paris, Armand Colin, 1932
BRUNNER, K. and MELTZER, A.H. (1967). Economies of Scale in Cash Balances Reconsidered. *Quarterly Journal of Economics* **81**, 422–436
CAIRNES, J.E. (1873). *Essays in Political Economy*. Repr. New York, A.M. Kelley, 1965
CANNAN, E. (1924). Limitation of Currency or Limitation of Credit? *Economic Journal* **34**, 52–64

CANTILLON, R. (1755). *Essai sur la Nature du Commerce en Général*. Repr. (trans. and ed. by H. Higgs), 143, 301–305. London, Cass, for the Royal Economic Society, 1959

CHRISTIERNIN, V.N. (1761). *Lectures on the High Price of Foreign Exchange in Sweden*. (Trans. and ed. by R.V. Eagly.) Philadelphia, American Philosophical Society, 1971

CLAYTON, G. (1962). British Financial Intermediaries in Theory and Practice. *Economic Journal* **72**, 869–886

COGHLAN, R. (1980). *The Theory of Money and Finance*. London, Macmillan

COGHLAN, R. and SYKES, C. (1980). Managing the Money Supply. *Lloyds Bank Review* **135**, 1–13

CRAMP, A.B. (1960). Radcliffe's Victorian Forebears. Liquidity and Money Supply in the 1850s. *The Banker* **110**, 593–599

CRICK, W.F. (1927). The Genesis of Bank Deposits. *Economica* **7**, 191–202

DAVIS, E. (1981). R.G. Hawtrey, 1879–1975. In *Pioneers of Modern Economics in Britain* (ed. by D.P. O'Brien and J.R. Presley), 203–233. London, Macmillan

DENNIS, G.E. (1981). *Monetary Economics*, pp. 178–201. London, Longman

DORFMAN, J. (1970). Some Documentary Notes on the Relations among J.M. Clark, N.A.L.J. Johannsen and J.M. Keynes. In *The Costs of the World War to the American People* (by J.M. Clark). Repr. New York, A.M. Kelley

DURBIN, E.F.M. (1935). *The Problem of Credit Policy*. London, Chapman and Hall

ENGLAND, M.T. (1912). Fisher's Theory of Crises: A Criticism. *Quarterly Journal of Economics* **27**, 95–106

ESHAG, E. (1963). *From Marshall to Keynes. An Essay on the Monetary Theory of the Cambridge School*. Oxford, Blackwell

FISHER, I. (1896). *Appreciation and Interest*. New York, Macmillan

FISHER, I. (1911). *The Purchasing Power of Money*, new edn. New York, Macmillan, 1920

FISHER, I. (1933). *Booms and Depressions*. London, Allen and Unwin

FOSTER, W.T. and CATCHINGS, W. (1924). *Money*. Boston, Houghton Mifflin

FOSTER, W.T. and CATCHINGS, W. (1928). *The Road to Plenty*. Boston, Houghton Mifflin

FRIEDMAN, M. (1969). *The Optimum Quantity of Money and other Essays*, pp. 58, 264. London, Macmillan

FRIEDMAN, M. (1970). A Theoretical Framework for Monetary Analysis. *Journal of Political Economy* **78**, 193–238

FRIEDMAN, M. (1971). A Monetary Theory of Nominal Income. *Journal of Political Economy* **79**, 323–337

FRIEDMAN, M. and SCHWARTZ, A.J. (1963). *A Monetary History of the United States 1867–1960*. Princeton, Princeton University Press

FRIEDMAN, M. and SCHWARTZ, A. (1969). The Definition of Money: Net Wealth and Neutrality as Criteria. *Journal of Money, Credit and Banking* **1**, 1–14

FULLARTON, J. (1845). *On the Regulation of Currencies*, pp. 44, 46–47, 2nd edn. Repr. New York, A.M. Kelley, 1969

GIFFEN, R. (1877). *Stock Exchange Securities*. London, Bell

GIFFEN, R. (1887). *Essays in Finance*, 2nd ser., 2nd edn. London, Bell

GOODHART, C. (1975). *Money, Information and Uncertainty*. London, Macmillan

GOSCHEN, G.J. (1864). *The Theory of the Foreign Exchanges*, 5th edn. London, Effingham Wilson

GURLEY, J.G. and SHAW, E.S. (1960). *Money in a Theory of Finance*. Washington, Brookings Institution

HABERLER, G.v. (1937). *Prosperity and Depression*. Geneva, League of Nations

HAWTREY, R.G. (1913). *Good and Bad Trade*. London, Constable

HAWTREY, R.G. (1919). *Currency and Credit*, 2nd edn 1923, 3rd edn 1928. London, Longman

HAWTREY, R.G. (1923). *Monetary Reconstruction*. London, Longman

HAWTREY, R.G. (1932). *The Art of Central Banking*. London, Longman

HAWTREY, R.G. (1938). *A Century of Bank Rate*. London, Longman

HAYEK, F.A.v. (1932). A Note on the Development of the Doctrine of 'Forced Saving'. *Quarterly Journal of Economics* **47**, 123–133

HAYEK, F.A.v. (1933). *Monetary Theory and the Trade Cycle*. London, Cape

HAYEK, F.A.v. (1935). *Prices and Production*. 2nd edn. London, Routledge

HEGELAND, H. (1954). *The Multiplier Theory*. Repr. New York, A.M. Kelley, 1966

HICKS, J.R. (1939). *Value and Capital*, 2nd edn. Oxford, The Clarendon Press, 1946

HICKS, J.R. (1967). *Critical Essays in Monetary Theory*. Oxford, The Clarendon Press

HICKS, J.R. (1969). Automatists, Hawtreyans, and Keynesians. *Journal of Money, Credit and Banking* **1**, 307–317

HOLTROP, M.W. (1929). Theories of the Velocity of Circulation of Money in Earlier Economic Literature. *Economic History* **I**, 503–524

HUGHES, J.R.T. (1960). *Fluctuations in Trade, Industry and Finance*. Oxford, The Clarendon Press

HUME, D. (1752). *Writings on Economics* (ed. by E. Rotwein), pp. 37–38. Edinburgh, Nelson, 1955

JAFFÉ, W. (1951). Walrasiana: the *Élements* and its Critics. *Econometrica* **19**, 327–328

JEVONS, W.S. (1875). *Money and the Mechanism of Exchange*, 23rd edn. London, Kegan Paul, 1910

JEVONS, W.S. (1884). *Investigations in Currency and Finance*. London, Macmillan

JOHNSON, H.G. (1969). Inside Money, Outside Money, Income, Wealth, and Welfare in Monetary Theory. *Journal of Money, Credit and Banking* **1**, 30–45

JOHNSON, H.G. (1970). Recent Developments in Monetary Theory—a Commentary. In *Money in Britain 1959–1969* (ed. by D.R. Croome and H.G. Johnson), pp. 83–114. Oxford, Oxford University Press

JOPLIN, T. (1844). *Currency Reform: Improvement not Depreciation*, p. 43. London, Richardson

KEYNES, J.M. (1911). Review of I. Fisher *The Purchasing Power of Money*. *Economic Journal* **21**, 393–398

KEYNES, J.M. (1923). *A Tract on Monetary Reform*. Repr. London, Macmillan, for the Royal Economic Society, 1971

KEYNES, J.M. (1924). A Comment on Professor Cannan's Article. *Economic Journal* **34**, 65–68

KEYNES, J.M. (1930). *A Treatise on Money*, 2 vols. Repr. London, Macmillan, for the Royal Economic Society, 1971

KEYNES, J.M. (1936). *The General Theory of Employment, Interest and Money*. Repr. London, Macmillan, for the Royal Economic Society, 1973

LAIDLER, D. (1969). The Definition of Money. Theoretical and Empirical Problems. *Journal of Money, Credit and Banking* **1**, 508–525

LAIDLER, D. (1973). *The Demand for Money*. Aylesbury, Intertext Books

LAVINGTON, F. (1911). The Social Importance of Banking. *Economic Journal* **21**, 53–60

LAVINGTON, F. (1921). *The English Capital Market*. London, Methuen

LAWRENCE, J.S. (1928a). Borrowed Reserves and Bank Expansion. *Quarterly Journal of Economics* **42**, 593–626

LAWRENCE, J.S. (1928b). *Stabilisation of Prices*, p. 368. New York, Macmillan

LEATHAM, W. (1840). *Letters on the Currency, Addressed to Charles Wood*. London, Richardson

LETWIN, W.O. (1963). *The Origins of Scientific Economics*. London, Methuen

LONGFIELD, M. (1840). Banking and Currency. *Dublin University Magazine*. Repr. in *Economic Writings* (ed. by R.D.C. Black). New York, A.M. Kelley, 1971

MACLEOD, H.D. (1863). *Dictionary of Political Economy*. London, Longman

MACLEOD, H.D. (1892–1893). *The Theory and Practice of Banking*, 5th edn, 2 vols. London, Longman

MARGET, A.W. (1931). Léon Walras and the 'Cash Balance' Approach to the Problem of the Value of Money. *Journal of Political Economy* **39**, 569–600

MARGET, A.W. (1935). The Monetary Aspects of the Walrasian System. *Journal of Political Economy* **43**, 145–186

MARGET, A.W. (1938–1942). *The Theory of Prices*, 2 vols. Repr. New York, A.M. Kelley, 1966

MARSHALL, A. and M.P. (1879). *The Economics of Industry*. Repr. London, Macmillan, 1888

MARSHALL, A. (1890). *Principles of Economics*, 9th (Variorum) edn. London, Macmillan, for the Royal Economic Society, 1961

MARSHALL, A. (1923). *Money, Credit and Commerce*, pp. 58, 59. London, Macmillan

MARSHALL, A. (1925). *Memorials of Alfred Marshall* (ed. by A.C. Pigou). London, Macmillan

MARSHALL, A. (1926). *Official Papers*. London, Macmillan

MARTIN, P.W. (1931). *The Problem of Maintaining Purchasing Power*, London, P. S. King

MILL, J. (1826). *Elements of Political Economy*, 3rd edn. Repr. in *Selected Economic Writings* (ed. by D. Winch). Edinburgh, Oliver and Boyd, 1966

MILL, J.S. (1844). *Essays on some Unsettled Questions of Political Economy*. Repr. London, London School of Economics, 1948

MILL, J.S. (1848). *Principles of Political Economy with some of their Applications to Social Philosophy* (ed. by W.J. Ashley). London, Longman, 1923

MISES, L.v. (1912). *The Theory of Money and Credit*, trans. H.E. Batson, p. 61. London, Cape, 1934

MITCHELL, W.C. (1928). *Business Cycles*. New York, National Bureau of Economic Research

MORGAN, E.V. (1969). The Essential Qualities of Money. *Manchester School* **37**, 237–248

MYRDAL, G. (1933). *Monetary Equilibrium*, trans. 1939. Repr. New York, A.M. Kelley, 1965

NEMMERS, E.E. (1956). *Hobson and Underconsumption*. Repr. New York, A.M. Kelley, 1972

NEWMARCH, W. (1857). *A History of Prices and of the State of the Circulation*, Vols V and VI (with T. Tooke). Repr. London, P.S. King, 1928

NORMAN, G.W. (1841). *Letter to Charles Wood, Esq., M.P. on Money and the Means of Economizing the Use of It*. London, Pelham Richardson

O'BRIEN, D.P. (1970). *J.R. McCulloch. A Study in Classical Economics*. London, Allen and Unwin

O'BRIEN, D.P. (1971). Introduction. In *The Correspondence of Lord Overstone* (Vol. I, pp. 1–144). Cambridge, Cambridge University Press

O'BRIEN, D.P. (1975). *The Classical Economists*. Oxford, The Clarendon Press

O'BRIEN, D.P. and DARNELL, A.C. (1982). *Authorship Puzzles in the History of Economics*. London, Macmillan

OVERSTONE, LORD (1857). *Tracts and other Publications on Metallic and Paper Currency*. London, privately printed

OVERSTONE, LORD (1971). *The Correspondence of Lord Overstone* (ed. by D.P. O'Brien), 3 vols. Cambridge, Cambridge University Press

PENNINGTON, J. (1829). Paper Communicated by Mr Pennington. In *A Letter to Lord Grenville* (by T. Tooke), pp. 117–127. London, Murray

PENNINGTON, J. (1838). Letter Addressed to the Author by James Pennington, Esq. In Tooke, T. (1838–1857) *History of Prices*, Vol. II, pp. 369–378

PESEK, B.P. and SAVING, T.R. (1967). *Money, Wealth, and Economic Theory*. New York, Macmillan

PETTY, SIR. W. (1899). *Economic Writings* (ed. by C.H. Hull). Cambridge, Cambridge University Press

PHILLIPS, C.A. (1921). *Bank Credit: A Study of the Principles and Factors underlying Advances made by Banks to Borrowers*. New York, Macmillan, 1926

PIGOU, A.C. (1917). The Value of Money. *Quarterly Journal of Economics* **32**, 38–65

PIGOU, A.C. (1923). *Essays in Applied Economics*. London, P.S. King

PIGOU, A.C. (1927). *Industrial Fluctuations*. London, Macmillan

PRESLEY, J.R. (1979). *Robertsonian Economics*. London, Macmillan

RADCLIFFE COMMITTEE (1959). *Report of the Committee on the Working of the Monetary System*, pp. 132, 135, 337. London, HMSO

RICARDO, D. (1951–1973). *Works and Correspondence*, 11 vols (ed. by P. Sraffa with M.H. Dobb). Cambridge, Cambridge University Press

ROBBINS, LORD (1958). *Robert Torrens and the Evolution of Classical Economics*. London, Macmillan

ROBERTSON, D.H. (1915). *A Study of Industrial Fluctuation*. Repr. London, London School of Economics, 1948

ROBERTSON, D.H. (1922). *Money*. London, Nisbett

ROBERTSON, D.H. (1926). *Banking Policy and the Price Level*, rev. edn. London, P.S. King, 1932

ROBERTSON, D.H. (1928). *Money*. Repr. London, Nisbett, 1946

ROBERTSON, D.H. (1940). *Essays in Monetary Theory*. London, P.S. King

ROBERTSON, D.H. (1948). New Introduction. In reprint of Robertson (1915), pp. vii–xvii.

ROBERTSON, D.H. (1963). *Lectures on Economic Principles*, 1 vol. London, Collins

ROTWEIN, E. (1955). Introduction. In *David Hume. Writings on Economics*, pp. ix–cxii. Edinburgh, Nelson, 1955

SAYERS, R.S. (1963). The Life and Work of James Pennington. In *Economic Writings of James Pennington*, pp. ix–xliv. London, London School of Economics

SENIOR, N.W. (1827–1840). *Three Lectures on the Value of Money*. Repr. in *Selected Writings on Economics*. New York, A.M. Kelley, 1966

SENIOR, N.W. (1829–1830). *Three Lectures on the Cost of Obtaining Money*. Repr. in *Selected Economic Writings*. New York, A.M. Kelley, 1966

SHACKLE, G.L.S. (1967). *The Years of High Theory*. Cambridge, Cambridge University Press

SIDGWICK, H. (1887). *The Principles of Political Economy*, 2nd edn. London, Macmillan

SMITH, A. (1776). *An Inquiry into the Nature and Causes of the Wealth of Nations* (ed. by E. Cannan). Repr. Chicago, University of Chicago Press, 1976. Readers should note that the pagination of this reprint does *not* correspond to the pagination of the Methuen *hardback* printing of the Cannan edition, which is the one most commonly cited.

SPRENKLE, C.M. (1969). Laidler's 'The Definition of Money', A Comment. *Journal of Money, Credit and Banking* **1**, 526–530

THORNTON, H. (1802). *An Enquiry into the Nature and Effects of the Paper Credit of Great Britain* (ed. by F.A. v. Hayek). London, Allen and Unwin, 1939

TOBIN, J. (1956). The Interest-elasticity of the Transactions Demand for Cash. *Review of Economics and Statistics* **38**, 241–247

TOBIN, J. (1958). Liquidity-preference as Behaviour towards Risk. *Review of Economic Studies* **25**, 65–86

TOBIN, J. (1963). Commercial Banks as Creators of Money. In *Banking and Monetary Studies* (ed. by D. Carson), pp. 408–419. Homewood, Ill., R.D. Irwin

TOBIN, J. (1965). The Theory of Portfolio Selection. In *The Theory of Interest Rates* (ed. by F. Hahn and F. Brechling), pp. 3–51. London, Macmillan

TOOKE, T. (1826). *Considerations on the State of the Currency*, 2nd edn. London, Murray

TOOKE, T. (1829). *A Letter to Lord Grenville on the Effects Ascribed to the Resumption of Cash Payments on the Value of the Currency*. London, Murray

TOOKE, T. (1838–1857). *A History of Prices and of the State of the Circulation from 1792 to 1856*, with W. Newmarch, 6 vols. Repr. London, P.S. King, 1928

TOOKE, T. (1844). *An Inquiry into the Currency Principle: the Connection of the Currency with Prices, and the Expediency of a Separation of Issue from Banking*, pp. 26–27, 31. London, Longman

TOOKE, T. (1856). *On the Bank Charter Act of 1844, its Principles and Operation*. London, Longman

TORRENS, R. (1837). *A Letter to the Right Honourable Lord Viscount Melbourne on the Causes of the Recent Derangement in the Money Market and on Bank Reform*. London, Longman

WADSWORTH, J.E. (1968). Banking Ratios Past and Present. In *Essays in Money and Banking* (ed. by C.R. Whittlesey and J.S.G. Wilson), pp. 229–251. Oxford, The Clarendon Press

WICKSELL, K. (1898). *Interest and Prices* (trans. R.F. Kahn). London, Macmillan, 1936

WICKSELL, K. (1906). *Lectures on Political Economy. Vol. 2, Money* (ed. by L. Robbins), pp. 6, 24, 142, 145. London, Routledge, 1935

WOOD, E. (1939). *English Theories of Central Banking Control 1819–58*. Cambridge, Mass., Harvard University Press

WRIGHT, A.H. (1956). The Genesis of the Multiplier Theory. *Oxford Economic Papers* **8**, 181–193

YEAGER, L.B. (1968). Essential Properties of the Medium of Exchange. *Kyklos* **21**, 45–69

Chapter Three

Welfare Economics

R.F. Hébert and R.B. Ekelund

3.1 Introduction

3.1.1 THE NATURE OF WELFARE ECONOMICS

Writing in 1776, Adam Smith confidently asserted that each individual, pursuing his own self-interest, was led as if by an invisible hand to promote the general welfare of all. As a rule, modern economists are much less sanguine about the 'automatic' prospects of social welfare, but the point is that the concern for collective well-being is practically as old as economics itself. In the days of the classical economists—Smith being the most prominent, but by no means the only one—economics was conceived in terms of 'political economy', which Smith defined as a branch of the art of legislation. In other words, the whole body of economics centred on the welfare problem. This point of view was sustained by Jeremy Bentham, the high priest of utilitarianism, and by his brilliant disciple, John Stuart Mill, whose writings formed the capstone of classical economics. Incremental improvements in analytical technique during the period notwithstanding, the driving force of classical economic theory seems to have been the establishment of principles capable of guiding economic policy.

Welfare economics may therefore be defined, with Scitovsky (1951), as that part of the general body of economic theory that is concerned primarily with policy. Although this kind of distinction would not have been necessary during the heyday of classical economics, the neoclassical period that began near the end of the nineteenth century was marked by a conscious retreat from open policy pronouncements and a concomitant move toward 'value-free' economic analysis. This is not to say that welfare economics was ignored in the neoclassical tradition, merely that it became compartmentalized into a subset of general economics. Partly as a result of intellectual division of labour and partly as a consequence of the desire to emulate the physical sciences, economists in the twentieth century have attempted to dichotomize their discipline into 'positive' and 'normative' domains. The former is analytical and descriptive in an ethically neutral sense—that is, without regard to specific value judgements. By contrast, the latter is intricately tied up with value judgements. Although in practice a clean division between these two is difficult to achieve, economists readily admit that welfare economics falls within the normative branch of economics.

3.1.2 WELFARE ECONOMICS AND VALUE JUDGEMENTS

Due to the somewhat controversial nature of what constitutes a value judgement, this chapter adopts the broad definition that a value judgement implies a recommendation of some kind (Nath, 1969). This definition covers all ethical judgements plus statements that may appear to be descriptive but are in certain contexts either persuasive or influential. The following statements are examples of value judgements: 'Redheads are hot-tempered'; 'the existing income distribution is unfair'; 'Russians make poor lovers'; and 'monopolies need to be regulated'. Each of these statements reflects an opinion that is not necessarily shared by all members of society; furthermore, each statement is not conducive to testing its validity in the strict, scientific sense. Positive economics, by contrast, confines itself to propositions that do submit readily to testing in an objective sense.

Value judgements are basic to welfare economics for a number of reasons. The first is that, as we have already seen, welfare economics confines itself to that branch of economics that deals with policy. Policy is, by its very nature, normative. No social prescriptions can ever be made without resort, either explicitly or implicitly, to some notion of what is beneficial or desirable. Policy must conform to the attainment of some social objective, which, by its very nature, is subjective. The second reason is that welfare economics deals with the rank ordering of social preferences. A basic notion in welfare economics is the social welfare function. In a loose sense, the social welfare function is a statement of the objectives of a society. But who decides what these objectives are? The answer is that either one member of the society (e.g. a dictator), every member of society (a pure democracy) or some part of society (e.g. a representative democracy) must choose, and to the extent that different tastes and values obtain, the choice is likely to be arbitrary. Moreover, the shape of the social welfare function depends on the relative weights attached to each individual's preferences when these are incorporated into the social preference function. Although it may seem intuitively desirable to give everyone's preferences equal weight, it is not at all clear that this should be the case. But even if it were, to determine the shape of the social welfare function would still involve a value judgement, namely the choice of a weighting scheme. The third reason, perhaps the most basic, is that welfare itself is an ethical concept. The language of welfare economics openly embraces subjective terms, such as welfare, utility, satisfaction, bliss. There is no objective way to measure these 'magnitudes' the way science can measure, for example, rainfall or a magnetic field.

3.1.3 THE PLAN OF THE CHAPTER

There are two distinct trends in welfare economics—the Pigovian and the Paretian. The first takes its name from A.C. Pigou (1877–1959), whose standard work on the subject was first published in 1920. The second takes its name from Vilfredo Pareto (1848–1923), whose major writings were published near the turn of the century. The two approaches have somewhat different ethical preconceptions, but their analytical structure is basically the same. An important difference, however, is that Pigovian welfare theory follows the partial equilibrium method endorsed by Alfred Marshall (Pigou's teacher at Cambridge), whereas Paretian welfare theory was inspired by the general equilibrium approach of Pareto's mentor at the University of Lausanne, Léon Walras. These distinctly British and European roots, respectively, played a role in shaping the concerns and emphases of the two independent strands of welfare theory.

This chapter is a concerted effort to trace the history of welfare economics from its roots in classical political economy to the present time. More attention is paid to the early period of welfare analysis for two reasons. The first is that the period prior to the twentieth century is far richer in 'sophisticated' analysis than is commonly recognized. The second is that the individual contributions of this period and their fundamental continuity have tended to be neglected in the literature on welfare economics.

The plan of presentation is as follows. Section 3.2 traces the early history of welfare economics that stretches roughly from Adam Smith to John Stuart Mill. Space constraints permit us only a broad sweep of major ideas and trends, but we have tried to stress the continuity of ideas and their filiations among and between different writers. Section 3.3 treats more modern concerns among welfare theorists, specifically the development and consequences of the theory of consumer's surplus. It is within this tradition that the Pigovian approach asserts itself most forcefully and that the Swedish tradition in welfare theory developed. Other issues that have occupied the attention of modern welfare theorists include the measurement of welfare and the development of various pricing rules to ensure allocative efficiency. These issues are also discussed in section 3.3 and their impact is traced on the development of modern welfare economics. Since most of the contemporary work in welfare economics is in the Paretian tradition, section 3.4 takes up some of the present issues that pose threats to the attainment of Pareto-optimal levels of economic welfare and examines proposed theoretical solutions. Compensation tests, social welfare functions and the problem of market failure form the chief concerns of this section. Finally, section 3.5 examines the politics of social choice, assesses the present condition of welfare economics, and tentatively judges its future prospects.

3.2 Welfare economics in the classical paradigm

By and large the classical economists, from Smith to Mill, conceived the economic problem as the struggle of man against nature in producing material wealth. Classical economic analysis was consequently based on a fundamental contrast between natural resources, taken as fixed, and labour, which was augmentable. It proceeded on a physical level to examine the means to increase material wealth either by increasing the supply of labour or by raising its physical productivity. Adam Smith, who cast the mould for the classical paradigm, emphasized the importance of capital accumulation and division of labour in augmenting labour's output and hence the material well-being of society. Beginning with a technical concept of production as the transformation of natural resources into physical products, Smith (1776, in 1937) placed division of labour at the centre of his theory. He laid it down as the most vigorous means of increasing the size of the national dividend. Thus he wrote:

> The annual labour of every nation is the fund which originally supplies it with all the necessaries and conveniencies of life which it annually consumes, and which consist always either in the immediate produce of that labour, or in what is purchased with that produce from other nations, Vol. I, p. 1.

And further:

> The greatest improvement in the productive powers of labour, and the greater part of the skill, dexterity, and judgment with which it is any where directed or applied, seem to have been the effects of the division of labour, 1776, Vol. I, p.1.

It is from such a view of economic welfare that Smith derived his basic criterion of economic policy: it should promote the growth of the annual produce of labour. Certain passages from the *Wealth of Nations* may suggest, especially to the neoclassical mind, that Smith's notion of economic welfare rests on the purely subjective gains that consumers derive from free exchange. For example, the primacy of consumption is laid down in the following passage:

> Consumption is the sole end and purpose of all production; and the interest of
> the producer ought to be attended to only so far as it may be necessary for
> promoting that of the consumer. The maxim is so self-evident, that it would be
> absurd to attempt to prove it, 1776, Vol. II, p. 179.

Furthermore, Smith was sensitive to subjective consumers' gains in
the modern sense. He noted that exchange 'gives a value to ...
superfluities by exchanging them for something else which may satisfy
a part of their [i.e., consumers'] wants and increase their enjoyments'.
But the importance of consumers' satisfactions notwithstanding,
Smith's analysis rested on the assumption that, barring shortage or
glut, consumers derive satisfaction from a commodity roughly in
proportion to its intrinsic physical properties (i.e. its 'value-in-use'),
so that magnitudes of satisfaction are more or less commensurate with
quantities of physical products. It is this notion of economic welfare,
rather than the alternative conception of allocative efficiency among
consumers and producers within a given productive framework, that
pervaded classical economics.

Following Smith, the aim of economic policy was to increase the
absolute level of social production. Incidentally, Smith's desire for
free trade finds its most logical expression in this context. Free trade,
he felt, would serve to increase physical productivity by widening the
scope of the division of labour and by bringing fresh natural resources
into the framework of production. Capital accumulation would
subsequently expand the opportunities for new divisions of labour,
without which the new investment opportunities offered by a greater
freedom of trade could not be exercised. Thus Myint (1948) is correct
when he suggests that for Smith 'free trade is a method of expanding
the economic horizon horizontally so as to reap the advantages of
increasing physical returns brought about by overcoming the technical indivisibilities of production'.

What Smith did not count on, but what his followers discovered, is
that production under increasing returns is apt to be the exception
rather than the rule. The impact of Ricardo, Malthus and the others
who discovered the principle of diminishing returns was to shift the
focus of economic policy toward measures to increase the *net* social
product rather than the absolute scale of output. The difference is
important. As long as economic welfare is synonymous with increased
output, a system of free and open exchange exists, and there are no
limits to the growth process. Economic progress implies unambiguous
gains in economic welfare for all members of society. Smith's analysis
implied as much, and because of it, he did not look deeply into the
effects of economic growth on the distribution of material products
among different resource owners in society.

The Ricardian theory of distribution curbed Smith's optimism by
showing that diminishing returns served to limit the growth of

population and of capital. Adopting for the moment Ricardo's expository device of considering society to be one giant firm that employs a single variable factor, labour, and produces a single commodity called 'corn', his argument reduces to the following terms. The increase in population brought about by progressive capital accumulation would extend the margin of cultivation to less fertile land, where a larger quantity of labour would be required to produce a standard measure of 'corn'. The price of output, reflected by higher production costs, would therefore rise, so that the owners of better-grade land would claim a higher rent than before. Since real wages could not permanently fall below the minimum subsistence level, money wages would rise, which would have the effect of lowering the rate of profit. Economic expansion would cease when the marginal product of labour had fallen so low as to leave nothing for the capitalists after wages and rents had been paid, because at this point there would be no further incentive for the capitalist either to accumulate capital or employ labour to increase production. On the strength of this argument, emphasis shifted from the absolute scale of social output to the social *net product*, which increases at a diminishing rate as the scale of production rises. Ricardo and his followers inferred that it was not enough to explain welfare in terms of aggregate gross revenue, as Smith had done. What was also required was to determine how much 'corn' was left after the expenses of production (i.e. wages) had been paid. This new viewpoint recognized that there were many different populations that were capable of producing the same net real income, rents and profits. Thus for any given level of labour productivity, the size of a nation's population was no longer an index of its wealth or welfare.

Although he was a co-discoverer of the principle of diminishing returns, Malthus was outside the mainstream of Ricardian orthodoxy. His contribution to the classical discussion of welfare was nevertheless important. It consisted in showing that society must be studied not only as a giant producing unit but also as a giant *consuming* unit. Unlike Ricardo and his followers, Malthus denied the automatic synchronization of society's capacity to produce with its capacity to consume. He believed that attempts to expand economic output by capital accumulation would break down because of oversupply long before the extreme limit of Ricardo's stationary state was reached. Malthus approached the notion of economic welfare within the context of effective demand rather than Ricardo's physical output approach, but in the end this merely served to shift attention to the savings–investment nexus rather than the subject of allocative efficiency in the consumption–production processes. The glut controversy, moreover, remained a burning issue well into the time of John Stuart Mill.

In the heyday of Mill's influence, technological considerations became dominant, a fact demonstrated by the celebrated arrangement of topics in his *Principles of Political Economy*. There Mill divided economics into areas of Production, Distribution and Exchange, in that order. The assertion on which the first branch of economics rests is that the size of the national product depends entirely on technology and the laws governing changes in the supply of productive factor. For their parts, Distribution and Exchange do not affect the size of the national product. Each plays the ancillary role of parcelling out a predetermined block of wealth among different groups or individuals according to the prevailing system of economic organization.

Although Karl Marx is not usually placed in the pantheon of classical economists, there is a paradoxically strong common bond between the two. Starting from classical premises, Marx ranged far afield and concluded his analysis with a denial of the proposition that a *laissez-faire*, competitive economy tends to maximize social welfare. But the 'materialist' bias of early welfare theory permeated Marx's entire effort. This is nowhere more evident than in his extension of the labour theory of value to the extreme. For Marx, value was an *objective* property that had to be rooted in something more substantial than the 'superficial' market forces of supply and demand. Consequently, purely subjective valuations (e.g. utility considerations) were as conspicuously absent from the Marxian framework as they were subsequently obtrusive in the neoclassical approach. The quantity of material wealth remained an important maximand for Marx as for the classical economists, but Marx was more preoccupied with the question of wealth distribution and the issue of inherent contradictions in capitalist society.

Despite his massive influence on political and social theory, Marx's impact on economic analysis was highly restricted. In the 1870s economics took a decidedly subjectivist turn as it was reconstructed on the twin pillars of utility and the mathematical concept of the margin. The new approach shunned questions of economic growth *per se* and concentrated instead on the question of allocative efficiency in a regimen of fixed resources. Besides a basic reorientation of value theory, the neoclassical approach spawned a new conception of economic welfare. Welfare became divorced from the mere notion of physical goods and reoriented toward considerations of 'satisfaction' and 'utility'—decidedly subjective maximands. The earliest and most impressive advances in this direction were made at the most unlikely of places, the School of Civil Engineering in Paris.

3.3 Post-classical developments in welfare economics

3.3.1 UTILITY THEORY: THE BEGINNINGS

While the roots of all economics, including welfare economics, may be said to have sprung from the concerns of the early English classical writers, refinements taking place in the post-classical era led to the emergence of welfare economics in its contemporary form. The great breakthrough was the specification and understanding of the significance of the concept of utility. Just as fuzzy and inaccurate prevailing notions of the word 'demand' were finally brought into focus by Augustin Cournot in 1838, the evolution and refinement of utility theory from its Latin meaning (*uti* = use or usefulness), through the Benthamite philosophical notion (utilitarianism) to its ultimate post-classical meaning of 'a subjective quantity of satisfaction' took numerous decades of polishing by able and, sometimes, not so able hands. Importantly, however, the subjective theory of utility forms the basis of virtually all branches of neoclassical and modern welfare economics. These branches shall be considered in detail following a brief categorization and outline of their origin.

The idea that there is a connection between utility and value was debated as early as Greek times. Medieval scholars were part of a lively tradition interrelating costs of production, utility and subjective notions of 'justice'. Smith's *Wealth of Nations* contained less vague notions of utility and its relation to price, although he did not at that time, with the mere concept of *total* utility, unlock the paradox that some goods (water) possess great value in use but low value in exchange, while others (diamonds) have small use value but enormous value in exchange[1].

The philosopher Jeremy Bentham took another tack. His *philosophy* of utilitarianism emphasized the importance of achieving aggregate welfare. This measure—the greatest good for the greatest number—could only be produced, in Bentham's view, by legal and/or legislative enactments to correct perceived market failures, or what today would be called 'externalities'. Specifically, property rights could be defined to set up artificial identities of interests, rather than rely on Smith's natural identity of interests to maximize social welfare[2]. It is noteworthy that Bentham was the earliest thinker of the classical era to question the welfare-maximizing property of *laissez-faire* as a guiding principle of market organization.

All post-classical and contemporary developments in welfare economics are therefore of two fundamental origins: (1) the development of subjective utility theory as the foundation of a theory of value, *including* the development of the marginal utility concept, and the consequent unlocking of the water–diamond paradox; and (2) the refinement and application of Bentham's utilitarian precepts and his suggestion, mainly through philosophical premises, that competitive markets and free exchange might not lead to global welfare maximization in society. These two developments, sometimes interrelated, spawned two distinct traditions in welfare economics, as noted in the introduction: the first, a Franco–Anglo-Saxon or 'partial equilibrium' development, and the second, a Paretian or 'general equilibrium' approach to welfare theory.

The Franco–Anglo-Saxon tradition in welfare theory is itself two 'traditions', both concerned with microanalytic developments in *particular markets*. More importantly, both employ a partial equilibrium framework.

The first line of theoretical development expanded upon Bentham's (1790) philosophical hint that free competition might not maximize efficiency or welfare. Bentham's early disciples, J.S. Mill, Henry Sidgwick and Edwin Chadwick toyed with concepts of externalities and market failure in certain industries, proposing a number of alternative methods of dealing with them. This continuing, and almost exclusively British, concern found its way, blended with subjective value theory, into Marshall's *Principles* (1890), although Marshall did not give market failure a central role in his text. Pigou (1912, 1920) amplified these 'Marshallian' welfare developments, inducing, four decades later, Ronald Coase's (1960) famous reaction to the problem of social cost. Much contemporary literature has in turn been nurtured by these ideas.

A second, and interrelated, reaction to the discovery of subjective marginal utility theory centred on an early tradition in public finance. This development emphasized problem-solving in terms of partial equilibrium, static analysis. French economists of the early nineteenth century originated this approach by the invention of subjective marginal utility theory and by the identification of marginal utility curves with individual and market demand curves. As is well known, the marginal utility theory of value gained wider acceptance as the nineteenth century wore on, both on the Continent and in England, in the writings of such economists as W. Stanley Jevons (1871), Léon Walras (1874), Alfred Marshall (1890) and Maffeo Pantaleoni (1898). The distinguishing feature of this second approach was the assessment of the effects of taxation or of particular kinds of market arrangements and institutions upon economic welfare in a partial equilibrium context. Welfare assessments of various types of taxation, of the effects of monopoly and price discrimination, and of marginal cost pricing constitute this tradition, and contemporary applications of cost–benefit analysis in particular markets and under particular sets of institutions have been spawned by the same concerns. Key figures in the development of this problem-solving approach include Jules Dupuit, Alfred Marshall, A.C. Pigou and Harold Hotelling. This approach is closely related to the one emphasizing market failure in that its emphasis is upon 'what can be done' when ubiquitous competitive conditions do not exist (as in the case of 'natural' monopoly). It differs from the externalities paradigm, however, in the emphasis it places upon the actual measurability or approximation of 'benefits'. The tradition rests, in other words, upon the invention of subjective utility theory rather than upon Benthamite philosophical distinctions of private versus social costs and benefits. Elements of both approaches, however, and their propagation, are found in the works of Marshall and Pigou.

A second major line of contemporary welfare theory also derives from early subjective utility theory but it is general equilibrium in character. This second variant combined utility theory with Léon Walras's famous contribution, which emphasized the welfare-maximizing properties of an integrated system of interrelated demanders and suppliers. Walras investigated the abilities of a competitive system to produce global equilibrium in a pure exchange model constrained by fixed inputs and individual utility functions. Building upon Walras's elegant structure, Vilfredo Pareto derived criteria for examining a social welfare function and for assessing the effects of aggregate changes in welfare.

A number of modern threads in welfare economics have developed from this theoretical perspective and can be found in the writings of such contemporary economists as Nicholas Kaldor, Tibor Scitovsky, James Meade, I.M.D. Little, Abram Bergson, Paul Samuelson and others, where the existence and legitimacy of a social welfare function is questioned and debated. Scandinavian and Italian economists such as Knut Wicksell, Erik Lindahl and Ugo Mazzola placed fiscal theory within the context of a broad structure of Walrasian interdependencies. The development of group decision rules, as in voting rules and constitution construction, is a large part of the contemporary quest to discover the impact of institutional structure upon aggregate welfare. In short, the Walrasian–Paretian tradition, spawned by the marriage of nineteenth-century subjective utility theory with general equilibrium interdependencies, has stimulated numerous inquiries into the nature of aggregate welfare and into how it might be produced and maximized.

Since the major branches of welfare theory developed concurrently, the order of discussion is somewhat arbitrary. In the following section we emphasize the impact of utility and demand upon partial-equilibrium welfare theory, reserving details of other developments for later sections of this chapter.

3.3.2 CONSUMERS' SURPLUS AND ITS APPLICATIONS

The long, complex, and tortuous origin of partial-equilibrium welfare theory was two-pronged. It required an understanding of the functioning and the effects of a competitive system and the resolution of the water–diamond paradox by resort to a theory of marginal utility. Both of these discoveries emerged, in effect, through the 'back door', on French soil, at the Ecole des Ponts et Chaussées.

The Ecole was an invention of the Corps des Ponts et Chaussées, which was instituted in 1716 under the regency of the Duc d'Orléans to supervise state projects. Given its official name by Turgot in 1775, the Ecole began instruction in 1747 under the direction of the French engineer Trudaine. One authority described it as 'the first well-organized school of civil engineering in the modern world' (Artz, 1966). Through its doors passed the most capable engineers of the eighteenth and nineteenth centuries, including selected students from foreign countries such as Austria, Great Britain and the United States.

The official journal of the Ecole—the *Annales des Ponts et Chaussées*—began publication in 1831 and, from the beginning, contained important articles relating to public works and to the measure of their economic value (Ekelund and Hébert, 1973). Prominent engineers, such as Henri Navier (1832) and Joseph Minard (1850), were proposing measures of the costs and benefits of specific public goods, e.g. bridges, highways, canals, and railroads, early in the nineteenth century. These first measures of 'public utility' were unsatisfactory for basically two reasons: (1) they relied upon a cost of production theory of value—one generally appropriate to a market of pure or perfect competition in the long run and not to the public works or public goods markets, that were the usual object of investigation, and (2) no theory of diminishing marginal utility was attached to the demand for public works, so that no adequate measure of 'benefits' could be derived. Jules Dupuit (1844, 1853) eventually filled these two voids and, in the process, supplied the foundations of modern welfare economics.

Dupuit (1844) believed that all earlier utility theories, including those advanced by Navier, were 'vague, incomplete, and often inaccurate', and consequently of little value in the measurement of public welfare. Accordingly, he set out to reshape the concept of utility into a tool of practical import. His sharpest criticisms were directed against Adam Smith's French disciple, J.B. Say. The major issue concerned the meaning of the word utility. Say defined utility as the 'faculty which things possess to be able to serve man in any possible way', and price as 'the measure of the utility which men judge the thing to have'. He further held that 'this price is the basis of the *demand* for products and consequently of their value' (quoted in Dupuit, 1844, 1853). But Say thought that value could not exceed costs of production, for if it did, it would pay the consumer to produce it for himself. In sum, utility was the basis for demand and value, and price (or value in exchange) was the measure of a commodity's utility, the stand taken by earlier writers such as Navier. Say approved and accepted Smith's distinction in the *Wealth of Nations* between value in use and value in exchange which amounted to asserting that *all* goods could not be treated under one theory of value.

Dupuit countered with the idea that the measure of the utility of any given quantity of a good was the maximum price consumers would be willing to offer for it. Utility was not synonymous with value in his view, it was merely one element of value. In Dupuit's (1853) words:

> ...utility and value are two different properties not independent, but having between them a coupled relationship in which enters another circumstance, which is rarity. In order for something to have value, two essential conditions are necessary: first, that it be useful...; second, that it not be in such great quantity as to satisfy completely all desires.

The solution to the water–diamond paradox was at hand; utility and scarcity provided the key. The exchange value of diamonds was high because quantity was restricted so that 'only those who are disposed to make the greatest sacrifices' could afford to procure them. Dupuit thus showed that water and diamonds both follow the same law of exchange value. This solution to the paradox of value was critical to the development of welfare economics because it enabled Dupuit to (1) give a starring role to marginal utility in price determination; (2) identify the marginal utility schedule with the demand curve; and (3) discover consumers' surplus and apply it to the solution of partial equilibrium welfare problems. These strikingly original insights, and Alfred Marshall's amendments, placed the theory of welfare economics on firm analytical ground.

3.3.3 MEASUREMENT PROBLEMS IN EARLY WELFARE ANALYSIS

To Dupuit and Marshall, consumers' surplus was the money measure of the difference between the price that the consumers would be willing to pay for a given quantity of a good and the price that the consumers actually pay for that quantity of the good. Marshall hedged this measure with protective assumptions, but his *concept* was identical to Dupuit's. *Figure 3.1*—Dupuit's (1844) demand curve, with

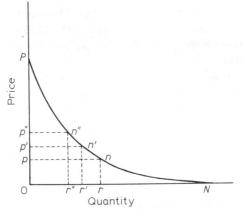

Figure 3.1 The demand curve as a welfare measure

axes reversed here for convenience—provides illustration of this measure.

Dupuit argued that the total utility of Or'' articles is equal to the area $(Or''n''P)$ under the demand curve. He defined this measure as absolute utility. From this quantum Dupuit deducted cost of production, which is represented by the price of the article multiplied by quantity consumed, or the area $Or''n''p''$. Dupuit's *relative utility*, or what is now called consumers' surplus, which accrued to consumers, is the difference between absolute utility and 'costs of production'. With reference to *Figure 3.1*, consumers' surplus is equal to the triangular area $p''n''P$, the difference between the amount of money that consumers would be willing to pay for r'' units of the commodity and the amount that they actually pay for r'' units.

To Dupuit (1853), the utility under any demand curve is 'always separated into three parts; the utility collected by the proprietor [total receipts or cost of production], the utility collected by the public [consumers' surplus], and lost utility'. At quantity Or'' in *Figure 3.1*, lost utility is represented by the triangle $Nn''r''$. Alternatively, it can be found by subtracting the area representing absolute utility from the total area under the demand curve.

A change in consumers' surplus could be calculated, according to Dupuit, in the following manner: assume that price falls from p'' to p' and that quantity taken increases from r'' to r'. After the price decline (i.e. drop in 'cost of production'), absolute utility is increased to $Or'n'P$, and this, less costs of production, $Op'n'r'$, yields a total consumers' surplus of $p'Pn'$, or a *net* gain in consumers' surplus represented by $p'n'n''p''$.

In this way Dupuit developed his measure of the utility (or 'benefit') of public works and of goods in general. Welfare became an area under a demand curve *identified* with a utility curve.

This identification and the definition of the money measure of consumers' surplus made its way into Marshall's *Principles*. We may, therefore, take Dupuit's measure as Marshall's so long as Marshall's protective assumptions are understood. These are best appreciated in the context of the welfare measurement problems that afflicted both Dupuit's and Marshall's measure. Indeed, some of the problems are inherent in any money measure of welfare benefits. Consequently, they must be dealt with in contemporary applications of the tool. Two major problems are: (1) the issue of 'additive' utility functions, and (2) the issue of measurability for the individual consumer.

The first issue centres on the so-called 'problem of the apostrophe'. Consumer's surplus implies an individual measure; consumers' surplus an aggregate measure. Demand curves may be added horizontally for all consumers of a product or service. But utility curves, whether or not identified with demand curves, cannot legitimately be added together in order to construct welfare measures. Such an addition is said to involve an illegitimate *interpersonal utility judgement*.

Since utility is a subjective quantum, either cardinal or ordinal measures will vary from individual to individual. Because incomes and other factors (tastes, etc.) vary from individual to individual, demand prices cannot be counted upon to carry the same 'utility weight' among individual demanders. A source of error is therefore introduced when money measures of consumer's surplus are calculated using market demand curves. This criticism does not deny the existence of a utility surplus; it simply means that money expenditures cannot be used to measure it accurately.

Dupuit (1844) attempted to handle this problem by noting that incomes were stratified, and that the utility within different classes of consumers of specific goods was enough alike to get meaningful measures. In other passages he maintained that income distribution did not matter with respect to utility calculations and that it was not in the province of political economy, but was the proper concern of the state. 'Because the losses and gains counterbalance each other,' said Dupuit (1844), changes in the distribution of wealth are not to be considered in utility calculations.

Marshall was more circumspect in recognizing the problem, but his defence was technically as inadequate as Dupuit's. In his chapter on consumers' surplus Marshall (1890) not only claimed that utility was measurable but was unreservedly prepared to make interpersonal comparisons (although there are passages elsewhere which seem to contradict this view). One passage in particular claims:

> On the whole ... it happens that by far the greater number of the events with which economics deals, affect in about equal proportions all the different classes of society; so that if the money measures of the happiness caused by two events are equal, there is not in general any very great difference between the amounts of happiness in the two cases. And it is on account of this fact that the exact measurement of the consumers' surplus in a market has already much theoretical interest, and may become of high practical importance (p. 131).

Thus Marshall had few qualms concerning utility measurement. It is equally obvious from the position of the apostrophe in 'consumers'', that Marshall, like his predecessor Dupuit, was not above interpersonal utility additions or comparisons. From a technical perspective, none of these 'defences' yields an accurate money measure of utility[3]. From a practical point of view, money measures are still used, are a great convenience to the economist and are defensible as approximations of benefits (Winch, 1965).

The measurability problem persists when calculating welfare measures from an individual's demand curve. If *money* income is held constant, as in the traditional Marshallian demand curve, *real* income will vary as the price of a good varies in partial equilibrium. A changing real income means that the marginal utility of money will also change. This means that, for the individual consumer, the utility value of the *numéraire* or of the units of the total amount of money spent on a good will itself vary. An 'income effect' guarantees this result, whether the good is normal or inferior.

Dupuit (1849) showed little appreciation for this point, other than to invoke a general *ceteris paribus* condition. Marshall's famous defence required an assumption of constancy of the marginal utility of money or that the consumer's surplus calculation be made for an 'unimportant' commodity in the consumer's budget. If the commodity (Marshall used tea) was 'unimportant', real income would not change significantly as the price of it changed. Use of consumer's (or s') surplus in practical matters would be severely restricted, however.

Most importantly, it is not obvious from Marshall's writings just what he wanted to hold constant—money income or real income. Research on demand curves in general, and upon Marshall's constancy assumption and consumer's surplus, specifically, has been wide-ranging in this century. Milton Friedman (1949) interpreted Marshall's demand curve as a real-income constant construction, offering several different interpretations of constancy. For example, constancy can be achieved by varying the prices of other goods in a consumer's array when the price of one good changes, thereby maintaining an initial level of real income. In support of his interpretation, Friedman argued that it makes Marshall's theory of consumer's surplus understandable, and, in principle, accurate.

In the 1930s and early 1940s, Sir John Hicks, following the Hicks and Allen (1934) 'reconsideration' of demand theory, re-examined Marshall's theory of consumers' surplus (1941, 1943). Hicks developed a set of adjustments to the traditional Marshallian demand curve (money income constant). Depending upon whether the good in question was normal or inferior, and whether price was raised or lowered, the consumer could be 'compensated' by removal or restoral of money income so as to maintain his initial marginal utility of real income. Such 'compensations' provided direct measurement of surpluses. In practice, however, it is questionable whether an individual would reveal his/her initial level of utility. In cases of income removal (restoral) the individual has an incentive to overreveal (underreveal) his or her initial level of welfare. In purely theoretical terms, however, Hicks' formulation was a definite advance. In a later section, we shall consider the idea of 'compensation' again, against the background of Paretian welfare economics.

3.3.4 MONOPOLY, PRICE DISCRIMINATION AND MARGINAL-COST PRICING

While an understanding of the problems involved in partial-equilibrium welfare measurement is important, it should be noted that they have never prevented economists from utilizing welfare theory as a practical tool for policy assessment and implementation.

In particular, welfare implications were subsequently developed in two important areas affiliated with the notion of consumer's surplus: (1) the theories of monopoly and price discrimination, and (2) the related theories of optimal taxation and marginal cost pricing. These applications of partial-equilibrium welfare theory originated in Dupuit's writings and remain the chief areas of welfare policy assessment today.

Utilizing the theory of diminishing marginal utility and thorough understanding of competition and monopoly, Dupuit devised an analytical apparatus for the evaluation of public works and, implicitly, for all markets. One aspect of that apparatus may be viewed in terms of *Figure 3.2*, in which a linear market demand for some good, service, or 'use' (e.g. crossings of a bridge) is represented along with a linear, constant per-unit cost function.

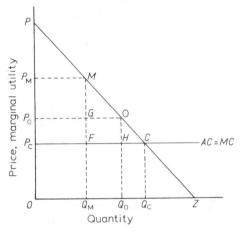

Figure 3.2 Monopoly, price discrimination and economic welfare

Under competition ($AR=AC$), the sum of consumers' surplus and sellers' receipts ('absolute utility') is maximized. In *Figure 3.2* this is equivalent to area $OPCO_C$. 'Lost utility' under competitive conditions (area $Q_C CZ$) is 'lost' because resources are scarce and because the marginal gain in utility for production past Q_C units of output is less than the marginal opportunity cost of the resources necessary to produce these units.

Consider the impact of monopoly upon welfare. Dupuit thought that most public utilities and some areas of the transportation industry (e.g. railroads) were monopolies and that monopoly existed in other areas of the French economy. The existence of monopoly imposes costs on society, as shown in *Figure 3.2*. Specifically, if monopoly price is P_M when quantity is reduced to Q_M, a 'deadweight loss' in consumers' surplus is identifiable, as in triangle FMC. There may be other losses as well. Resources that would have been devoted to the production of this good are redirected to other, presumably less valued, uses. Monopoly profits, area P_CP_MMF, are maximized at the expense of consumers' surplus.

An important point made by Dupuit, later elaborated upon by Joan Robinson (1933), was that the introduction of price discrimination, when compared to simple monopoly pricing, may have positive welfare effects. Consider *Figure 3.2* once more and suppose that the seller is a railroad with the ability to introduce different 'classes' of service so that (second-degree) discrimination could be instituted. This means, in effect, that the demand curve would be partitioned into segments. With regard to *Figure 3.2*, suppose that OQ_O-OQ_M consumers could be identified as willing to pay at least P_O but not more than P_M for railway transportation. If these consumers can be placed into 'second-class' carriages, a two-price discrimination can be set up with one group of consumers (first class) paying P_M for OQ_M units of travel, and another group paying P_O for Q_MQ_O units of transportation. The point is that, if discrimination increases output, it also reduces the lost utility to society. In the case described in *Figure 3.2*, the total utility produced by the good after the introduction of discrimination increases by an amount Q_MMOQ_O. Profits are increased by $FGOH$ and consumer welfare is enhanced by the area of triangle GMO. Whatever other distortive economic effects discrimination might have when compared to simple monopoly pricing, it will increase welfare if output is increased by its introduction. Although the resulting outcome is 'second best', it is interesting that demand theory, subjective utility theory and welfare theory all arose in considerations of monopoly, not competition.

Modern partial-equilibrium welfare theory, including that related to monopoly, taxation and marginal cost pricing, ultimately rests upon the *Dupuit taxation theorem*. Dupuit (1844) pointed out that 'where a tax is small relative to the cost of manufacture ... it is legitimate to suppose a uniform rate of decrease [in quantity consumed]', and further, that 'it may thus be said that the loss in utility is proportional to the square of the tax'. This may be shown in relation to *Figure 3.3*, which depicts a linear demand curve and zero costs. The negatively sloped linear demand function is constructed so that $P_m = mP_1$ and $AQ_m = mAQ_1$, where P_m and Q_m can take on any values of price and quantity, respectively. Dupuit's theorem states that the loss in utility, ΔU_m, is proportional to the square of the tax (or price), P_m, above marginal cost (which is zero in *Figure 3.3*). Formally, the condition is:

$$\Delta U_m = \tfrac{1}{2}AQ_mP_m$$

Making use of the relations $P_m = mP_1$ and $AQ_m = mAQ_1$, and multiplying the numerator and denominator of the above expression by P_1, the obtained result is $\Delta U_m = \alpha P_m^2$, where $\alpha = AQ_1/2P_1$ is the constant factor of proportionality. This result holds for any linear

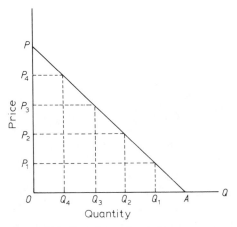

Figure 3.3 The Dupuit taxation theorem

demand curve and approximates the loss of utility for small incre-
ments in price under conditions of non-linear demand.

The taxation theorem leads directly to some fundamental propositions relating to the welfare effects of taxes, some of them drawn by
Dupuit and some of them supplied later by such economists as
Marshall (1890), Edgeworth (1912), Pigou (1920) and Hotelling
(1938). The three most significant propositions are:

(1) The welfare loss will always be greater when per-unit taxes as
    opposed to lump-sum taxes are imposed in non-competitive
    markets. This conclusion follows because lump-sum taxes do not
    alter the position or slope of the firm's marginal cost function.
    True lump-sum taxes are merely transfers of welfare from mono-
    polists to government. Impositions of excise, sales or other
    per-unit taxes alter the marginal-cost functions of firms, causing
    price and quantity alterations and losses in the aggregate utility
    (absolute utility) provided by the production and sale of goods
    and services.
(2) If a given amount of revenue is to be collected by excise or
    per-unit taxes, the loss in welfare will be less if the taxes are
    spread out over a large number of commodities. This conclusion
    follows directly from the taxation theorem. Depending, of course,
    upon demand and supply elasticities, the welfare loss will
    approach zero as a given excise tax burden is spread across larger
    and larger arrays of commodities, since the loss is always
    proportionate to the square of the tax imposed.
(3) In the absence of externalities, maximum social welfare consists
    of the sale of all commodities and services at marginal costs. This
    argument rose to prominence in the 1930s and 1940s. It amounts
    to the assertion that monopoly and discriminatory prices—i.e.

prices above marginal costs—have effects analogous to excise taxes, in that they reduce welfare in a amount proportionate to the square of the excess of price above marginal cost. In a powerful generalization of the Dupuit taxation theorem, Hotelling (1938) argued that public utilities (which he presumed to be 'natural monopolies') should be nationalized and forced to price at marginal cost in order to maximize economic welfare. Hotelling thought that socialization of these industries was necessary because losses would be incurred under natural monopoly conditions—marginal costs would be below average costs, forcing the firm to incur losses.

Nationalization and marginal cost pricing would, in other words, imply taxation and subsidies in order to maintain natural monopolies at marginal cost. Hotelling therefore attempted to design an optimal system of taxes so that marginal cost conditions would not be disturbed within the interrelated economic system. His mathematical proof, given a virgin set of prices unaffected by prior market interferences, required that *lump-sum* taxes (Hotelling thought that land taxes and income taxes fit the bill) be imposed in order to subsidize the utilities. While Hotelling's proof was challenged on a number of technical points (Frisch, 1939; Morrison and Pfouts, 1981), it became obvious that income taxes were not true lump-sum taxes, since they distort the marginal relation between work and leisure. For this and other reasons, Hotelling's proposal did not solve the issue of welfare distribution. Taxation of any sort conjoined with subsidization of some consumers requires an interpersonal judgement of utility gains and losses. Problems of interpersonal comparisons and of income distribution have continued to be a bugbear for welfare economists of both traditions.

While Hotelling was unable to conquer all of the difficulties associated with the welfare concept of marginal cost pricing, his famous attempt illustrates the degree and intensity of interest in applications of the tool in partial and general equilibrium situations. Much of the economic analysis stimulated by Hotelling's contribution, generalizing Dupuit's approach and blending it with the Paretian welfare tradition, subsequently developed in the context of public goods, a more complete discussion of which appears in a later section of this chapter.

3.4 Modern issues in welfare economics

3.4.1 ORIGINS: THE PARETIAN VALUE JUDGEMENTS

Most of the conventional theory of welfare economics today rests on the assumed value judgement that welfare is increased if one person is made better off while no-one is made worse off. This implies that welfare is an increasing function of individuals' utilities. The assumption was first made explicit by Vilfredo Pareto (1906), who created a new framework to analyse welfare considerations, one that combined the subjective theory of utility with Léon Walras' elegant general equilibrium theory of value and exchange. Three particular propositions reside at the centre of the Paretian tradition.

(1) Concern is with the welfare of all members of society. This implies an ordinal social welfare function of the form, $W = W(U_1, U_2,...,U_n)$, where W represents social welfare and $U_1, U_2,...,U_n$ represents the level of utility of each of the n individuals who together comprise the society under consideration. Commodities are relevant to social welfare only insofar as they affect the utilities of individual members of society.
(2) An individual is considered the best judge of his own welfare, which is viewed entirely subjectively. Minors and lunatics are sometimes (uneasily) excluded from this important value judgement, but no other exceptions are allowed. In other words, no individual may impose his or her own preferences upon any other individual.
(3) Any change in the allocation of resources that increases the welfare of at least one individual without reducing the welfare of any other individual is said to increase social welfare.

These Paretian value judgements are in no sense trivial, nor universally acceptable, but they have come to dominate contemporary welfare economics. As Rowley and Peacock (1975) have noted, the approach is fundamentally conservative because it is silent on the welfare effects of any change that improves the welfare of some at the expense of others. In the Paretian approach, a single objection to a proposed reallocation is sufficient to cloud the welfare issue and to render unambiguous policy judgement impossible. In due course, we shall see how other writers have attempted to improve on the Paretian approach.

3.4.2 THE NECESSARY CONDITIONS FOR PARETO OPTIMALITY

Following the Walrasian general-equilibrium theory, Paretian optimality requires the simultaneous achievement of efficiency conditions (equilibria) in exchange and in production. Formally, this requires the satisfaction of several marginal conditions. Most modern texts on welfare economics contain comprehensive analyses of the necessary conditions for Pareto optimality (e.g. Henderson and Quandt, 1958;

Just *et al.*, 1982; Nath, 1969; Quirk and Saposnik, 1968; Winch, 1971); consequently space is confined here to a summary review.

To begin with, the marginal rate of substitution (number of units of one good that can be sacrificed for another without changing the level of utility) between any pair of consumer goods must be the same for all individuals who consume both goods. This assures efficiency in exchange. If this condition does not hold, some consumer(s) could benefit from further exchange without harming other consumers. The second condition guarantees efficiency in production. It states that the marginal rate of technical substitution (number of units of one input that can be substituted for another without changing the level of output) between any pair of factor inputs must be the same for all producers who use both factors. If this condition does not hold, a reallocation of factor inputs is possible which would result in greater aggregate output without reducing the output of any single commodity.

The above conditions guarantee the achievement of sub-optima in each of the major sectors of the economy. The final (general-equilibrium) condition is that for every pair of commodities the marginal rate of transformation in production must be equal to the common marginal rate of substitution in consumption. If this condition does not hold, a shift in the pattern of commodity production could benefit some consumers without injuring others.

The achievement of the above three conditions constitutes a 'top-level' optimum, which is the highest level of social welfare that can be defined by reference to Paretian criteria, given the initial distribution of property rights in society. A number of writers have demonstrated mathematically that the existence of perfect competition guarantees satisfaction of the above conditions (Mishan, 1960). However, even if perfect competition were universally present (it is not), and even if the Paretian value judgements were unanimously accepted (they are not), the simultaneous attainment of efficiency in exchange and in production does not necessarily imply the best attainable solution. It only does so for a particular distribution of property rights. With an infinite number of distributions of property rights there also exists an infinite number of Paretian optima, each located on the 'utility possibility frontier' of the economy in question. Given the Paretian prohibition against interpersonal utility comparisons, it is possible neither to compare alternative efficiency points nor to assume that any efficiency point is necessarily better than inefficient points associated with different distributions of property rights. In order to determine an 'optimum optimorum', a specific social welfare function must be employed which ranks alternative property-right distributions. We shall soon see, however, that for those who cling to the individualistic approach embodied in the Paretian tradition, social welfare functions pose a number of serious problems.

3.4.3 COMPENSATION CRITERIA

In an early attempt to establish a more complete criterion on which to base welfare decisions, Nicholas Kaldor (1939) and J.R. Hicks (1939) developed the *compensation principle*. This principle asserts that state B is preferred to state A if all individuals *could* be made better off at state B, whether or not they are actually made better off. In terms of the Paretian framework, the compensation principle states that B is preferred to A if, in moving from A to B, the gainers can compensate the losers such that everyone can be better off. Unlike the Paretian principle, the Kaldor–Hicks criterion does not require the *actual* payment of compensation. Kaldor and Hicks eschewed this stipulation because in their view the actual payment of compensation involves a value judgement (as though the Paretian criterion does not!). The ultimate question posed by the compensation principle, of course, is what constitutes the ideal distribution of income, a question Kaldor and Hicks were understandably reluctant to tackle.

Although the compensation principle was a theoretical advance of some importance, it was not without problems of its own. One class of problems it engendered falls under the general heading of the reversal paradox, first defined by Tibor Scitovsky. Scitovsky (1941) pointed out that the conclusion of welfare superiority is not always warranted when gainers can potentially compensate losers. It must also be shown that losers cannot bribe gainers not to make the move. In some cases, application of the Kaldor–Hicks compensation test alone produces ambiguous results where both states A and B are preferred to each other. This 'reversal' of conclusions occurs because in each case a given distribution of the initial goods-bundle is compared with all possible distributions of the alternative bundle. The reversal paradox suggests that all distributions of the initial bundle must also be considered. In order to avoid the reversal problem, Scitovsky suggested a new criterion that supplements the Kaldor–Hicks principle. This states that it be determined, first, that gainers can bribe losers to make a change, and second, that losers cannot bribe gainers not to make the change. Unless the Scitovsky test is passed in addition to the Kaldor–Hicks compensation test, it is illegitimate to conclude that one state is even potentially preferred to another.

It should be pointed out that the reversal problem does not arise in all instances, but even where it does not, a further obstacle may be encountered. This additional problem was pointed out by Gorman (1955) as a possible outcome when more than two states are being compared in a Kaldor–Hicks setting. The specific issue is one of intransitivity, which arises when one must choose among several states where all of the alternative policies are of a less-preferred (i.e. second-best) nature—in other words, where no single policy in the policy set satisfies the Paretian efficiency criterion. When the compensation test does not lead to a ranking of policy sets containing more than one first-best state, intransitive welfare rankings are a distinct possibility.

Kaldor, Hicks and Scitovsky were all seeking a criterion that would be neutral on the question of income distribution (or utility levels), yet still allow meaningful comparisons of alternative economic policies. Their compensation criteria were subsequently challenged by Paul Samuelson (1950), who maintained that even if the Kaldor–Hicks and Scitovsky criteria are met, a potential gain in welfare is not necessarily attained. Samuelson contended that one has to consider all possible bundles and all possible distributions of these bundles before statements can be made about potential gains. This amounts to selecting among many first-best situations from which no solution can be obtained unless a social ranking of first-best utility possibilities can be determined. Attempts to determine such a social ranking of utilities take us into the realm of the social welfare function, which is the subject of the next section.

Before examining the notion and specification of the social welfare function, it is desirable to conclude the present discussion with a review of Little's contribution. Little (1957) advanced a welfare criterion shortly after Samuelson's criticism of the compensation criteria appeared. He declared the Kaldor–Hicks and Scitovsky criteria inadequate because they did not admit income distribution as an *ethical* variable and because they were concerned with *potential* rather than actual superiority of a point. Little's criterion builds on the Kaldor–Hicks–Scitovsky advances by inserting a third condition. The basic statement of Little's approach is as follows.

(1) Is the Kaldor–Hicks criterion satisfied?
(2) Is the Scitovsky criterion satisfied?
(3) Is any resulting redistribution good or bad?

The difficulty, of course, comes in determining what constitutes 'good' or 'bad'. Little's contribution has been the subject of different interpretations and considerable controversy, with at least one writer (Nath, 1969) finding it unsatisfactory on any possible interpretation. Its chief value therefore seems to have been in openly broaching the subject of ethical considerations, albeit without solving any of the major problems introduced to welfare economics by such an issue. To some welfare theorists, pursuit of a specifiable social welfare function seemed a more promising avenue of progress.

3.4.4 SOCIAL WELFARE FUNCTIONS

The modern notion of a social welfare function was first introduced by Abram Bergson (1938), who built upon the Paretian formulation of welfare as a function of individual utilities. Specifically, Bergson's social welfare function postulated that (1) an increase in the utility of any one individual, *ceteris paribus*, increases social welfare; (2) if one individual is made worse off, then another individual must be made better off in order to retain the same level of social welfare; and (3) if some individual has a very high level of utility and another has a very low level of utility, then society is willing to give up some of the former's utility to obtain an increase in the latter's, with the intensity of this trade-off depending on the degree of inequality.

The first of these postulates is a straightforward adoption of the Pareto principle, but the second two went beyond Pareto in an important sense. The second postulate implies that the social welfare function is additive, and the third that a particular set of weights is attached to the individual preference functions that make up the collective welfare. Accepting all of these propositions for the moment, the properties described suggest the existence of a welfare contour that corresponds conceptually to a typical indifference curve for an individual. *Figure 3.4* depicts such a curve, labelled W_o. By property

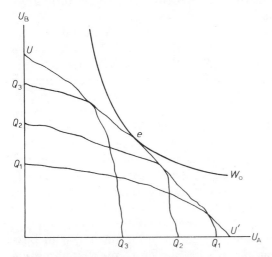

Figure 3.4 The social welfare function and utility-possibilities frontier

(1), social welfare increases with movement to higher social welfare contours located to the right of W_o. By property (2), the social welfare contours have negative slope; and by property (3), the welfare contours are convex to the origin. Social welfare is maximized by moving to the highest attainable social welfare contour that makes a tangent with the grand utility possibilities frontier—i.e. the envelope curve (UU') connecting the many individual utility possibilities curves associated with different individuals or different bundles of goods.

Insofar as the above discussion seems to be a straightforward application of indifference-curve analysis, the social welfare function appears to be a desirable theoretical concept. Nevertheless, its practicality has been illusory for two main reasons. The first is that little hope exists for determining a social welfare function on which everyone can agree. Early utilitarians such as Bentham believed that changes in happiness should simply be added up. If the net gain was positive, policy implementation was recommended[4]. This approach ignored the question of whether different utility weights should be assigned to different individuals. After Bergson, some economists argued that what is needed is a social welfare function calculated in such a way that the happier individual A is relative to individual B, the less socially valuable is an addition to A's happiness compared with an addition to B's happiness. The problem is that such questions involve a morass of interpersonal utility comparisons that are impossible to resolve on purely objective grounds. Welfare weights must be assigned to different groups of individuals in order to make such interpersonal comparisons. Among modern welfare theorists, the tendency is to give equal weights to each group. Obviously, the choice of such weights is highly controversial, because their choice ultimately determines income distribution.

The second reason for the illusory nature of the social welfare function is that the logical existence of a general rule for determining such a function has been seriously questioned. Kenneth Arrow (1951) set out to explore whether there was some non-contradictory method of aggregating individual preferences in a society not characterized by dictatorship, and he concluded that there can be no such rule under reasonable requirements. Arrow's impossibility theorem seemed quite startling at first, due to his unusual use of the phrase 'social welfare function'. But what he proved was that, on his conditions, there is no general rule for aggregating individual orderings to reach a master-ordering that will always be consistent (among other things it argues that majority rule can lead to intransitive decisions). Although the impossibility theorem does not deny the possibility, in principle, of developing a logically consistent master-ordering on which to base democratic decisions, it has placed the burden of proof squarely on those who espouse the existence of master-ordering schemes. Subsequent approaches to the welfare calculus have tended to admit interpersonal comparisons of utility on *ethical* grounds, which takes the whole matter somewhat beyond the limits of economics.

It is usually at this juncture that theories of justice impinge on the economics of welfare. In his recent theory of justice, for example, John Rawls (1971) contends that public policy should be evaluated by the welfare of the most miserable person in society. In Rawls' theory, making this person better off, even though others are made worse off, is socially desirable. His method, of course, requires comparing the levels of utility of different people in different circumstances, a baldly ethical manoeuvre. Nozick (1974), in a widely acclaimed rebuttal

Rawls, rejected the Rawlsian value judgement in favour of an entitlement theory—an idea more congenial to those who support the individualistic (e.g. Paretian) approach to welfare economics.

Although widespread disagreement on the concept of the social welfare function persists, Arnold Harberger (1971) recently attempted to recast the idea in the mould of positive economics. Harberger pleaded for the acceptance of a 'conventional framework' for all applied welfare analysis. Practically speaking, this means general acceptance of the following basic postulates:

(1) The competitive demand price for a given unit measures the value of that unit to the demander;
(2) The competitive supply price for a given unit measures the value of the unit to the supplier;
(3) When evaluating the net benefits or costs of a given action (project, programme or policy), the costs and benefits accruing to each member of the relevant group (e.g. a nation) should normally be added without regard to the individual(s) to whom they accrue.

Harberger points out that these postulates underlie most analyses that use the concepts of consumer and producer surplus, either in a partial equilibrium or a Paretian framework. His plea is for the general acceptance by the economics profession of a social welfare function that maximizes the sum of consumers' and producers' surplus over competitive cost and which is neutral with respect to income distribution. This is, in effect, an argument for a social welfare function of the following form:

$$W = TR + S - (TC - R)$$

where W = net economic welfare, TR = total revenue, S = consumers' surplus, TC = total cost and R = infra-marginal rent. In the event that all factors are available in completely elastic supply, infra-marginal rents will be zero and the above equation collapses to $W = TR + S - TC$, where the necessary and sufficient conditions for a net welfare maximum are that the first derivative of the equation be equal to zero (i.e. price = marginal cost) and that the second derivative of the equation be less than zero (W is not a monotonically increasing function). This last point flies in the face of Paretian theory, which asserts the opposite; namely, that the only unambiguous gain in social welfare results when no one individual is made worse off in order to make another individual better off—a theorem that implies that W is a monotonically increasing function of any level of utility. In other words, Harberger's proposed social welfare function accepts the individualistic thrust of the first two Paretian value assumptions while rejecting the policy constraint imposed by the third. Rowley and

Peacock (1975) interpret Harberger's argument to mean that public policy analysis should be concerned principally with issues of efficiency in resource allocation, leaving equity considerations in the hands of the fiscal authorities.

From the vantage point of a mere decade, Harberger's plea seems to have had little impact on theoretical welfare economics. Many economists today think it is chimerical to believe that social welfare functions can be translated into useful economic advice. According to Mishan (1973),

> Even if there were no fundamental obstacles to its construction, or even if one could think up reasonable conditions under which a social welfare function could exist, there would remain the virtually impossible task of arranging for society to rank unambiguously all conceivable combinations of the individual welfares and moreover—in order to utilize this massive apparatus—to discover (without much cost) the effect on the welfare of each person in society (in terms of utilities, goods, or money) of the introduction of alternative economic organizations (p. 747).

3.4.5 MARKET FAILURE

It is possible to apply the marginal equivalencies of Paretian optimality on a *ceteris paribus* basis if and only if the following assumptions hold: that the goods in question are private goods only; that the acts of factor supply, production, exchange and consumption are matters of indifference to all but the immediate participants; and that all production and utility functions are continuously differentiable. In other words, the Paretian criterion finds its legitimate application in a world without joint products, externalities, indivisibilities or public goods. The real world, of course, is not like that.

We have chosen to group these issues under the general heading of market failure and, because of space constraints, we have confined the discussion to two major categories of market failure that give rise to welfare problems: externalities and public goods.

The notion of externality goes back at least as far as Alfred Marshall (1890), but it was Marshall's student, A.C. Pigou (1912, 1920), who pioneered the economic analysis of control of external effects. Marshall recognized the conceptual existence of certain economies or diseconomies that are external to a firm but internal to an industry. He further showed that the presence of external economies or diseconomies result in firms' long-run supply curves having negative or positive slope. His famous treatment combined the theory of decreasing, increasing and constant costs with the theory of consumers' surplus to propose a pattern of taxes and subsidies that would increase welfare. Specifically, Marshall considered a tax on increasing-cost industries and a simultaneous subsidy to decreasing-cost industries.

Marshall's theoretical insights stirred up a protracted debate over the identification of increasing, decreasing and constant cost industries (Clapham, 1922; Pigou, 1922; Robertson, 1924), which subsequently served to focus welfare economists' attention on *technological* rather than pecuniary externalities[5]. Pigou's seminal work on welfare economics abounds with examples of the former, mostly *negative* externalities, such as smoke, slag or water pollution—the unwanted side-effects of private production. Pigou's major theme was that the market fails in those instances in which external costs or external benefits are not charged to or paid to the initiator of the externality. As a consequence, marginal *social* costs diverge from marginal *private* costs, introducing distortion in the allocation of productive resources.

Pigou argued that a simple modification of private contractual arrangements would not be sufficient to remove the external effects, opting instead for a Marshallian solution of corrective taxes and subsidies. The Pigovian approach is illustrated in *Figure 3.5*, which

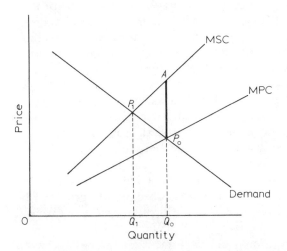

Figure 3.5 Pigovian externalities

shows the marginal private cost, marginal social cost and demand curve of a good that produces stream pollution as a by-product. If the polluter is not made to bear social costs, the MPC is relevant to decision-making. Quantity Q_o is produced and society is forced to bear marginal pollution costs in the amount AP_o. From society's viewpoint, too much output is produced.

Pigou's solution was to tax the offending industry so that its decision curve became the MSC function. A lower quantity, Q_1, would be produced and sold at a higher price, P_1. Pigovian taxes thus addressed the externality problem, but contemplated an enlarged role of government in the form of legislative or regulatory action.

Later writers like Kneese and Bower (1968), Mishan (1971) and Ruff (1970) followed the Pigovian approach in analysing externalities, but an early attack was launched by Frank Knight (1924), who took issue with Pigou's claim that externalities could not be internalized through private, contractual agreements. Knight argued that the market was not inherently incapable of dealing efficiently with externalities, that instead it was the absence of well-defined property rights which gives rise to the problem. A redefinition of property rights would thereby allow externalities to be internalized. This Knightian idea was further extended by Ronald Coase (1960), who pointed out the reciprocal nature of externalities. According to Coase, certain residents may put themselves 'in harm's way' by locating near a smoky factory or by refusing to move after the fact. In some cases it may cost less to relocate residents than to reduce smoke emissions. Therefore Coase (1960) argued that 'A tax system...confined to a tax on the producer for damages could tend to lead to unduly high costs being incurred for the prevention of damage' because it would not provide appropriate incentives for damaged parties to protect themselves from harm. In Coase's view, a system of bilateral taxes or subsidies is more efficient than a unilateral one. Recent welfare theorists who have defended this approach in one fashion or another include Buchanan and Stubblebine (1962), Ralph Turvey (1963) and Mohring and Boyd (1971).

Major relief from the polarization of views into unilateral versus bilateral tax schemes to correct externalities was eventually provided by W.J. Baumol (1972), who demonstrated that in large-numbers cases (where many parties are affected and bargaining is unlikely or impossible), a unilateral tax is efficient, whereas in small-numbers cases where bargaining is possible the same kind of tax may be inefficient. Support for Baumol's view was subsequently provided by Edgar Browning (1977), who offered an improved measure of external harm.

Baumol based his argument in part on the analogy between externalities and public goods, which takes us into the second realm of market failure. When the market fails because of externalities, goods are at least produced, albeit in inefficient quantities and at distorted prices. The ultimate market failure occurs when some kinds of desired goods—called public goods—are not produced at all in the private sector.

The unique nature of this problem can be seen in a brief list of the characteristics of a *pure* public good, first identified by Bowen (1943) and later by Samuelson (1954). These characteristics include:

(1) *Non-competing consumption.* This means that an additional unit of a public good, e.g. an additional nuclear missile supplied to one

user, does not reduce the benefits of other users. Rather, the production of an additional missile increases *all* consumers' protection by an *additional* missile. This feature of public goods means that demand curves for pure public goods must be added *vertically*, not horizontally, as in the case of private goods;

(2) *Non-excludability*. Another public goods characteristic, related to the 'free rider' principle, is that non-paying individuals cannot be excluded from consumption of the good. Barring minor locational factors, an underground missile or the establishment of a local police patrol cannot be supplied to one individual without simultaneously benefiting others. At base, one of the reasons for market failure is the 'free rider'. Why would anyone correctly reveal a demand for national defence if he thought that others would provide it? He could then 'free ride' on others' expenditures, since there would be no practical low-cost way to exclude non-payers. But if all consumers have an incentive to 'free ride', the good will *not* be produced. This is the source of market failure in the case of public goods.

The Bowen–Samuelson description of public goods equilibrium is abstract and perfectly general in nature, but problems arise in trying to make it operational. In the first place, few goods are exactly described by the Bowen–Samuelson conditions. Education and medical care are, at some times and in some places, treated as 'public goods' but they do not conform to the definition of a *pure* public good. In the second place, determination of the true individual demand for a public good is extremely difficult because individuals have incentives not to reveal their true preferences. In the former case, it is perhaps enough to say that goods such as education share some of the characteristics of pure public goods. But the latter case is much less tractable.

One of the earliest schemes to incorporate individual preferences into the supply of public goods was advanced by Knut Wicksell (1896), who proposed that decisions concerning the provision of public goods be made simultaneously with decisions as to how public expenditures would be financed, and that each such joint decision receive the unanimous approval of those affected. Although this rule has serious drawbacks, it nevertheless has served as an important impetus to much work on revealed preference for public goods.

Another proposal along Wicksellian lines was advanced by Erik Lindahl (1919), who asserted that the democratic voting process could, under certain circumstances, accurately register preferences for public goods. Lindahl described a public goods equilibrium where tax shares were distributed by free agreement in a political process influenced by the relative power of the conflicting parties (well-to-do versus poor voters, for instance). In such a process, the pro-rata tax share paid by each group could be equivalent to its respective marginal evaluation of the public good. Lindahl also noted cases where the well-to-do demanders would try to foist off part of the burden on the poor, or vice versa. The result is not predictable unless an exact set of political institutions is specified, which is something Lindahl's successors have set themselves to do.

Following Lindahl, Howard Bowen (1943) described an equilibrium in a democratic community wherein everyone is assumed to vote and thereby reveal his or her preferences for public goods. Insofar as individuals choose public goods on the same grounds that they demand private goods, i.e. calculations of benefits received versus costs incurred, Bowen assumed that each citizen would pay a pro-rata tax share for the public good. If the demand curves revealed by this willingness to pay are clustered around some median according to some normal degree of error, the preferences of the *median voter* will determine the quantity of public goods produced. Multiple voting issues or agenda manipulation by politicians will tend to upset the Bowen equilibrium, but it is noteworthy that the analysis provides a potential means of preference registration through the voting process.

More recent and elaborate proposals for soliciting accurate evaluations of public goods have concentrated on bidding. Recent schemes have been put forth with varying degrees of success by E.A. Thompson (1965), Peter Bohm (1971), Dreze and de la Valle Poussin (1971), J.M. Buchanan (1973), Tideman and Tullock (1976) and by A.H. Barnett (1981). Despite the theoretical insights gained by these contributions, however, the development of a practical proposal for eliciting accurate evaluations of public goods remains an elusive goal.

3.5 The present condition and future prospects of welfare economics

3.5.1 THE POLITICS OF SOCIAL CHOICE

Most of the contemporary discussion in the theory of welfare economics proceeds under the assumption that there exists a social welfare function. The focus of attention is consequently on the process of maximizing a known objective in the presence of various constraints and the properties and corollaries of the optimum solution. The whole edifice has relevance only insofar as the concept of collective rationality is meaningful. Unless there is some definable objective that a society seeks to achieve, it makes no sense to inquire into the method of pursuing it. To many, this fact argues most powerfully for the existence of a State and for its extension into economic activities.

At the same time, market failure of any kind is often regarded as a necessary and sufficient condition for collective action. Orthodox economic theory holds that the state is an efficient, omniscient and impartial servant of the public good and that the nature and scope of its intervention in instances of market failure are to be determined by cost-effectiveness considerations. But social welfare functions are subject to severe analytical drawbacks and market failure has proven to be an elusive concept. Even where outright market failure exists, government intervention may not be a desirable automatic response. For some people (e.g. libertarians), the concentration of power in collective hands evokes negative marginal utility, thus implying that efficiency losses due to market failure must be weighed against welfare losses due to expanded collective choice. Symptomatic of this issue is the contemporary debate as to the appropriate institutional framework of collective choice within the democratic societies. Most prominent—and in many cases most vocal—among the debaters is a group of writers led by James Buchanan: the public-choice Paretians.

The public-choice Paretians have adopted a fundamentalist approach to welfare economics that combines aspects of collective choice with market performance. The framework within which they operate is the classical 'social contract' approach of Locke, Rousseau, Kant and others. This approach holds that all individuals in a free society are bound in their interactions by an implicit social agreement (i.e. constitution), which defines the rights and responsibilities of the individuals in society. Implicit in this approach is the belief that the individual need not take part in the writing of a constitution governing his actions; all that is required is his tacit agreement to the terms of the social contract.

In *The Calculus of Consent* Buchanan and Tullock (1965) distinguish between decision-making at the constitutional and post-constitutional levels. At the former level they follow Pareto (1906) and Wicksell (1896) in advocating the unanimity principle, that is, individuals must unanimously accept the rules that govern social interactions. Agreement is not necessary at the post-constitutional level, however. Many people might disapprove of the actions of some individual or group, but as long as the latter acts within the provisions of the constitution, the social contract is being upheld. Indeed, since the costs of arriving at unanimous agreement are so high, the constitution should be expected to provide for many cases involving less than unanimous approval. John Rawls adopts the same point of view in his *Theory of Justice* (1971), suggesting that the rules of society should be those that could be unanimously agreed upon before each individual knows what position in society he will occupy in the post-constitutional stage. This stipulation is required to raise the probability of a unanimous outcome and also to avoid the promulgation of biased rules.

In a sense, the social contract theory views the State as a type of club where all individuals agree in principle to become club members and adhere to the club rules. Members volunteer to join the club, and by that action they imply agreement with the club's set of rules. The analogy is imperfect, however, since individuals are born into society whether they like it or not, and, once there, they must adhere to the rules of the existing social contract.

One logical extension of Buchanan's thought is that the Pareto criterion is more meaningful when applied to the *classification* of social constraints within which individuals act than when it is applied merely to the results of those actions, as is the custom of the orthodox Paretians. The public-choice paradigm admits that optimal rules do not always produce optimal results (Buchanan, 1962). To be at all relevant to discussions of policy, the Pareto criterion should be applied to positions attainable through *changes* in the existing set of societal rules. Each change in the set of rules produces a potential situation in which some one or group can be made better off without making any individual or group worse off. Modifications of the constitution, however, remain subject to the Wicksellian unanimity principle.

At least in part, the public-choice approach to collective decision-making is a reaction against the deficiencies of the social welfare function, especially its inability to avoid interpersonal utility comparisons. The public-choice Paretians hold that social choices in a free society do not exist apart from individual values. Buchanan's (1962) specific complaint is that the use of a social welfare function tends to reduce the concept of Pareto optimality to a meaningless state because any change in the set of social value judgements will change the definition of optimality with regard to changes in the rules.

3.5.2 PERSISTENT PROBLEMS

In terms of the technical virtuosity of its practitioners, welfare economics has come a long way from its formal inception over two centuries ago. Despite the growing elegance of its theoretical structure, however, many persistent problems continue to plague this branch of economic analysis. The list is both long and varied. Some of the problems have been recounted in the foregoing pages, while others have not been mentioned because of a binding space constraint. There are the fundamental problems of whether society should be conceived as a hodgepodge of individuals or as an organic whole; of the optimum set of rules, or constitution; of the ultimate role of ethics in the decision calculus—whether individual or collective. In a meaningful sense, these problems transcend economics, and for that reason, as well as their inherently complex nature, they are likely to persist.

On a narrower plane, a host of problems surrounding the measurability of welfare remain. Our survey has noted several measurability problems that are identifiable due to the subjective nature of the maximand. These problems are part and parcel of the Paretian framework—a framework that assumes, somewhat naively, that individual utility functions are independent of each other. Once it is admitted that some utility functions are interdependent (i.e. A's happiness depends in part on B's happiness) the common problems of measurability are greatly multiplied. A closely related problem involves the inability to determine, *a priori*, intergenerational differences in utility. Policy decisions made today will often have far-reaching effects on generations to come, yet there seems to be no clear way to include the preference functions of people yet unborn. This criticism particularly plagues the public-choice approach to constitution-making.

Another set of problems arises when one leaves the rarified atmosphere of the perfectly competitive model. The standard, static model of welfare economics becomes inapplicable once the inevitable imperfections of knowledge which are likely to exist in any real-world situation are recognized. In particular, uncertainty has three major consequences for welfare analysis. The first is that the price of each commodity may no longer be equal to its marginal cost, so that the market mechanism will not produce an allocation of resources which is optimal in the Paretian sense. The second problem is that the presence of generalized uncertainty removes the guarantee that a unique price will always emerge for a homogeneous product. Closely related is the fact that, with uncertainty, the important interdepencies of the profitability of some economic ventures may remain unknown to individual producers, so that they fail to expand in a way that would extend society to its technological frontier. The third consequence of generalized uncertainty is that information itself becomes a commodity, the free flow of which is restrained by institutional impediments such as patent rights and/or trade secrets. In theory at least, each of these three difficulties can be removed by state intervention (Nath 1969), although past experiments with government programmes designed to reduce uncertainty give little cause for hope of a favourable outcome in this regard.

A different, though no less serious, problem in welfare economics has been formally recognized now for close to three decades. Lancaster and Lipsey (1956) questioned the legitimacy of 'piecemeal' applications of welfare principles, a common practice prior to their formal presentation of the general theory of second-best. Their theory successfully overturned the assumption that any movement towards satisfying the necessary conditions for Pareto optimality must lead to an improvement in overall efficiency, even if not all of the conditions can be met. In other words, the theory of second-best condemned piecemeal policy prescriptions under the Paretian banner as futile and inappropriate. According to its authors (Lancaster and Lipsey, 1956–1957)

...the attainment of a Paretian optimum requires the simultaneous fulfillment of all the optimum conditions. The general theorem for the second best optimum states that if there is introduced into a general equilibrium system a constraint which prevents the attainment of one of the Paretian conditions, the other Paretian conditions, although still attainable, are, in general, no longer desirable. In other words, given that one of the Paretian optimum conditions cannot be fulfilled, then an optimum situation can be achieved only by departing from all the other Paretian conditions. The optimum situation finally attained may be termed a second best optimum because it is achieved subject to a constraint which, by definition, prevents the attainment of a Paretian optimum (p. 11).

3.5.3 FUTURE PROSPECTS

From its first faltering steps as a new, independent discipline to the present day, economics has been concerned in one fashion or another with the form and prospects of economic welfare. There seems no reason to think otherwise about future development of the discipline. Welfare considerations of one kind or another lie at the very heart of economic analysis and policy. In the future, therefore, the development of welfare economics is not likely to be retarded by a failure of interest or of relevance. However, welfare economics, like general economics, seems to have got itself in the position that Leontief (1971) described over a decade ago, namely that its analytical superstructure has outstripped its empirical foundations. Indeed, Leontief's indictment seems even more appropriate to welfare theory, where measurement problems abound and have proved most recalcitrant.

One overriding observation is that welfare economics in the twentieth century has never strayed far from the Paretian design, nor is it likely to do so in the foreseeable future. But some interesting extensions have taken place in the development of the property-rights literature and in the search for the theoretical underpinnings of optimal constitutions. It is predicted that most of the new insights in future welfare economics will stem from this 'new institutionalism' rather than from more refined applications of neoclassical design. If this view is correct, a re-reading of the classic treatises on political economy and political theory may become more than a harmless diversion for welfare economists.

Notes

1. In his *Lectures* Smith had, however, solved the diamonds and water paradox on the basis of relative scarcity; see O'Brien (1975, pp. 78–80).
2. This natural identity required, however, a framework of Justice; see O'Brien (1975, pp. 31, 32, 51) and Samuels (1966).
3. On Marshall's treatment of consumer surplus, see O'Brien (1981, pp. 41–43).

4. This same notion, coincidentally, underpins the Hicks–Kaldor criterion.
5. Pecuniary externalities result from increased factor scarcity. Technological externalities are non-priced modifications of the environment. In modern usage, the term 'externality' is reserved solely for the latter.

References

ARROW, K.J. (1951). *Social Choice and Individual Values*. New York, John Wiley and Sons

ARTZ, F.B. (1966). *The Development of Technical Education in France, 1500–1850*, p. 110. Cambridge, Mass., MIT Press

BARNETT, A.H. (1981). Soliciting Accurate Evaluations of Public Goods. *Public Finance Quarterly* **9**, 221–234

BAUMOL, W.J. (1972). On Taxation and the Control of Externalities. *American Economic Review* **62**, 307–322

BENTHAM, J. (1790). *An Introduction to the Principles of Morals and Legislation*. Oxford, The Clarendon Press, 1879

BERGSON, A. (1938). A Reformulation of Certain Aspects of Welfare Economics. *Quarterly Journal of Economics* **52**, 310–334

BOHM, P.J.G. (1971). An Approach to the Problem of Estimating Demand for Public Goods. *Swedish Journal of Economics* **73**, 55–66

BOWEN, H.R. (1943) The Interpretation of Voting in the Allocation of Economic Resources. *Quarterly Journal of Economics* **58**, 27–48

BROWNING, E.K. (1977). External Diseconomies, Compensation, and the Measure of Damage. *Southern Economic Journal* **43**, 1279–1287

BUCHANAN, J.M. (1962). The Relevance of Pareto Optimality. *Journal of Conflict Resolution* **6**, 341–354

BUCHANAN, J.M. (1973). The Institutional Structure of Externality. *Public Choice* **14**, 69–82

BUCHANAN, J.M. and STUBBLEBINE, W.C. (1962). Externality. *Economica* **29**, 371–384

BUCHANAN, J.M. and TULLOCK, G. (1965). *The Calculus of Consent*. Ann Arbor, University of Michigan Press

CLAPHAM, J.H. (1922). Of Empty Economic Boxes. *The Economic Journal* **32**, 305–314

COASE, R.H. (1960). The Problem of Social Cost. *Journal of Law and Economics* **3**, 1–44

DREZE, J.H. and DE LA VALLE POUSSIN (1971). A *tâtonnement* Process for Public Goods. *Review of Economic Studies* **38**, 133–150

DUPUIT, J. (1844). On the Measurement of the Utility of Public Works. In *Transport: Selected Readings* (ed. by D. Munby), pp. 19–57. Baltimore, Penguin Books, 1968

DUPUIT, J. (1849). De l'influence des péages sur l'utilité des voies de communication. *Annales des ponts et chaussées. Mémoirs et documents*, 2d Ser. **17**, 170–248

DUPUIT, J. (1853). De utilité et sa mesure. *Journal des économistes*, 1st Ser. **36**, 1–27

EDGEWORTH, F.Y. (1912). Contributions to the Theory of Railway Rates. *The Economic Journal* **21**, 346–370, 551–571; **22**, 198–218; **23**, 206–226

EKELUND, R.B. and HÉBERT, R.F. (1973). Public Economics at the Ecole des Ponts et Chaussées: 1830–1850. *Journal of Public Economics* **2**, 241–256

FRIEDMAN, M. (1949). The Marshallian Demand Curve. *Journal of Political Economy* **47**, 463–495

FRISCH, R. (1939). The Dupuit Taxation Theorem. *Econometrica* **7**, 145–150; 156–157

GORMAN, W.M. (1955). The Intransitivity of Certain Criteria Used in Welfare Economics. *Oxford Economic Papers* **7**, 25–35

HARBERGER, A.C. (1971). Three Basic Postulates for Applied Welfare Economics: An Interpretive Essay. *Journal of Economic Literature* **9**, 785–797

HENDERSON, J.M. and QUANDT, R.E. (1958). *Microeconomic Theory*. New York, McGraw-Hill

HICKS, J.R. (1939). The Foundations of Welfare Economics. *The Economic Journal* **49**, 696–712

HICKS, J.R. (1941). The Rehabilitation of Consumer's Surplus. *Review of Economic Studies* **8**, 108–116

HICKS, J.R. (1943). The Four Consumer's Surpluses. *Review of Economic Studies* **11**, 31–41

HICKS, J.R. and ALLEN, R.G.D. (1934). A Reconsideration of the Theory of Value. *Economica* **1**, 52–76, 196–219

HOTELLING, H. (1938). The General Welfare in Relation to Problems of Taxation and of Railway and Utility Rates. *Econometrica* **6**, 242–269

JEVONS, W.S. (1871). *Theory of Political Economy*. New York, Augustus M. Kelley, 1965

JUST, R.E., HUETH, D.L. and SCHMITZ, A. (1982). *Applied Welfare Economics and Public Policy*. Englewood Cliffs, NJ, Prentice-Hall

KALDOR, N. (1939). Welfare Propositions of Economics and Interpersonal Comparisons of Utility. *The Economic Journal* **49**, 549–552

KNEESE, A.V. and BOWER, B.T. (1968). *Managing Water Quality: Economics, Technology, Institutions*. Baltimore, Johns Hopkins University Press

KNIGHT, F. (1924). Some Fallacies in the Interpretation of Social Cost. *The Quarterly Journal of Economics* **38**, 582–606

LANCASTER, R.K. and LIPSEY, R.G. (1956–1957). The General Theory of the Second-best. *Review of Economic Studies* **24**, 11–32

LEONTIEF, W. (1971). Theoretical Assumptions and Non-observed Facts. *American Economic Review* **61**, 1–7

LINDAHL, E. (1919). Just taxation—a Positive Solution. In *Classics in the Theory of Public Finance* (ed. by R.A. Musgrave and A.T. Peacock), pp. 168–176. London, Macmillan, 1967

LITTLE, I.M.D. (1957). *A Critique of Welfare Economics*, 2nd edn. Oxford, Oxford University Press

MARSHALL, A. (1890). *Principles of Economics* 9th(Variorum) edn (ed. by C.W. Guillebaud), pp. 100, 131. London, Macmillan, 1963

MAZZOLA, U. (1890). The Formation of the Prices of Public Goods. Trans. E. Henderson and repr. in *Classics in The Theory of Public Finance* (ed. by R.A. Musgrave and A. Peacock). London, Macmillan, 1967

MINARD, J. (1850). Notions élémentaires d'economie politique appliquées aux travaux publique. *Annales des ponts et chaussees, Memoirs et Documents*, 2d Ser. **19**, 1–125

MISHAN, E.J. (1960). A Survey of Welfare Economics, 1939–59. *The Economic Journal* **70**, 197–256

MISHAN, E.J. (1971). The Postwar Literature on Externalities: An Interpretive Essay. *Journal of Economic Literature* **9**, 1–28

MISHAN, E.J. (1973). Welfare Criteria: Resolution of a Paradox. *The Economic Journal* **83**, 747–767

MOHRING, H. and BOYD, J.H. (1971). Analyzing 'Externalities': 'Direct Interaction' vs. 'Asset Utilization' Frameworks. *Economica* **38**, 347–361

MORRISON, C.C. and PFOUTS, R.W. (1981). Hotelling's Proof of the Marginal Cost Pricing Theorem. *Atlantic Economic Journal* **9**, 34–37

MYINT, H. (1948). *Theories of Welfare Economics*, p. 3. Cambridge, Mass., Harvard University Press

NATH, S.K. (1969). *A Reappraisal of Welfare Economics*, pp. 106ff., 230. New York, Augustus M. Kelley

NAVIER, H. (1832). De l'execution des travaux publique, et particulierment des concessions. *Annales des ponts et chaussées, Mémoirs et Documents*, 1st Ser. **3**, 1–31

NOZICK, R. (1974). *Anarchy, State, and Utopia*. New York, Basic Books

O'BRIEN, D.P. (1975). *The Classical Economists*. Oxford, The Clarendon Press

O'BRIEN, D.P. (1981). A. Marshall, 1842–1924, In *Pioneers of Modern Economics in Britain*, (ed. by D.P. O'Brien and J.R. Presley), pp. 36–71. London, Macmillan

PANTALEONI, M. (1898). *Pure Economics*, trans. by T.B. Bruce. London, Macmillan

PARETO, V. (1906). *Manual of Political Economy*, English trans., 1971. New York, Augustus M. Kelley

PIGOU, A.C. (1912). *Wealth and Welfare*. London, Macmillan

PIGOU, A.C. (1920). *The Economics of Welfare*. London, Macmillan

PIGOU, A.C. (1922). Empty Economic Boxes: A Reply. *The Economic Journal* **32**, 458–465

QUIRK, J. and SAPOSNIK, R. (1968). *Introduction to General Equilibrium Theory and Welfare Economics*. New York, McGraw-Hill

RAWLS, J. (1971). *A Theory of Justice*. New York, Oxford University Press

ROBERTSON, D.H. (1924). Those Empty Boxes. *The Economic Journal* **34**, 16–30

ROBINSON, J. (1933). *The Economics of Imperfect Competition*. London, Macmillan

ROWLEY, C.K. and PEACOCK, A.T. (1975). *Welfare Economics: A Liberal Restatement*, pp. 10, 60. New York, John Wiley and Sons

RUFF, L.E. (1970). The Common Sense of Pollution. *The Public Interest* **19**, 69–85

SAMUELS, W.J. (1966). *The Classical Theory of Economic Policy*. Cleveland, Ohio, World Publishing

SAMUELSON, P.A. (1950). Evaluation of Real National Income. *Oxford Economic Papers* **2**, 98–117

SAMUELSON, P.A. (1954). The Pure Theory of Public Expenditure. *Review of Economics and Statistics* **36**, 387–389

SCITOVSKY, T. (1941). A Note on Welfare Propositions in Economics. *Review of Economic Studies* **9**, 77–88

SCITOVSKY, T. (1951). The State of Welfare Economics. In *Papers on Welfare and Growth*, pp. 174–189. Stanford, Stanford University Press

SMITH, A. (1776). *An Inquiry into the Nature and Causes of the Wealth of Nations*, p. 625. New York, Random House, 1937

THOMPSON, E.A. (1965). A Pareto-optimal Group Decision Process. *Papers on Non-Market Decision Making* **1**, 133–140

TIDEMAN, T.N. and TULLOCK, G. (1976). A New and Superior Process for Making Social Choices. *Journal of Political Economy* **84**, 1145–1159

TURVEY, R. (1963). On Divergence Between Social Cost and Private Cost. *Economica* **30**, 309–313

WALRAS, L. (1874). *Elements of Pure Economics*, trans. by W. Jaffé. Homewood, Ill., R.D. Irwin, 1954

WICKSELL, K. (1896). A New Principle of Just Taxation. In *Classics in the Theory of Public Finance* (ed. by R.A. Musgrave and A.T. Peacock), pp. 72–118. London, Macmillan, 1967

WINCH, D.M. (1965). Consumer's Surplus and the Compensation Principle. *American Economic Review* **55**, 395–423

WINCH, D.M. (1971). *Analytical Welfare Economics*. Baltimore, Penguin

Chapter Four

Public Finance

J. Creedy

4.1 Introduction

Public finance is concerned with the very broad range of issues relating to government expenditure and the methods used to finance that expenditure. It examines the economic role of the State in the allocation of resources by considering both the effects of specified expenditure and revenue policies and the nature of policies which are required in order to achieve efficiency and equity objectives. The methods used to raise revenue, and the purposes for which it is required, have varied considerably over time and from country to country. The subject acquires additional interest, since, nothing shows so clearly the character of a society and of a civilization as does the fiscal policy that its political sector adopts, (Schumpeter, 1954, p. 769)[1].

A further interesting, although complicating, feature of public finance is the strong interdependence between expenditure and revenue policies. The ability of governments to raise revenue by various methods depends significantly on the way in which the revenue is spent[2]. Obvious examples include expenditure on health, education, public transport and other measures which may increase growth and earning capacity. Conversely, the particular methods chosen to raise revenue may, for example, harm work incentives, create distortions in the economy or raise unemployment. These responses impair the ability of governments to spend in the way in which they had originally planned[3].

Public finance has sometimes been compared with 'private' finance, by suggesting that whereas the individual's problem is to allocate a fixed budget, the government's problem is to devise ways of raising revenue to meet a specified amount of expenditure[4]. While this comparison does not really do justice either to individual or to public finance, it is nevertheless true to say that in formal analysis the problems have often been constructed in this way. This procedure reflects an understandable need to take problems 'one at a time'. But just as models of household demand *and* labour supply have recently been developed, so the interdependence .between revenue and expenditure has gradually been given more explicit attention[5].

4.1.1 GOVERNMENT CONTROL OF APPROPRIATIONS

The statement that public finance is concerned with *government* revenue and expenditure requires further comment. Although a large variety of methods of raising revenue was used by English monarchs before the Revolution of 1688, largely to finance wars and personal expenditure, the economic analysis of such methods could now hardly be described under the modern heading of public finance[6]. Those who object to current taxes may gain some solace by considering the methods used under the right of seignory. Sir John Sinclair (1790) suggested that

> this system, originally intended for the public protection and security, was afterwards made a pretext to introduce a plan of tyranny and oppression hardly to be equalled in history (p. 19).

The Revolution of 1688 involved the rejection of the absolute concept of the monarchy, when Parliament replaced James II with William III. At the same time Parliament took more effective control of the nation's finances, so that this marks a crucial stage in the gradual development of English public finance. Earlier concessions by the monarchy, made in order to gain additional revenues, are to be found (for example, in the Magna Carta of John), but it was not until after 1688 that systematic accounts were prepared which facilitated control over the appropriation of revenue. The struggle with the monarchy to obtain control of public revenue and expenditure can, of course, be traced in many countries[7]. Indeed, the establishment of a constitutional or, rather, elected government within a country may be regarded as a prerequisite for public finance, according to its modern meaning[8].

The development of public expenditure and systems of taxation may also be related to Parliamentary reform and the widening of the franchise. The establishment of representative government has not, in fact, been associated with a reduction in expenditure but has been an important element in the dramatic increase in public expenditure. This is partly related to factors such as the increased recognition of possible benefits arising from some forms of expenditure (when not simply devoted to the aggrandisement of the monarchy), the greater expense of more complex public administration and increased demands for transfer payments[9]. Furthermore, the greater stability of

Parliament (the legislature) allows a much greater use of government long-term borrowing, whereas most of the borrowing of monarchs was of a very short-term nature, at high rates of interest, and was based on the expected proceeds of tax revenues. Indeed, the establishment of a National Debt began with the long-term loan of £1.2m from, and the deliberate establishment for that purpose of, the Bank of England in 1694. Other early large loans were associated with the granting of special monopoly privileges to companies such as the New East India Company and the South Sea Company (which had much to gain from victory in the wars against the French). It is often claimed that England's more highly developed financial system and government borrowing played a large part in the victory over the French at the beginning of the eighteenth-century, which gained control over important overseas markets. The ability to finance the huge expenditure on the war effort, with the use of loans, enabled England to gain victory over a country which, in terms of population and wealth, was much more powerful[10].

Public expenditure in times of war has, in fact, dominated much of the course of the system of taxation which now operates in Britain, and has been a major influence on the growth of public expenditure from the late seventeenth century[11]. While it may be thought that war expenditure is a prime example of the interdependence between government expenditure and revenue, it may also be suggested that the importance of 'necessary' war expenditure partly explains the approach of earlier tax writers. This approach took the level of expenditure as exogenously given and regarded the benefits as indivisible and impossible to allocate to individuals.

4.1.2 PUBLIC FINANCE IN THE MONETARY ECONOMY

It may perhaps be thought that if the subject of public finance is largely concerned with the allocation of resources, the use of the term *finance* is not quite accurate. However, the government control of resources on a significant scale requires payments to be made in money rather than in kind. Without the ability to collect taxes in money, the division of the 'burden' of taxation in what might be regarded as an 'equitable' way is almost impossible. As Musgrave (1959) clearly stated, 'the need for securing a cost distribution independently of the particular resource transfer is *the* function and *raison d'être* of taxation'. The sophisticated development of a monetary economy is therefore a prerequisite for a significant amount of government expenditure. The earlier attempts by the English monarchy, engaged in overseas crusades and wars and maintaining troops for long periods, to convert payments in kind to money in an economy where specie was scarce, created great difficulties. These attempts were, furthermore, frustrated by earlier debasements of the currency.

It is therefore no accident that the growth of public expenditure, and serious thought about public finance matters after the Revolution of 1688, coincided with a significant development of monetary institutions. Despite this importance, and the fact that the National Debt is prominent in public finance literature, the wider financial implications of government borrowing and the printing of money are not examined in this chapter.

4.1.3 PUBLIC FINANCE AND STATISTICS

Connected with the increasing control and administration by Parliament of the national finances, and the very large increase in war-related expenditure in the late 1600s and early 1700s, were early attempts to measure the National Income. These attempts were facilitated by the data generated in the process of assessing and collecting tax revenue, and were stimulated by the desire on the part of the investigators to show that the nation was not suffering an intolerable burden arising from the increase in government expenditure occasioned by the wars. The first estimates were those of William Petty, and it is known that

> In estimating the National Income and resources of England, Petty had several objectives in mind. First of all, he wanted to prove mathematically that the State could raise a much larger revenue from taxes to finance its peace and wartime needs, and that it could do so by more equitable and less burdensome forms of taxation...Secondly, Petty wanted to disprove the notion that England had been ruined by the Revolution and foreign wars (Studenski, 1958, p. 27)[13].

A further interesting connection between the recurrence of 'crises', the stimulus to data collection and analysis in order to place the current situation in perspective, and public use of the techniques developed, may be mentioned at this point. These factors are actually associated with a link between demography and public finance. The *Bills of Mortality* (of deaths occurring in London) were initially produced to give warning, or to allay false apprehensions, of outbreaks of the plague. These data stimulated the development of actuarial techniques in the late seventeenth century, exemplified by the production by Graunt of the first set of life tables in 1662. Such information was used as the basis of offers of State annuities in order to raise long-term loans. They were, in fact, first used by the Dutch in 1671, but were adopted several times by the government of William III. It is of interest that these methods were first applied primarily to government finance; that is, before the beginning of true life-insurance by joint-stock companies. The use of state annuities nevertheless represented a distinct improvement over the loans which were made on the basis of a lottery, and which were devised in order to make use of the great popular interest in gambling[14].

4.2 Public expenditure

4.2.1 BRITISH CLASSICAL VIEWS

When the early classical economists were considering the role of public expenditure at the end of the eighteenth century, that expenditure was already dominated by war finance, the importance of which was to increase to unprecedented levels during the Napoleonic wars. Much of the later technical discussion of public finance therefore concentrated on methods of war finance, in particular on the problem of interest charges on the national debt. It is perhaps not really surprising that the classical economists did not take seriously the possibility of dividing the benefits of public expenditure among the taxpayers. Concern was mainly with the 'fiscal problem' of raising a given amount of revenue in the most equitable way, involving (in a way which was not really clarified until much later) the 'least sacrifice'. Taxation was regarded neither as an 'insurance premium' nor as payment for a *quid pro quo*[15]. The prevailing view is stated most clearly by McCulloch (1845), who accepted the need for expenditure, but argued that

> it is no part of our business to inquire whether the revenue raised by the State exceeds its necessary wants, or whether it be judiciously expended. These questions, how important soever, do not affect the principles on which taxes should be imposed, or the method of their imposition (p. 16).

It is true that to the modern reader Smith's (1776) earlier statement of his famous first maxim of taxation seems highly ambiguous. He suggested that

> The subjects of every State ought to contribute towards the support of the government, as nearly as possible, in proportion to their respective abilities; that is, in proportion to the revenue which they respectively enjoy under the protection of the State (p. 350).

The first half of this sentence may be interpreted as saying that taxation should be according to the individual's 'ability to pay', while the second half suggests that taxation should be according to the 'benefits' received. The more likely interpretation arises, however, from a consideration of the views of the role of the State held by others, like Hobbes, Locke, Hume and Rousseau, who are generally thought to have held a 'benefit' view of taxation[16]. They saw the main role of the State, within a contractarian model, as protection, and taxation was regarded as the 'price' of protection. Since 'income' was regarded as the best measure of the benefits of protection, the two principles amounted to the same thing and were indeed indistinguishable in the minds of the earlier authors[17]. Nevertheless the main view taken during the first three quarters of the nineteenth century is that reflected in McCulloch's statement quoted above (see also Edgeworth, 1925).

Despite the fact that the view of Smith as a leading proponent of extreme *laisser-faire* is really a caricature, it is nevertheless the case that the role which Smith set out was limited. It has been easy for later critics to suggest that Smith had no 'theory of public expenditure'; that the only theory held, and vigorously pursued by later chancellors such as Gladstone, was one of retrenchment[18]. However, it is necessary to appreciate that much of Smith's discussion of government expenditure was concerned with the issues surrounding the *formation* of constitutional government. These issues were being fiercely debated at the time, and, of course, the French and American Revolutions were to follow very soon after the appearance in 1776 of the *Wealth of Nations*. The later theories of government expenditure are either positive theories in post-constitutional frameworks (involving the politics of choice and voting procedures) or concerned with the optimal allocation of public expenditure in a static framework, using methods of analysis and a subjective theory of demand developed by the neoclassical writers[19].

The rejection of a *quid pro quo* view of taxation by the British writers on public finance naturally led to an emphasis on taxation as a compulsory levy. The taxes selected to raise a given revenue should therefore impose the least sacrifice, and a great deal of attention was paid to aspects such as the 'convenience', the 'certainty' of tax levies and the administrative costs. These were given considerable emphasis in the remaining three of Smith's famous maxims. The British writers, and most politicians, were strongly opposed to any system which to them contained 'inquisitorial' elements.

4.2.2 THE VOLUNTARY EXCHANGE APPROACH

The American, French and later European Revolutions in the middle of the nineteenth century took, however, a rather different form from the earlier English Revolution. The establishment of representative government was achieved with considerably more violence, and was much more evident to the majority of the population than in England. Indeed, Bagehot (1865) refers to a characteristic English dislike of government and authority, and explains this by a history of *resistance* to executive government. He argued that

> By the very nature of our Government our executive cannot be liked and trusted as the Swiss or the American is liked and trusted (p. 378).

Thus to 'continental' writers the close connection between politics and government expenditure and taxation became much more evident, and there was clearly a need for a 'new principle' of taxation. The principle must not only recognize explicitly the benefits from government expenditure which accrue to different individuals, but also the ability of the electorate to reject a government whose policies it dislikes. Therefore it was necessary to specify not only the conditions for an efficient allocation between private and public expenditure, but also those under which stability would be maintained in the sense that any policy decision would not be rejected by the electorate. Although a number of European writers examined these problems, the clearest statement of a 'new principle' came from the important contribution of Wicksell in 1896[20].

Instead of emphasizing the compulsory aspects of taxation Wicksell was concerned with the nature of taxation as 'voluntary exchange', similar to the exchange of private goods and amenable to the same kind of analysis. Taxes were to be regarded as indirect payments for the subjective benefits gained from government expenditure[21]. Wicksell suggested that individuals should be able to vote for a set of fully specified tax and expenditure plans (each expenditure plan could, of course, be financed by a variety of schemes of taxation) and only those which receive unanimous support should be adopted. Thus:

> The practical realisation of the principle of voluntary consent and unanimity…requires first of all that no public expenditures ever be voted upon without simultaneous determination of the means of covering their cost (Wicksell, 1896, in Musgrave and Peacock, 1958, p. 91).

This principle clearly satisfies (what was later to be called) the Pareto criterion, and a policy which satisfied this condition would not subsequently be outvoted. It must be stressed that Wicksell's principle presumes that the distribution of income is in some sense optimal. This does not mean that Wicksell did not believe that redistribution is a legitimate function of governments; indeed there was increasing acceptance of a redistributive role in the late nineteenth century[22]. What Wicksell suggested was that the 'social welfare' aspects could be examined separately from the 'allocative' aspects of government policy[23]. Nevertheless, he recognized that in practice the distribution of income at any time would not be 'ideal', and he was prepared to relax his principle to being one of 'almost' unanimity.

The explicit introduction of the benefits of public expenditure in a voluntary exchange context was later extended, particularly by Lindahl in 1919, to show that the 'just' solution to taxation would be to set the tax price equal to each individual's marginal valuation of the public good. The partial equilibrium demand curve for a public good was, furthermore, shown to be obtained as the vertical (rather than horizontal) sum of individual demand curves[24].

4.2.3 THE MODERN THEORY OF PUBLIC GOODS

There are, however, two major difficulties with Wicksell's principle. The first concerns the problem of distribution and the analytical separation of the 'social welfare' and 'allocative' branches of public finance. The second relates to the problem that because of the property of non-excludability of public goods, there is generally no clear incentive for individuals to reveal their true preferences. These issues will be treated in turn.

The extension of the standard general equilibrium model to allow for public goods, by Samuelson (1954), represents in a very clear way the application of the theorems of Pareto optimality to public expenditure. For each pair of private goods it is required that the marginal rates of substitution of all individuals are equal, and that the common marginal rate of substitution is equal to the marginal rate of transformation. However, the extended first-order conditions require that the *sum* over all individuals of the marginal rate of substitution between public and private goods should be equal to the marginal rate of transformation between the goods. But the important point about these extended conditions for Pareto optimality is that, just as in the case of private goods, they do not define a *unique* position. A range of efficient positions for variations in the distribution of income is defined (along a utility possibility curve), and the choice among these depends on explicit views about the desired distribution; views which underlie a social welfare function. The optimal position requires *simultaneous* choice of income distribution and the allocation of resources between private and public goods. The former is to be achieved, in principle at least, by lump sum transfers[25]. The implication is that there is no strict separation between the problems of distribution and of optimal provision of public goods. Thus this analysis rejects the claim made by the benefit theorists of the end of the nineteenth century that their treatment provided expenditure policies and a set of tax 'prices' which do not (unlike the 'sacrifice' approach) require interpersonal comparisons.

It is worth stressing at this point that the 'voluntary exchange' theories, and the Samuelson (1954) analysis of public goods, follow the conventional utility theory of demand and are therefore entirely individualistic in their approach. The problem, as specified, is to determine the optimal amount of public expenditure based on social choice, where that choice is regarded as the outcome or 'aggregate' of individual preferences. The conditions required for the consistent aggregation of preferences, and the possibility of obtaining social choice functions, have, of course, given rise to an extensive literature[26]. However, critics of the theory have suggested that public goods do not enter individual utility functions in the same way as do private goods, and that views concerning public expenditure are based on a 'group-minded' attitude. The orthodox response to such criticisms has usually been rather peremptory and dismissive, preferring to regard such a view as a value judgement that social choice *should* be concerned with individual values, rather than as a statement about the way in which certain groups do, in fact, behave[27].

The difficulty of inducing individuals to reveal their true preferences for public goods, of overcoming the so-called 'free rider' problem so clearly stated by Samuelson (1954), has been investigated at length since the late 1950s. A seminal contribution is that of Vickrey (1961), which provides a method of allocating the tax payments and simultaneously generating preference revelation. What is surprising is that the application of Vickrey's method to public goods was not made until the early 1970s[28]. The suggestion is that in voting for two alternatives, each individual must state the value in money terms of the benefits. The system is such that a person pays tax only if his vote (in terms of the statement of his pecuniary benefits) is decisive in changing the outcome (given all other individuals' votes). The tax paid is equal to the amount needed to balance the benefits in aggregate. For example, suppose that the total stated benefits for projects denoted A and B are 120 and 140, respectively, and that a further individual has stated benefits of 30 for project A. The latter individual's preferences are decisive in favour of project A; he would therefore pay tax, but only 20 units. The tax paid is always less than the benefits received by any individual, there is no incentive to understate the gain (and incur the risk of foregoing the chance to cast the decisive vote) and there is no incentive to overstate the gain (as this would lead to excessive tax payments which could outweigh the actual gain). The basic framework has been much extended, though there are clearly many problems. These include the incentive to form coalitions, the appropriate treatment of income distribution (since the possibility of 'bankruptcy' exists) and the possibility that subsequent voting is affected by outcomes. Furthermore, the costs of reaching agreement may well be prohibitive.

4.2.4 POSITIVE THEORIES OF PUBLIC EXPENDITURE

In contrast to the various normative theories of public expenditure, there has also been considerable interest, since the late 1950s, in positive theories of the growth of total government expenditure, often associated with the so-called 'law of increasing expenditure' of Wagner[29]. This kind of work, too voluminous to be examined in detail here, has involved a variety of approaches. These range from the view that the State is controlled by a ruling class which attempts to maximize revenues by creating a 'fiscal illusion' (arising from the uncertainty inherent in general financing rather than 'earmarking'), to models of bureaucracies, to an approach which assumes that governments try to maximize expenditure and regards the tax structure as an attempt to *control* that behaviour. Other studies include econometric tests of the 'median voter' model[30].

A broad empirical analysis of the growth of public expenditure in Britain since 1790, which has stimulated much subsequent research, was carried out by Peacock and Wiseman (1967)[31]. While their study does not contain a formal model, they synthesize in an interesting way a number of factors associated with what they called the 'displacement effect' of war (that is, a discontinuous shift in the trend of expenditure growth). They argue that individuals have views about public expenditure which are not necessarily compatible with their views about reasonable tax burdens. These views are rather unsteadily balanced in times of peace, initially by the active policy of retrenchment which was later replaced by the concept of taxable capacity. In periods of upheaval, exemplified by war, taxable capacity increases as the usual constraints are relaxed. The increase in expenditure is maintained after war by what are called 'inspection' and 'concentration' effects. The former concept relates to the greater awareness of social conditions (especially health, housing and education) which is brought about by war. Concentration effects refer to the increasing movement towards central government control (away from local authorities) which is required in wartime planning. The attempts in recent years (especially in Britain) to reduce public expenditure clearly show the difficulties of pursuing a policy of retrenchment, compared with one of expansion[33].

4.3 Personal taxation

The study of the history of personal taxation, and in particular of income taxation, exemplifies a number of themes which recur in all aspects of public finance. These include the considerable importance of prevailing attitudes towards inequality and redistribution, the strong connection between financial policy and political reform and the fact that in matters of government revenue 'necessity is the parent of invention'.

The unprecedented costs of the Napoleonic wars, quickly following the wars of the middle and late eighteenth century, were directly influential in Pitt's introduction of the income tax in 1799 as a temporary device to raise revenue. This was repealed after the peace of Amiens, but promptly reintroduced in 1803 by Addington, and was not repealed again until 1816. The income tax was again introduced as an emergency measure by Peel in 1842, but with Gladstone's strong desire to eliminate it, the tax did not really become firmly established until the late 1880s[34]. The introduction of Pay-As-You-Earn (PAYE) during the Second World War came less than one year after a government White Paper had rejected the idea[35]. In America the introduction of an income tax did not occur on a permanent basis until 1913.

Popular objection to the income tax was largely associated with what was regarded as its 'inquisitorial' nature, rather than with any formal economic arguments. The feeling against the tax was, however, not always as strong as sometimes suggested. Indeed, the principles involved in the schedule adopted by Pitt represented no very significant departure from recent practice, and previous years had seen a considerable increase in the use of 'assessed' taxes. These included taxes on personal property such as luxuries, including coaches, racehorses, plate, perfumes and many other items. It may be added here that the use of the term 'assessed' taxes is in some ways preferable to the term 'direct taxation', which, despite its ambiguities, is more commonly used. The distinction between 'direct' and 'indirect' taxation has varied somewhat over time, but the former is perhaps best defined as including those taxes which may be adjusted to the individual characteristics of the taxpayer, and the latter as those levied on transactions irrespective of the circumstances of buyer or seller[36].

In the analysis of taxation it is clearly necessary to specify the *base* on which the tax is to be levied, and also the *rate structure* which applies to the base. Both aspects, involving technical and equity problems, have given rise to much controversy in the field of personal taxation.

4.3.1 SOME RECURRENT ISSUES

A great deal of the serious discussion of issues relating to the choice of the tax base and the rate structure was associated with the various Select Committees which were appointed by Gladstone, during his protracted attempt to repeal the income tax reintroduced by Peel. In the present century considerable debate has been stimulated by two Royal Commissions, under the Chairmanship of Colwyn (1920) and

Radcliffe (1955), respectively. The income tax was regarded for many years as a tax on various sources of income rather than a personal tax. Indeed the famous schedules (from A to E, covering different income sources) were first introduced in 1803 and were in operation for over 150 years. Early debate therefore concerned the question of 'differentiation' according to source, since initially the same tax rate applied to all sources. This issue was discussed 'with a sophistry comparable only to that of later scholastic logic' (Shehab, 1953).

The debate on differentiation partly involved the question of the appropriate taxation of savings, which raised in an early form the question of whether the tax base should be defined by some concept of income or of total expenditure (that is, a base which excludes savings). Although an expenditure tax was supported in theory by Mill (1848), it did not receive fully articulated support until the work of Fisher (1937). Prest (1979) has commented that since then, 'the controversy has a curious twenty-year periodicity with Irving Fisher in the 30s, Kaldor in the 50s and the Meade Committee in the 1970s'.

The choice of the appropriate tax base, between expenditure and some concept of income, is sometimes coupled with the question of whether taxation should be levied according to the benefits received from public expenditure or according to ability to pay. It is possible to link the choice of base with the benefit approach, for in the benefit approach either income or expenditure could be regarded as approximations to benefits received. Although the approach strictly requires equal treatment of people who have the same effective demand for public goods, it has been seen that this is non-operational, because it requires knowledge of true preferences. Since this is not available, it might be argued that income is a good approximation, especially if public goods involve substantial capital outlays.

Nevertheless it is true that the large majority of the literature on the choice of the tax base has compared the bases from the point of view of ability to pay and 'equal sacrifice'[38]. Furthermore, the question of the progressivity of the rate structure has been discussed in terms of *income* taxation, and has involved the implications of alternative interpretations of the expression 'equal sacrifice'. Nevertheless, taxes on total expenditure may also display any required degree of progression. Some aspects of these issues—differentiation, the choice of tax base, and progression—are examined in turn in this section.

4.3.2 DIFFERENTIATION AND THE TREATMENT OF SAVINGS

It has been seen that from the earliest form of the income tax in Britain the meaning of 'income' has been defined by reference to its source, rather than according to a rigorous economic definition. The general question of 'differentiation' was first examined in terms of the difference between 'permanent' and 'transitory' incomes. In practice, the distinction between these types of income stream was made by distinguishing between sources; for example, property and interest income on the one hand and income from employment on the other. One argument concerned the effort of work, and the suggestion that a greater sacrifice is involved in paying the same amount of tax on earned income as compared with property income.

A major critic of the income tax, McCulloch, actually based part of his criticism on the argument that it should in principle be based on the capitalized value of the income stream, rather than on the annual flow of income. Otherwise, he argued, temporary incomes would pay proportionately more tax than permanent incomes. But, of course, this argument must be based on the assumption that the income tax is itself temporary (as indeed many people had hoped it would be), otherwise permanent incomes pay tax over a longer period and the capitalized values of the tax payments would be in the appropriate proportion[39]. As an extension of his argument, McCulloch argued that the tax on earnings should be based on their capitalized value, using estimates of life expectancy. But because of the inadequacy of life tables for such purposes, the difficulty of treating educational expenses, and of separating the different elements of self-employment income, this condition could never be met in practice. Thus, by stating such rigid requirements for an income tax, it was not difficult for McCulloch to dismiss it as impracticable.

Mill's main concern, however, was with the need of those with temporary incomes (exemplified by wages and salaries) to save for their retirement. The need for such saving would be lower for those with permanent incomes. Therefore a greater sacrifice is involved in paying tax on a given amount of 'temporary' income, since part of that income must be saved for the future. These arguments for differentiation were actually supplemented by the rather different argument that savings were subject, under a conventional income tax, to what was unfortunately named 'double taxation'. Mill (1848) argued that since the income from which savings are made are subject to tax, and then the interest from the savings subsequently taxed, savings are effectively 'double' taxed. Thus

> the proper mode of assessing an income tax would be to tax only the part of income devoted to expenditure, exempting that which is saved (p. 813)[40].

Mill suggested that in practice it would not be possible to assess people on the basis of their expenditure, so that differentiation should be used as a practical compromise. Then

> if no plan can be devised for the exemption of actual savings, ... it is necessary ... to take into account ... what the different classes of contributors *ought* to save (p. 815).

When differentiation was eventually adopted in the legislation, earnings from employment were taxed at two thirds of the rate imposed on interest and property income[41]. This difference was, in fact, based on a contemporary estimate of the *actual* propensity to save out of the different sources. Furthermore, life insurance payments, up to specified limits, could be deducted from income for tax purposes.

Mill's argument failed, however, to acknowledge that the interest arises from what is essentially a new source of income. More explicit arguments for the exemption of savings are based either on the deliberate desire to stimulate saving in order, for example, to increase growth, or on the value judgement that inequality is reflected in differences between consumption rather than differences in the *power* to consume[42]. The modern proponents of expenditure taxes nevertheless continue to be attracted by what must be thought to be the persuasive power of the expression 'double taxation'[43]. Furthermore, although the income tax contains many accepted limitations which make reform long overdue, there has been a tendency to compare an ideal expenditure tax with an imperfect income tax[44].

4.3.3 THE CONCEPT OF INCOME

Much of the (English) literature has tended to emphasize a concept of income (such as Hicks, 1939) which depends on each individual's expectations, and is therefore impossible to measure. Furthermore, when several Royal Commissions have been reluctant to define income, it has been easy to criticize the conceptual basis of the income tax. However, the American literature has concentrated on what is called an *accretion* concept of income; that is, the accretion of economic power between two specified dates. This more comprehensive concept can actually be traced to 1889, and is referred to as the 'Schanz–Haig –Simons' definition (after its three major proponents)[45]. Simons (1938) defined income for tax purposes as

the algebraic sum of (1) the market value of rights exercised in consumption and (2) the change in the value of the store of property rights between the beginning and end of the period in question ... In other words, it is merely the result obtained by adding consumption during the period to 'wealth' at the end of the period and then subtracting 'wealth' at the beginning (p. 50).

A major implication of this definition is that it includes all capital gains in the calculation of net worth at the beginning and end of the period, along with all transfers. But in practice it would be impossible to administer a tax based on valuations rather than realizations, so that a further problem arises over the timing of realizations. To overcome this difficulty, Vickrey (1939) proposed a scheme of lifetime averaging (or lifetime cumulation)[46]. There are, of course, many issues which have been discussed at length in the literature, including the appropriate allowance for inflation, the treatment of the costs of obtaining income, household production and imputed rents[47].

4.3.4 PROGRESSION AND OPTIMAL INCOME TAXATION

It has been seen that much of the discussion of income taxation after its reintroduction in 1842 concerned the question of differentiation according to the source rather than the amount[48]. With few exceptions, there was strong opposition to any form of progression, and after twenty years of wrangling over income taxation there were few significant discussions from 1862 until the end of the nineteenth century[49]. This quiet period was associated with the large reductions in expenditure, after Palmerston's expensive foreign policy, which allowed the tax rate to be reduced from a level of 16d in the pound during the Crimean war to 2d in the pound in 1874.

The statement that most economists objected to progression must, however, be qualified to some extent because of the fact that certain lower incomes were exempted. Initially the level of exemption was set on humanitarian grounds at what was regarded as a subsistence minimum, combined with the argument that a tax on lower incomes would be passed on to employers. But it is important to recognize that, unlike the present system, all other incomes were taxed at a fixed proportion of *gross* income. In order to avoid hardship at the lower limit a system of abatements was used. Thus, specified income ranges, *below* the level at which proportional taxation applied, were taxed at *lower* rates. That system is better described as having 'degressive graduation'. In the case of 'progressive graduation' the tax rate *increases* as income increases *above* a threshold. For the large majority of taxpayers the marginal and average rates were therefore equal. Mill (1848) was one of the first to argue that income tax should be based on the excess of income above the 'subsistence' level[50]. Thus Mill could be said to be strongly against *graduation*, but not against progression, since his proposal implied average tax rates lower than the constant marginal rate.

While a system in which the marginal tax rates exceed average tax rates (so that average rates increase with income) is generally regarded as a minimum requirement for progressivity, the precise measurement of progression is far from being a simple matter. This is now well recognized, and in comparing the progressivity of alternative tax systems, modern treatments would prefer to compare systems by their effects on a measure of dispersion of the distribution of income. High marginal tax rates are, of course, meaningless if there are no incomes to tax in the specified ranges[51].

With the widening of the franchise and increasing government expenditure towards the end of the nineteenth century, there was greater acceptance of progressive taxation, in terms of graduation of the rate structure. Chamberlain's *Radical Programme* in favour of graduation was issued in 1885, and, only one month after Gladstone's retirement in 1894, Sir William Harcourt introduced his famous budget which proposed progressive death duties, and which he had originally intended should include a graduated income tax (see Shehab, 1953). An 'economic' rationale for progressive taxation was first clearly stated by Cohen-Stuart (1889, with excerpts in Musgrave and Peacock, 1958) and Edgeworth (1897). It was explicitly based on a reinterpretation of Mill's requirement of 'equal sacrifice' and a broadening of this aspect of public finance to allow for wider considerations of social welfare[52].

Edgeworth's concern was to examine the nature of the tax system which produces the utilitarian maximum, and in this context it was natural to interpret equal sacrifice as equal *marginal* sacrifice, which implies *minimum total* sacrifice. Edgeworth showed that with equal utility functions and diminishing marginal utility of income, the requirement of raising a given revenue with equal marginal sacrifice gives the result that income taxes should be progressive. Other interpretations, such as equal absolute sacrifice or equal proportional sacrifice, only lead to progression under specific assumptions about the nature of the utility function[53]. However, Edgeworth did not himself favour highly progressive taxes; he was very conscious of the strong nature of the assumptions, was not prepared to make explicit assumptions about the form of utility functions and was aware of the possible effects on incentives.

The basic utilitarian approach to taxation in terms of minimum sacrifice was, of course, criticized, for what are now familiar reasons, in the 1920s and 1930s[54]. But in view of later analyses it is worth emphasizing the special nature of Edgeworth's approach to taxation, and in particular his use of utilitarianism, which is quite different from that of his contemporaries. In 1881 Edgeworth had used utilitarianism as a principle of *arbitration* in the context of indeterminate contract. He had shown that the utilitarian solution gave a position on the contract curve of efficient exchanges, and had argued that contractors would in general agree to accept the utilitarian arrangement. From the consideration of hypothetical 'repeated experiences', Edgeworth (1881) suggested that

it may seem to each that as he cannot have his own way, in the absence of any definite principle of selection, he has about as good a chance of one of the arrangements as another ... both parties may agree to commute their chance of any of the arrangements for ... the utilitarian arrangement (p. 55).

In the context of taxation, Edgeworth clearly saw this in terms of a principle of justice in a *social contract* between government and taxpayers. In deciding on the appropriate tax burden

> each party may reflect that, in the long run of various cases ... of all the
> principles of distribution which would afford him now a greater, now a smaller
> proportion of the sum-total ability obtainable ... the principle that the
> collective utility should be on each occasion a maximum is most likely to afford
> the greatest utility in the long run to him individually (1897, in 1925, p. 102).

Edgeworth therefore clearly viewed justice in terms of choice under uncertainty, with each individual taking the *a priori* view that any outcome is *equally likely*. This 'deeper and more roundabout justification of utilitarianism' (Rawls, 1971) was later stated more rigorously by Harsanyi (1955)and Vickrey (1960) in terms of a social contract theory, following the development of the von Neumann –Morgenstern approach to choice under uncertainty[55]. It is therefore of much interest that the (maxi–min) 'theory of justice' developed by Rawls (1971), whereby the objective is to make the least well-off person as well-off as possible, may be interpreted in similar terms; but with choice, behind the 'veil of ignorance', made with each person fearing the worst and with extreme aversion to risk[56].

It is in the context of examining in rigorous terms the implications for taxation of adopting such alternative views, or principles, of distributive justice that the 'optimal tax' analyses are best regarded. The work on optimal income taxation, from Mirrlees (1971) onwards, is thus really a direct descendant of, though broader than, that of Edgeworth. Furthermore, the optimal tax literature of more recent years is distinguished by the explicit inclusion of the possible incentive effects of taxation; and it has clearly demonstrated the considerable sensitivity of the tax structure to assumptions about labour supply behaviour[57]. The specification of the limits of *feasible* redistribution, whatever the desired amount of redistribution implied in any 'social welfare function', continues to be extremely difficult[58].

4.4 Indirect taxation

Although indirect taxes include import tariffs, this section concentrates on internally traded goods and services. Unlike personal taxation, there seems to be little, if any, connection between economic analysis and the adoption by governments of specific policies or principles (most policy debates have, in fact, been concerned with tariffs). It has been seen that the classical economists were generally opposed to direct taxation, especially in the form of income taxes, and preferred the use of a broad base which would enable the rates of taxation to be kept relatively low (high rates would encourage smuggling and other forms of evasion). They argued that indirect taxes were more 'convenient', consumers were less conscious of payment, they did not face 'inquisitions' about their personal circumstances and they avoided other compliance costs associated with personal taxation[59].

4.4.1 WELFARE LOSSES: DIRECT VERSUS INDIRECT TAXES

A further argument was that individual consumers can always avoid paying high indirect taxes simply by reducing purchases of those goods and services which are most heavily taxed. However, it does not follow that consumers are no worse-off after the imposition of indirect taxes. Comparisons should really be made between tax structures yielding the same total revenue. More importantly, later analysis showed that substitution away from more heavily taxed goods and services leads to a 'deadweight' loss, even after allowing for the government expenditure of tax revenue.

This result was clearly shown by Dupuit (1844), using partial-equilibrium analysis and the concept of consumers' surplus. An *ad valorem* tax leads to an upward shift in the supply curve by the amount of the tax, and the loss of consumers' and producers' surplus exceeds the tax revenue. The net loss of producers' and consumers' surplus is (for small taxes) approximately equal to one half of the product of the reduction in consumption and the *ad valorem* rate[60]. The same basic approach was used to argue that the rate of taxation should be inversely related to the elasticities of demand and supply, and to provide an early formal analysis of the incidence of indirect taxes[61] (incidence is discussed further in section 5.5).

The partial analysis necessarily ignores the interrelationships between commodities. An early treatment, following clarification of the concepts of substitutes and complements, was provided by Edgeworth (1897), who showed that where the supply of two or more non-independent commodities is controlled by a single monopolist, a tax on one of the goods may lead to a *reduction* in the equilibrium prices of *all* the goods[62]. This paradoxical result was extended by Hotelling (1932), who obtained the precise conditions under which it would also occur in competitive markets. Hotelling (1938) later extended his analysis of commodity taxes to provide the first really rigorous statement of the principle of 'marginal cost' pricing. Any deviation of price from marginal cost was treated as an indirect tax.

Hotelling's analysis depended on the assumption that income taxes can be treated as 'lump sum' taxes; that is, they do not involve any substitution of leisure for work. The apparent 'inferiority' of indirect taxes compared with direct taxes (exemplified by income tax) has been 'demonstrated' by numerous writers, using either indifference curve analysis for single individuals or the general equilibrium statement in terms of the resulting inequality between marginal rates of substitution and marginal rates of transformation[63]. The subsequent recognition that direct taxes could also have substitution effects led initially to a rather agnostic view about the relative merits of indirect taxes and income taxation. However, the analysis of Corlett and Hague (1953) showed that welfare increases if taxes are imposed on goods which are complementary with leisure[64].

4.4.2 'SECOND-BEST' TAXATION

From the middle 1950s the analysis of taxation thereby became more clearly seen as a problem in the economic theory of the 'second-best'. Since leisure cannot be taxed, the second-best policy does not involve attempting to obtain the 'first-best' conditions elsewhere, but a set of differential rates of taxation. The explicit analysis of indirect taxation as a subject in welfare economics was considerably formalized and extended in the 1970s. However, it is interesting that this work, from the contribution of Baumol and Bradford (1970), initially involved a 'rediscovery' of the highly original but neglected paper by Ramsey (1927). Ramsey derived the result that the appropriate system of taxation to minimize welfare loss involves an equal proportionate reduction in the consumption of all goods[65]. The approach has been extended, particularly by Atkinson and Stiglitz (1972, 1976), in order to relax many of the assumptions required by Ramsey. The practical application of the rules obtained by the use of more sophisticated models requires considerable detailed knowledge of demand and supply elasticities[66].

In discussing indirect taxation it has always been recognized that in practice a trade-off must be made between the objectives of efficiency and equity. Since costless 'lump-sum' transfers cannot actually be made, it becomes important to establish the likely redistributive effects of any tax and expenditure policy. This awkward problem is the subject of the next section.

4.5 Income redistribution

4.5.1 ALTERNATIVE APPROACHES

The question of who receives the benefits from public expenditure and who bears the 'burden' of raising the required revenue is extremely complex, and continues to be the subject of much lively debate. Governments may deliberately wish to redistribute resources between individuals, or they may wish to design policies which avoid any systematic changes in income distribution. In each case it may be argued that policy statements should ideally contain some discussion of the estimated redistributive effects.

With the early emphasis in public finance literature on revenue aspects it is not surprising that the classical economists were concerned mainly with the burden of taxation. Their discussions usually concentrated on the *type* of person expected to bear the burden; for example, they took consumers, producers and landlords as separate groups. However, the burden is ultimately borne by individuals, who may receive income from a variety of sources. With the greater availability of data relating to incomes following the permanent establishment of income taxation, and the acceptance of graduation, the question of the differential burden between *income groups* began to receive serious attention in the early years of the present century[67].

Most industrial countries have seen the increasing use of direct transfers to specified individuals and a considerable increase in the state provision of goods which are to a large extent private, although they contain a certain amount of publicness. This category includes, for example, health care and education. A number of more recent studies have therefore attempted to provide statistical information about the overall redistributive effect of government expenditure and taxation policies. There may, for example, be good grounds for suggesting that individuals who receive sickness and unemployment benefits should also pay direct taxation on those benefits (in addition to indirect taxes arising from purchases, using the benefits). In these cases the analysis of taxation alone would provide a spurious indication of the progressivity of the system as a whole.

There is a fundamental problem in considering redistribution which should be mentioned here. This arises from the strong interdependence between revenue and expenditure policies which was stressed at the beginning of this chapter. There is obviously little sense in allocating taxes and benefits to income groups and describing the difference between the observed distributions of gross income and a resulting measure of 'net' income as the 'redistributive effect of government' as a whole. Much government expenditure directly gives rise to incomes, for example, of government employees, and, of course, government intervention has important indirect effects on the process of income generation. The same qualification applies to specific policies, such as a state pension scheme, since the absence of the State scheme would not be expected to imply a complete lack of private provision. Studies of redistribution must therefore be very careful to specify the nature of the comparisons being made. It seems that an appropriate approach would compare the effects of 'marginal' changes in policy, with the additional condition imposed that the marginal changes are 'revenue-neutral'. However, it is no simple matter to ensure that these conditions are satisfied[68].

4.5.2 THE INCIDENCE OF TAXES

The question of incidence arises from the recognition that the ultimate effects of a tax depend on the possibility that the individual who is in direct contact with the Inland Revenue authorities (and bears the legal or 'formal' incidence) may 'shift' the tax 'backwards' to suppliers or 'forwards' to consumers. The classical economists' views of incidence were based on the subsistence theory of labour supply and on a fairly informal distinction between luxuries and necessities. They generally assumed that indirect taxes would raise the price by the amount of the tax, and objected to a tax on necessities because, with wages at subsistence levels, it would lead to a rise in wages and thereby a reduction in profits. Similarly, wage taxes would be passed on to producers and would inhibit growth, although McCulloch did not accept that a wage tax would necessarily be shifted.

It has also been seen that a simple view of incidence initially influenced the distinction between direct and indirect taxation, and during the second half of the nineteenth century it was generally (though not universally) accepted that income taxation was not passed on (remembering that this did not involve the taxation of low or subsistence wages)[69]. However, it became clear that the effects of taxes extend far beyond the question, for example, of whether the price of a good is raised by the full extent of the tax; the producer may nevertheless suffer a reduction in profits. The precise interpretation of 'incidence' was far from clear, and despite the extensive taxonomy of shifting and incidence provided by Seligman (1899), the issue still required careful clarification by Musgrave (1959), who described 'effective' incidence in terms of resource transfer, output effects and distribution changes[70].

4.5.3 THE MEASUREMENT OF REDISTRIBUTION

Although much work remains to be done on the subject of incidence, it has been extremely tempting to examine statistically the redistributive effect of taxation and expenditure, using specific incidence assumptions. The majority of studies have assumed that income taxes are borne in full by employees and that commodity taxes are fully passed on to consumers. However, these assumptions are not strictly compatible, since inelastic commodity demands are not consistent with an inelastic supply of labour[71].

The allocation of the benefits from public expenditure also raises severe difficulties, and consequently most studies have allocated to households a much smaller proportion of expenditure than revenue. An immediate problem arises from the need to place a value on government-provided activities such as education, health and roads, and the use of costs to measure benefits is clearly unsatisfactory. Pure public goods can only be allocated in an arbitrary manner or by making explicit assumptions about individuals' utility functions, as in Aaron and McGuire (1970)[72].

It is worth stressing that the majority of studies of redistribution have been based on annual incomes (usually of specified types of household). However, it may often be the case that policies redistribute income between different stages in the life cycle, so that there may be very little redistribution of lifetime incomes, however measured. Many transfers such as sickness and unemployment benefits, and especially State pensions, are best viewed using a lifetime perspective[73]. Furthermore, some schemes may involve substantial redistribution between generations. The analysis of these wider aspects of redistribution, which are in many ways more important than redistribution of annual income, raises interesting conceptual and practical issues for researchers to grapple with in the future.

4.6 Conclusions

Within the small space available, this chapter has examined only a limited number of aspects of public finance. Topics which have not been discussed, or have been mentioned only briefly, include the National Debt, company taxation, land and wealth taxes (including death duties), local taxation (including local public goods), international aspects (including mobility, and fiscal harmonization), the wider questions concerning 'fiscal welfare', administrative problems and theories of tax reform. Nevertheless it is hoped that by examining some major aspects of public expenditure and taxation, sufficient indication has been given of the kinds of attitude to public finance issues which have been taken by economists over a fairly long period.

Although public finance has always been an important area of economics it has more recently been absorbed much more into 'mainstream' economic analysis. An important feature, which has been stressed above, is that discussion of alternative policies has gradually been brought within the general framework of 'welfare economics', involving standard efficiency criteria (rather than a set of special 'maxims') and explicit treatment of the relevant trade-offs between equity and efficiency.

Notes

1. Schumpeter was Minister of Finance in Austria for a brief period in 1919. Indeed, it was traditional for economists in Austria to take part in practical affairs. Böhm-Bawerk was three times Minister of Finance, Wieser was Minister of Commerce, and Menger had earlier been influential in bringing about the currency reform in the 1890s.

2. This has been stated in very general form by Lorenz von Stein in 1885: 'The State must use its power to create the conditions which are the absolute prerequisite of the economic capacity which is the source of taxation'. (Translated and reprinted in Musgrave and Peacock, 1958, p. 34.)

3. McCulloch, the author of the first really systematic treatise on taxation (1845), argued that in some circumstances taxation can have a stimulating effect on savings and growth, which remains even after the particular tax has been reduced. (On McCulloch's views on taxation see O'Brien (1970, pp. 229–270; 1975a, pp. 240–271; 1975b), and Leroy-Beaulieu (1906, reprinted in Musgrave and Peacock, 1958, p. 159).

4. This distinction is stated in qualified form in Hicks (1947, p. 17) and criticized by Pantaleoni (Musgrave and Peacock, 1958, p.20), and de Viti de Marco (1936, p. 35).

5. The distinction, in national accounting terms, between taxation and expenditure is far from clear. For example, should a tax allowance or tax refund be treated as a negative tax receipt or as positive expenditure? For discussion of expenditure and national income measurement see Musgrave (1959, pp. 184–204), Peacock and Wiseman (1967, pp. 4–8), Hicks (1946), Haberler and Hagen (1946).

6. For details of early forms of revenue and the finances of the English monarchy, see the studies by Harriss (1975), Chandaman (1975) and the classic works of Sinclair (1790) and Dowell (1888).

7. This is stressed by many writers on public finance; but see, for example, de Viti de Marco (1936, pp. 33, 64, n. 1), Hicks (1947, p. 10), Buxton (1888, p. viii), Wicksell (1896, in Musgrave and Peacock, 1958, p. 83, n. 1). The well-known cry of the American revolution, 'Taxation without representation is tyranny' is a further example.

8. This view is clearly stated by Stein in 1885: 'taxation ... occurs only when the will of the people, acting through legislation, confers upon the State the rig' t to intervene in the economy' (Musgrave and Peacock, 1958, pp. 29, 30).

9. A clear statement of the latter point by de Viti de Marco (1936, p.70) may be noted: 'Power tends to pass from the classes possessing wealth to the democracy of the many; and the latter use the power to increase expenditures for their own advantage and taxes at the expense of the rich.' See also Musgrave (1976, p. 310).

10. For detailed discussion of this point, see Dickson (1967). England was, after 1688, helped by the alliance with the Dutch, whose earlier strength may perhaps also be linked to a more highly developed financial system.

11. Sinclair (1790, p. 2) commented: 'Wars are perpetually arising and the contest generally is, who can first drain the Exchequer, and destroy the credit of the enemy.' Its importance is a vital element in the thesis of Peacock and Wiseman (1961), discussed in section 4.2, and can be seen in the studies of British budgets by Buxton (1888), Mallet (1913), Mallet and George (1933) and Sabine (1970). The literature on war finance is too extensive to list here, but see, for example, Nicholson (1917) and Sayers (1956).

12. These developments were perhaps helped by price stability over a long period. Early Exchequer receipts for loans were in the form of wooden 'tallies'. The burning of obsolete tallies in 1834 led to the two Houses of Parliament, except for Westminster Hall, being destroyed by fire; see Buxton (1888, p. 93).

13. The same interest in taxation and national income was displayed by Baxter, the main investigator in the middle of the nineteenth century (see Schumpeter, 1954, p. 522; Studenski, 1958). Sinclair (1790) compiled an antidote to despondency in the form of a list of quotations from earlier periods showing how the nation had been ruined. The early investigations were entirely in the spirit of empirical scientific enquiry of the age of Newton; see, for example, Clark (1949, pp. 119–146).

14. The loans were conducted by selling tickets (£10 each) and after the draw, holders were given specified sums for sixteen years; see Dickson (1967, p. 48) and Hargreaves (1930). As shown in Chapter 6 of this volume, important developments in statistical theory were made in connection with the widespread interest in gambling.

15. However, Seligman (1909, p. 166) and Myrdal (1953, p. 164) suggest that McCulloch held the 'insurance' view of taxation. This is repeated by Musgrave (1959, p. 68). But see O'Brien (1970, p. 232). For discussion and criticism of the insurance and other views see Leroy-Beaulieu in Musgrave and Peacock (1958, pp. 154–156).

16. See Musgrave (1959, p. 63) for further discussion of these authors. Musgrave (1959, p. 66) points out that William Petty's views are stated in almost the same form as Smith's first maxim, but almost a hundred years earlier. Hicks (1947, p. 133) suggests that Smith's

maxims, 'have had a fame which perhaps they hardly deserve, since they appear to have been mainly a reflexion of contemporary opinion'.

17. Mill later criticized the benefit approach on the grounds that those who benefited most from protection were the weak, sick and poor (Mill, 1848, p. 804). (All page references to Mill are to the Ashley edition, 1920.) Mill also made the interesting point that 'If a person or class of persons receive so small a share of the benefits as makes it necessary to raise the question, there is something else than taxation which is amiss, and the thing to be done is to remedy the defect, instead ... of making it a ground for demanding less taxes' (1848, p. 805).

18. Giffen (1880, p. 225) remarked that Gladstone's views were 'coloured with a passion against the waste of money, with which experience has taught him to identify almost any government expenditure'. For a valuable analysis of Smith's views in this context see Viner (1927).

19. This aspect of Smith's approach is discussed by West (1976), and Buchanan (1976, p. 281). Prest (1976, p. 321) commented on Musgrave's discussion of Smith's views as follows, 'Perhaps the difference between Professor Musgrave and myself is that he is inclined to characterize a glass which contains half the quantity of liquid which it might hold as half-empty; I should say it was half-full.'

20. This is translated and reprinted in Musgrave and Peacock (1958). See also the introduction to Musgrave and Peacock (1958, pp. ix–xix) and Musgrave (1959, pp. 61–89).

21. Pigou's brief discussion is worth noting, though he does not refer to the European writers and his comment follows discussion of the view of the State as a 'unitary being'. 'The government is not, therefore, simply an agent for carrying out on behalf of its citizens their several separate instructions; it cannot simply balance at the margin each man's desire to buy battleships against his desire to buy clothes ... As the agent of its citizens collectively, it must exercise coercion upon them individually' (1947, p. 34).

22. A clear statement of the 'social welfare' aspect of public finance is given by Wagner (1883, translated and reprinted in Musgrave and Peacock, 1958, pp. 1–15).

23. The clearest modern statement of this position is that of Musgrave (1959, pp. 84–86), who recognized its difficulties in general equilibrium terms but suggested that it is useful for pragmatic purposes.

24. For discussion of Lindahl's contribution see Musgrave (1939 and 1959, pp. 74–78). Lindahl (1919) is translated and reprinted in Musgrave and Peacock (1958). The partial-demand curve was also obtained by Bowen (1948). The 'tax price' was noted by Mazzola in 1890 (reprinted in Musgrave and Peacock, 1958, p. 37), who was discussed by Wicksell (in Musgrave and Peacock, 1958, pp. 80–82).

25. The effects of non-lump sum taxation on the Samuelson (1954) condition, and on the optimal provision of public goods, has been examined by Atkinson and Stern (1974). See also Atkinson and Stiglitz (1980, pp. 490–497). For a survey of public goods theory, see Milleron (1972).

26. Much of the literature stems from Arrow (1951). A useful survey of public choice is Mueller (1979). The link between public finance and public choice is examined by Buchanan (1975).

27. For early comments on Samuelson's (1954) paper, see Margolis (1954) and Colm (1956). On alternative approaches, see Musgrave (1959, pp. 10, 11, 87), and Samuelson (1955, p. 350). For an interesting analysis of self-esteem, sympathy and public policy from different perspectives, see Wilson (1976).

28. The subsequent literature is examined in Mueller (1979). The rather different role of cost-benefit analysis in planning public expenditure is examined in Musgrave (1969).

29. For discussion of Wagner's law, which dates from 1890, see Peacock and Wiseman (1967, pp. 16–20).

30. For a recent analysis of the theory of tax illusion (which dates from the turn of the century), see Wagner (1976). Bureaucratic models are examined in Tulloch (1965), Downs (1967), Breton (1974) and Borcherding (1977). On the 'bureaucratic Leviathan', see Brennan and Buchanan (1980). Under certain conditions, majority voting ensures that the preferences of the median voter determine public policy; see, for example, Bergstrom and Goodman (1973).

31. This was first published in 1961, but the 2nd edition of 1967 contains an additional introduction. Supplementary data are given in Mitchell and Deane (1962), Deane and Cole (1962) and Veverka (1963).

32. See Peacock and Wiseman (1967, p. 66). For discussions of taxable capacity, see Stamp (1922), Clark (1945) and Kuznets (1942).

33. The practical problems of managing public expenditure have recently been discussed by Lord Diamond (1975) and Clarke (1978).
34. The introduction of the tax is examined in Hope-Jones (1939). For a history of income taxation, see Sabine (1966) and Shehab (1953). See also Buxton (1888) for discussion of parliamentary debates.
35. Details of the introduction of PAYE are given in Sayers (1956). See also Prest (1968a). A more recent example of expediency is provided by the introduction of an employers' National Insurance surcharge. Mill (1848, p. 831) said that 'taxes on income should be reserved for great national emergencies'.
36. See Atkinson and Stiglitz (1980, p. 427) and the discussion in Hicks (1946). A common distinction revolved around a difference between the person or persons who actually bore the 'burden' (see Mill, 1848, p. 822), but see section 4.5.
37. Fisher's contribution includes Fisher and Fisher (1942); the other references are to Kaldor (1955) and Meade (1978). Prest (1979, p. 245, n. 2) adds that Meade (1978) is 'remarkably silent about previous writers, especially American ones, in the fields it considers'.
38. However, there is also a tendency to support an expenditure base on the argument that people should be taxed according to what they 'take out' of the system. See Kaldor (1955).
39. See Mill (1848, p. 811) for criticism of the argument that temporary incomes pay proportionately more tax than permanent incomes. It was suggested by Farr (1853) that the only 'lump sum' income tax is one which is based on 'potential income'.
40. Mill (1848, p. 814) argued that, 'no income tax is really just from which savings are not exempted'. Kaldor (1955, p. 81)later criticized this for confusing the issues of the choice of tax base. The confusion in the minds of some witnesses to the Select Committee of 1861 is discussed in Shehab (1953, pp. 145–154). A proposed 'tax return' for the assessment of an expenditure tax is given by Kaldor (1955, p. 192).
41. The different rates finally adopted were based on contemporary estimates of *actual* propensities to save from different sources (see Shehab, 1953, pp. 125, 140). The estimates were used by Hubbard (Chairman of the Select Committee of 1861) in support of differentiation. Hubbard was complemented by Mill (1848, p. 815), who ignored the difference between amounts which people *ought* to save for retirement and the amount they *actually* saved under a given tax system. It is unlikely that the latter amount would equal the former. On Hubbard's later partial success in achieving differentiation, see Shehab (1953, pp. 180–182).
42. However, Meade (1978) and Kay and King (1978, p. 248) favour an expenditure tax as a stimulus to small businesses, and object to the increasing institutionalization of savings. On equity comparisons, see Musgrave (1959, pp. 161–164).
43. For example, the term is used throughout Kay and King (1978) without qualification. Similarly the term 'under-taxation' should not be applied to an expenditure tax. On 'double taxation' see Fisher (1937, 1939), Black (1939, pp. 269–284), Shehab (1953, p. 134) and Musgrave (1959, p. 162).
44. This criticism was made by Vickrey (1957, p. 1) in discussion of Kaldor (1955) and by Prest (1979, p. 246) in discussion of Meade (1978).
45. The contributions of Schanz are discussed by Simons (1938) and noted by Kaldor (1955, p. 54, n. 2), Goode (1977, p. 7, n. 18) and Musgrave (1959, p. 165, n. 1). The main American contributions are Haig (1921) and Simons (1938). See also Vickrey (1947) and Pechman (1977).
46. For general discussion of capital gains taxation, see David (1968). When discussing the timing of realized gains, Kay and King (1978, pp. 79–81) do not mention Vickrey's (1939, 1947) important contributions, although they later propose a lifetime expenditure tax. On income averaging, see also Creedy (1979).
47. For clear discussions of the problems involved, see Musgrave (1959, pp. 164–173) and Goode (1977). The gradual erosion of the income tax base through various reliefs and exemptions has given rise to the concept of 'Tax Expenditure'; see Surrey (1973) and Willis and Hardwick (1978). The problem of inflation has led to much discussion of indexation and the 'built-in flexibility' of progressive taxes; see Aaron (1976).
48. Critics of unlimited differentiation argued that it would penalize unfairly the recipients of low-interest incomes compared with those of high industrial incomes. The discussion of differentiation was muddled by the lack of a clear distinction between the choice of appropriate tax *base* and choice of *rates*.
49. Smith (1776, p. 327) had supported slight progression, though see Seligman (1908, p. 165). For objections, see Mill (1848, p. 808) and McCulloch (1845, p. 143).

50. Mill's suggestion was partially adopted by Gladstone, but the principle was not extended to all incomes until after the Royal Commission of 1920; see Shehab (1953, pp. 93, n. 1, 246). It still does not apply to all forms of personal taxes. For example, National Insurance contributions in Britain are based on gross income; see Creedy (1981b, 1982a).

51. For an early analysis, see Musgrave and Thin (1948). Recent treatments of progressivity measurement are Kakwani (1977), Suits (1977) and Formby *et al.* (1981).

52. See also Carver (1904). There is a brief reference to Mill's principle of minimum sacrifice in Edgeworth (1881, p. 95, n. 2). On Edgeworth's work on taxation, see Doresamienger (1929) and Creedy (1981a). Edgeworth's interpretation was endorsed by Pigou (1947). On the general welfare approach taken, see Musgrave (1959, p. 311) and Atkinson (1976, p. 325).

53. The required conditions, in terms of the elasticity of the marginal utility of income, are included in most texts on public finance; see, for example, Musgrave (1959, pp. 98–102).

54. For early criticism of the hypothesis of declining marginal utility of *income*, see Chapman (1913). It was explicitly rejected by Mill (1848, p. 807). For general sceptical discussions of the arguments for progression, see Fagan (1938) and Blum and Kalven (1953).

55. See also Vickrey (1961a). The problems with these approaches have been examined by Pattanaik (1968). Rawls (1971, pp. 170–171) criticizes Edgeworth for being 'extremely unrealistic', though the social contract theories of justice describe only hypothetical choice.

56. Some support for this interpretation seems to be given in Rawls (1967, p.61, n. 2), but he later rejects such a view (1971, p. 172). For discussion of maxi–min as extreme risk aversion, see Atkinson (1973), Atkinson and Stiglitz (1980, pp. 339, 420) and Phelps (1973, pp. 418–423).

57. For an analysis of the specification of such models, see Stern (1976) and Sandmo (1976).

58. For recent treatments of this problem, see Collard *et al.* (1980).

59. Indirect taxes were also generally supported for sumptuary purposes. For discussion of the classical economists' views on indirect taxation, see O'Brien (1975a, pp. 225–259).

60. This approximates the triangular area of the welfare loss; see also Chapter 3. Dupuit's work (1844, 1849) was admired by Edgeworth, and both these writers influenced the work of Hotelling, discussed later in this section.

61. For discussion of the elasticity conditions see Hicks (1947, pp. 167–172). An early and original treatment of incidence is by Jenkin (1871) who, like Dupuit, was an engineer.

62. Edgeworth's paper on monopoly was not available in English until 1925. His papers on taxation also appeared in 1897, and were described by Schumpeter (1954, p. 946) as 'the peak performance of its field and age'. For discussion of Edgeworth's tax paradox, see Creedy (1981a, pp. 88–90).

63. An early criticism of indirect taxation using indifference curves was by Joseph (1938), with an early 'counter-attack' by Wald (1945), and important contributions by Little (1951) and Friedman (1952). The controversy is surveyed by Walker (1955). Hotelling's (1938) paper stimulated controversy with Frisch, published in *Econometrica* in the following year.

64. A non-mathematical discussion of this result is given by Meade (1955, pp. 112–118).

65. Ramsey's work was discussed by Pigou (1947), who first posed the problem. The approach is examined, and rejected, by Musgrave (1959, pp. 148, n. 1).

66. It is probably the difficulty of applying the theory that prompted Prest's (1977, p. 53, n. 1) reference to 'a recrudescence of interest latterly in this problem'. But this work, with the other related work on optimal taxation, is really best regarded as attempting 'to explore the "grammar of arguments"' (Atkinson and Stiglitz, 1980, p. 456). This is surely a necessary step in the development of the subject.

67. Earlier studies of taxation and redistribution in Britain include Samuel (1919), Shiras and Rostas (1942), Barna (1945), Nicholson (1964), Merrett and Monk (1966). Important American studies include Musgrave *et al.* (1951), Pechman and Ockner (1974).

68. For extensive criticism of redistribution studies, see Prest (1955, 1968b, 1976). For general brief comments, see Musgrave (1976) and Atkinson (1976).

69. The Colwyn (1920) Report later gave rise to much discussion about the incidence of income tax. For extensive treatment of this issue, see Black (1939).

70. See also Hicks (1946), and the survey by Mieszkowki (1969). Edgeworth's (1897) paper provides a detailed discussion of views on incidence.

71. Musgrave *et al.* (1951) provides results for alternative incidence assumptions. The extent to which the elasticity assumptions are mutually incompatible depends on differences in factor intensities across industries (Atkinson and Stiglitz, 1980, p. 291). The incidence of National Insurance contributions raises problems in Britain, and official estimates have used different assumptions at different times; see O'Higgins (1980) and Nicholson and Britton (1974).

72. A recent study, following the general approach of Aaron and McGuire (1970), is by Gevers and Rouyer (1980). For a treatment of the redistributive effects of social service expenditure, see Le Grand (1982), and for a general discussion of the treatment of expenditure in redistribution studies, see Peacock (1974).
73. For an analysis of pension schemes using a lifetime perspective, see Creedy (1982a) and the references cited there. Even where annual income is used there is a problem that in comparing summary measures changes in the rankings of individuals may be ignored; see Atkinson (1979).

References

AARON, H.J. (ed.) (1976). *Inflation and the Income Tax*. Washington, The Brookings Institution

AARON, H. and MCGUIRE, M. (1970). Public Goods and Income Distribution. *Econometrica* **38**, 907–920

ARROW, K.J. (1951). *Social Choice and Individual Values*. Cowles Foundation Research Monograph 12, 2nd edn, 1963. New Haven, Yale University Press

ATKINSON, A.B. (1973). How Progressive should Income Tax be? In *Essays in Modern Economics* (ed. by M. Parkin and A.R. Nobay). London, Longman

ATKINSON, A.B. (1976). Comment on Paper by R.A. Musgrave. In *The Market and the State, Essays in Honour of Adam Smith* (ed. by T. Wilson and A.S. Skinner), pp. 324–329. Oxford, The Clarendon Press

ATKINSON, A.B. (1979). Horizontal Equity and the Distribution of the Tax Burden. *Taxation Incentives and the Distribution of Income Working Paper*, No. 3

ATKINSON, A.B. and STERN, W.H. (1974). Pigou, Taxation and Public Goods. *Review of Economic Studies* **41**, 119–128

ATKINSON, A.B. and STIGLITZ, J.E. (1972). The Structure of Indirect Taxation and Economic Efficiency. *Journal of Public Economics* **1**, 97–119

ATKINSON, A.B. and STIGLITZ, J.E. (1976). The Design of Tax Structure: Direct Versus Indirect Taxation. *Journal of Public Economics* **6**, 55–75

ATKINSON, A.B. and STIGLITZ, J.E. (1980). *Lectures on Public Economics*. London, McGraw-Hill

BAGEHOT, W. (1865). *The English Constitution*, p. 378

BARNA, T. (1945). *Redistribution of Income through Public Finance in 1937*. Oxford, Oxford University Press

BAUMOL, W.J. and BRADFORD, D.F. (1970). Optimal Departures from Marginal Cost Pricing. *American Economic Review* **60**, 265–283

BERGSTROM, T.C. and GOODMAN, R.P. (1973). Private Demands for Public Goods. *American Economic Review* **63**, 280–296

BLACK, D. (1939). *The Incidence of Income Taxes*. London, Macmillan

BLUM, W.J. and KALVEN, H. (1953). *The Uneasy Case for Progressive Taxation*. Chicago, University of Chicago Press

BORCHERDING, T.E. (ed.) (1977). *Budgets and Bureaucrats*. Durham, Duke University Press

BOWEN, H.R. (1948). *Towards Social Economy*. New York, Rinehart

BRENNAN, G. and BUCHANAN, J.M. (1980). *The Power to Tax*. Cambridge, Cambridge University Press

BRETON, A. (1974). *The Economic Theory of Representative Government*. London, Macmillan

BUCHANAN, J.M. (1975). Public Finance and Public Choice. *National Tax Journal* **28**, 383–394

BUCHANAN, J.M. (1976). Public Goods and Natural Liberty. In *The Market and the State. Essays in Honour of Adam Smith* (ed. by T. Wilson and A.S. Skinner), pp. 271–286. Oxford, The Clarendon Press

BUXTON, S. (1888). *Finance and Politics, An Historical Study 1789–1885*. London, John Murray. Repr. 1966, New York, Augustus M. Kelley

CARVER, T.N. (1904). The Minimum Sacrifice Theory of Taxation. *Political Science Quarterly* **19**, 66–79

CHANDAMAN, C.D. (1975). *The English Public Revenue 1660–1688*. Oxford, The Clarendon Press

CHAPMAN, S.J. (1913). The Utility of Income and Progressive Taxation. *Economic Journal* **23**, 25–35

CLARK, C. (1945). Public Finances and Changes in the Value of Money. *Economic Journal* **55**, 371–389

CLARK, G. (1949). *Science and Social Welfare in the Age of Newton*. Oxford, The Clarendon Press

CLARKE, R. (1978). *Public Expenditure, Management and Control. The Development of the Public Expenditure Survey Committee (PESC)*. London, Macmillan

COLLARD, D., LECOMBER, R. and SLATER, M. (eds) (1980). *Income Distribution: The Limits to Redistribution*. Bristol, Scientechnica

COLM, G. (1956). Comments on Samuelson's Theory of Public Finance. *Review of Economics and Statistics* **38**, 408–412

COLWYN, LORD (Chairman) (1920). *Report of the Royal Commission on the Income Tax*, Cmnd. 615. London, HMSO

CORLETT, W.J. and HAGUE, D.C. (1953). Complementarity and the Excess Burden of Taxation. *Review of Economic Studies* **21**, 21–31

CREEDY, J. (1979). Income Averaging and Progressive Taxation. *Journal of Public Economics* **12**, 387–397

CREEDY, J. (1981a). F.Y. Edgeworth, 1845–1926. In *Pioneers of Modern Economics in Britain* (ed. by D.P. O'Brien and J.R. Presley), pp. 72–104. London, Macmillan

CREEDY, J. (1981b). Taxation and National Insurance Contributions in Britain. *Journal of Public Economics* **15**, 379–388

CREEDY, J. (1982a). The Changing Burden of National Insurance Contributions and Income Taxation in Britain. *Scottish Journal of Political Economy* **29**, 127–138

CREEDY, J. (1982b). *State Pensions in Britain*. Cambridge, Cambridge University Press

DAVID, M. (1968). *Alternative Approaches to Capital Gains Taxation*. Washington, The Brookings Institution

DE VITI DE MARCO, A. (1936). *First Principles of Public Finance*, trans. from the Italian by Edith Pavlo Marget. London, Jonathan Cape

DEANE, P. and COLE, W.A. (1962). *British Economic Growth 1688–1959: Trends and Structure*. Cambridge, Cambridge University Press

DIAMOND, LORD (Chairman) (1975). *Royal Commission on the Distribution of Income and Wealth. Report No. 1. Initial Report on the Standing Reference*, Cmnd. 6171. London, HMSO

DIAMOND, LORD (1975). *Public Expenditure in Practice*. London, George Allen and Unwin

DICKSON, P.G.M. (1967). *The Financial Revolution in England. A Study in the Development of Public Credit 1688–1756*. New York, Macmillan

DORESAMIENGER, M.R. (1929). Some Recent Developments in the Mathematical Theory of Taxation due to Edgeworth. *Indian Journal of Economics* **10**, 317–31

DOWELL, S. (1888). *A History of Taxation and Taxes in England*, 4 vols. London, Longmans, Green and Co

DOWNS, A. (1967). *Inside Bureaucracy*. Boston, Little, Brown

DUPUIT, J. (1844). De le mesure de l'utilité des travaux publics. *Annales des Ponts et Chaussées* **8**. Trans. and repr. in *International Economic Papers* **2**, 83–110

DUPUIT, J. (1849). De l'influence des péages sur l'utilité de voies de communication. *Annales des Ponts et Chaussées* **13**, 207–248. Trans. and repr. in *International Economic Papers* **11**, 7–31

EDGEWORTH, F.Y. (1881). *Mathematical Psychics*, p. 55. London, Kegan Paul

EDGEWORTH, F.Y. (1897). Teoria pura del monopolio. *Giornale degli Economisti*. Trans. and repr. in *Papers Relating to Political Economy* I, pp. 111–140. London, Macmillan

EDGEWORTH, F.Y. (1897). The Pure Theory of Taxation. *Economic Journal* 7, 46–70, 226–238, 550–571. Repr. in *Papers Relating to Political Economy* II, pp. 63–125. London, Macmillan, 1925

FAGAN, E.D. (1938). Recent and Contemporary Theories of Progressive Taxation. *Journal of Political Economy* 46, 457–498. Repr. in *Readings in the Economics of Taxation* (ed. by R.A. Musgrave and C.S. Shoup), pp. 19–53. London, George Allen and Unwin.

FARR, N. (1853). Equitable Taxation of Property. *Journal of the Royal Statistical Society* 16, 1–45

FISHER, I. (1937). Income Theory and Income Taxation in Practice. *Econometrica* 5, 1–56

FISHER, I. (1939). Double Taxation of Savings. *American Economic Review* 29, 16–34

FISHER, I. and FISHER, H.W. (1942). *Constructive Income Taxation*. New York, Harper

FORMBY, J.P., SEAKS, T.G. and SMITH, W.J. (1981). A Comparison of Two New Measures of Tax Progressivity. *Economic Journal* 91, 1015–1019

FRIEDMAN, M. (1952). The 'Welfare' Effects of an Income Tax and an Excise Tax. *Journal of Political Economy* 60, 25–34

GEVERS, L. and ROUYER, J. (1980). Efficiency and Income Equality: some American Tradeoffs. In *Income Distribution: The Limits to Redistribution* (ed. by D. Collard, R. Lecomber and M. Slater), pp. 31–49. Bristol, Scientechnica

GIFFEN, R. (1880). *Essays in Finance*, 2nd edn. London, George Bell and Sons

GOODE, R. (1964). *The Individual Income Tax*. Washington, The Brookings Institution

GOODE, R. (1977). The Economic Definition of Income. In *Comprehensive Income Taxation* (ed. by J.A. Pechman), pp. 1–30. Washington, The Brookings Institution

HABERLER, G. and HAGEN, E.E. (1946). Taxes, Government Expenditures and National Income. In *Studies in Income and Wealth*, Vol. VIII. New York, National Bureau of Economic Research

HAIG, R.M. (1921). The Concept of Income—Economic and Legal Aspects. In *The Federal Income Tax* (ed. by R.M. Haig), pp. 1–28. New York, Columbia University Press

HARGREAVES, E.L. (1930). *The National Debt*. London, Edward Arnold

HARRISS, G.L. (1975). *King, Parliament and Public Finance in Medieval England to 1369*. Oxford, The Clarendon Press

HARSANYI, J. (1955). Cardinal Welfare, Individualistic Ethics, and Interpersonal Comparisons of Utility. *Journal of Political Economy* 63, 309–321

HICKS, J.R. (1939). *Value and Capital*, pp. 171, 188. Oxford, Oxford University Press

HICKS, U.K. (1946). The Terminology of Tax Analysis. *Economic Journal* 56, 38–51. Repr. in *Readings in the Economics of Taxation* (ed. by R.A. Musgrave and C.S. Shoup), pp. 214–226. London, George Allen and Unwin

HICKS, U.K. (1947). *Public Finance*. London, Nisbet

HOPE-JONES, A. (1939). *Income Tax in the Napoleonic Wars*. Cambridge, Cambridge University Press

HOTELLING, H. (1932). Edgeworth's Taxation Paradox and the Nature of Demand and Supply Functions. *Journal of Political Economy* 40, 577–616

HOTELLING, H. (1938). The General Welfare in Relation to Problems of Taxation and of Railway and Utility Rates. *Econometrica* 7, 151–155

JENKIN, F. (1871). On the Principles which Regulate the Incidence of Taxes. *Proceedings of the Royal Society of Edinburgh*. Repr. in *Readings in the Economics of Taxation* (ed. by R.A. Musgrave and C.S. Shoup), pp. 227–239. London, George Allen and Unwin

JOSEPH, M.F.W. (1938). The Excess Burden of Indirect Taxation. *Review of Economic Studies* 6, 226–231

KAKWANI, N.C. (1977). Measurement of Tax Progressivity: An International Comparison. *Economic Journal* **87**, 71–80

KALDOR, N. (1955). *An Expenditure Tax*. London, Unwin University Books

KAY, J.A. and KING, M.A. (1978). *The British Tax System*. Oxford, Oxford University Press

KUZNETS, S. (1942). National Income and Taxable Capacity. *American Economic Review* **32**, 37–76

LE GRAND, J. (1982). *The Strategy of Equality: Redistribution and the Social Services*. London, George Allen and Unwin

LITTLE, I.M.D. (1951). Direct versus Indirect Taxes. *Economic Journal* **61**, 577–585

MALLET, B. (1913). *British Budgets 1887–88 to 1912–13*. London, Macmillan

MALLET, B. and GEORGE, C.O. (1929). *British Budgets 1913–14 to 1920–21*. London, Macmillan

MALLET, B. and GEORGE, C.O. (1933). *British Budgets 1921–22 to 1932–33*. London, Macmillan

MARGOLIS, J. (1954). A Comment on the Pure Theory of Public Expenditure. *Review of Economics and Statistics* **37**, 347–349

MCCULLOCH, J.R. (1845). *A Treatise on the Principles and Practical Influence of Taxation and the Funding System*. Edinburgh, Adam and Charles Black. All page references are to the O'Brien (1975) edition

MEADE, J.E. (1955). *Trade and Welfare*. Oxford, Oxford University Press

MEADE, J.E. *et al.* (1978). *The Structure and Reform of Direct Taxation*. London, George Allen and Unwin

MERRETT, A.J. and MONK, D.A.G. (1966). The Structure of U.K. Taxation 1962–63. *Oxford Bulletin of Economics and Statistics* **28**, 145–162

MIESZKOWSKI, P. (1969). Tax Incidence Theory: The Effects of Taxes on the Distribution of Income. *Journal of Economic Literature* **7**, 1103–1123

MILL, J.S. (1848). *Principles of Political Economy*, pp. 806, 813, 815. Repr. in 1920, with editorial material by W.J. Ashley. London, Longmans, Green & Co.

MILLERON, J.C. (1972). Theory of Value with Public Goods; A Survey Article. *Journal of Economic Theory* **5**, 419–477

MIRRLEES, J.A. (1971). An Exploration in the Theory of Optimum Income Taxation. *Review of Economic Studies* **38**, 175–208

MITCHELL, B.R. with DEANE, P. (1962). *Abstract of British Historical Statistics*. Cambridge, Cambridge University Press

MITCHELL, B.R. and JONES, H.G. (1971). *Second Abstract of British Historical Statistics*. Cambridge, Cambridge University Press

MUELLER, D.C. (1979). *Public Choice*. Cambridge, Cambridge University Press

MUSGRAVE, R.A., CARROLL, J.J., COOK, L.D. and FRANE, L. (1951). Distribution of Tax Payments by Income Groups: A Case Study for 1948. *National Tax Journal* **4**, 1–54

MUSGRAVE, R.A. (1939). The Voluntary Exchange Theory of Public Economy. *Quarterly Journal of Economics* **53**, 213–238

MUSGRAVE, R.A. (1959). *The Theory of Public Finance*, pp. 16, 227–231. New York, McGraw-Hill

MUSGRAVE, R.A. (1969). Cost Benefit Analysis and the Theory of Public Finance. *Journal of Economic Literature* **7**, 797–806

MUSGRAVE, R.A. (1976). Adam Smith on Public Finance and Distribution. In *The Market and the State. Essays in Honour of Adam Smith* (ed. by T. Wilson and A.S. Skinner), pp. 297–319. Oxford, The Clarendon Press

MUSGRAVE, R.A. and PEACOCK, A.T. (1958). *Classics in the Theory of Public Finance*, pp. 48–71, 91. London, Macmillan for the International Economic Association

MUSGRAVE, R.A. and THIN, T. (1948). Income Tax Progression. *Journal of Political Economy* **56**, 498–515

MYRDAL, G. (1953). *The Political Element in the Development of Economic Theory*, trans. by P. Streeton. London,

NICHOLSON, J.L. (1964). *Redistribution of Income in the United Kingdom in 1959, 1957 and 1953*. London, Bowes and Bowes

NICHOLSON, J.L. and BRITTON, A.J.C. (1976). The Redistribution of Income. In *The Personal Distribution of Incomes* (ed. by A.B. Atkinson), pp. 313–334. London, George Allen and Unwin

NICHOLSON, J.S. (1917). *War Finance*. London, P.S. King

O'BRIEN, D.P. (1970). *J.R. McCulloch: A Study in Classical Economics*. London, George Allen and Unwin

O'BRIEN, D.P. (1975a). *The Classical Economists*. Oxford, The Clarendon Press

O'BRIEN, D.P. (ed.) (1975b). *McCulloch's Treatise on the Principles and Practical Influence of Taxation and the Funding System*. Edinburgh, Scottish Academic Press

O'HIGGINS, M. (1980). The Distributive Effects of Public Expenditure and Taxation: An Agnostic View of the CSO Analyses. In *Taxation and Social Policy* (ed. by C. Sandford, C. Pond, and R. Walker), pp. 28–45. London, Heinemann

PATTANIAK, P.K. (1968). Risk, Impersonality and the Social Welfare Function. *Journal of Political Economy*. Repr. in *Economic Justice* (ed. by E.S. Phelps), 1973, pp. 298–318. Harmondsworth, Penguin

PEACOCK, A.T. (1974). The Treatment of Government Expenditure in Studies of Income Redistribution. In *Public Finance and Stabilization Policy: Essays in Honour of Richard Musgrave* (ed. by W.L. Smith and J.M. Cuthbertson), pp. 151–167. Amsterdam, North-Holland

PEACOCK, A.T. and WISEMAN, J. (1967). *The Growth of Public Expenditure in the United Kingdom*, 2nd edn. London, George Allen and Unwin

PECHMAN, J.A. (ed.) (1977). *Comprehensive Income Taxation*. Washington, The Brookings Institution

PECHMAN, J.A. and OKNER, B.A. (1974). *Who Bears the Tax Burden?* Washington, The Brookings Institution

PHELPS, E.S. (ed.) (1973). *Economic Justice*. London, Penguin Education

PIGOU, A.C. (1947). *A Study in Public Finance*, 3rd edn. London, Macmillan

PREST, A.R. (1955). Statistical Calculations of Tax Incidence. *Economica* **22**, 234–245

PREST, A.R. (ed.). (1968a). *Public Sector Economics*. Manchester, Manchester University Press

PREST, A.R. (1968b). The Budget and Interpersonal Distribution. *Public Finance* **23**, 80–98

PREST, A.R. (1976). Comment on Paper by R.A. Musgrave. In *The Market and the State* (ed. by T. Wilson and A.S. Skinner), pp. 319–323. Oxford, The Clarendon Press

PREST, A.R. (1977). *Public Finance in Theory and Practice*, 5th edn. London, Weidenfeld and Nicolson

PREST, A.R. (1979). The Structure and Reform of Direct Taxation. *Economic Journal* **89**, 243–260

RADCLIFFE, LORD (Chairman) (1955). *Report of the Royal Commission on the Taxation of Profits and Incomes*, Cmnd. 9474. London, HMSO

RAMSEY, F. (1927). A Contribution to the Theory of Taxation. *Economic Journal* **37**, 46–61

RAWLS, J. (1969). Distributive Justice. In *Philosophy, Politics and Society* (ed. by P. Laslett and W.G. Runciman), pp. 58–82. Oxford, Basil Blackwell

RAWLS, J. (1971). *A Theory of Justice*, p. 29. Oxford, Oxford University Press

SABINE, B.E.V. (1966). *A History of Income Tax*. London, George Allen and Unwin

SABINE, B.E.V. (1970). *British Budgets in Peace and War 1932–1945*. London, George Allen and Unwin

SAMUEL, LORD (1919). The Taxation of the Various Classes of the People. *Journal of the Royal Statistical Society* **82**, 143–182

SAMUELSON, P.A. (1954). The Pure Theory of Public Expenditure. *Review of Economics and Statistics* **36**, 387–389

SAMUELSON, P.A. (1955). Diagrammatic Exposition of a Theory of Public Expenditure. *Review of Economics and Statistics* **37**, 350–356

SANDMO, A. (1976). Optimal Taxation—An Introduction to the Literature. *Journal of Public Economics* **6**, 37–54

SAYERS, R.S. (1956). *Financial Policy 1939–1945*. London, HMSO and Longmans, Green and Co

SCHUMPETER, J.A. (1954). *History of Economic Analysis*, p. 764. London, George Allen and Unwin

SELIGMAN, E.R.A. (1899). *The Shifting and Incidence of Taxation*. New York, Macmillan. Repr. 1969, New York, Augustus M. Kelley

SELIGMAN, E.R.A. (1908). *Progressive Taxation in Theory and Practice*. Princeton, Princeton University Press

SHEHAB, F. (1953). *Progressive Taxation: A Study in the Development of the Progressive Principle in the British Income Tax*, pp. 5, 197. Oxford, The Clarendon Press

SHIRRAS, G.F. and ROSTAS, L. (1942). *The Burden of British Taxation*. Cambridge, Cambridge University Press

SINCLAIR, J. (1790). *The History of the Public Revenue of the British Empire*, 2nd Edition), p. 19. London, T. Cadell. Repr. by Gregg International Publishers, Farnborough, 1970

SIMONS, H.C. (1938). *Personal Taxation: The Definition of Income as a Problem of Fiscal Policy*, p. 50. Chicago, University of Chicago Press

SMITH, A. (1776). *An Inquiry into the Nature and Causes of the Wealth of Nations*, p. 350. Ed. by E. Cannan and repr. 1976 by University of Chicago Press

STAMP, J. (1922). *Wealth and Taxable Capacity*. London, P.S. King

STERN, N.H. (1976). On the Specification of Models of Optimum Income Taxation. *Journal of Public Economics* **6**, 123–162

STUDENSKI, P. (1958). *The Income of Nations. Theory, Measurement and Analysis: Past and Present*, p. 27. Washington, New York University Press

SUITS, D. (1977). Measurement of Tax Progressivity. *American Economic Review* **67**, 747–752

SURREY, S.S. (1973). *Pathways to Tax Reform: The Concept of Tax Expenditures*. Cambridge, Mass., Harvard University Press

TULLOCH, G. (1965). *The Politics of Bureaucracy*. Washington, Public Affairs Press

VEVERKA, J. (1963). The Growth of Government Expenditure in the United Kingdom since 1790. In *Public Expenditure, Appraisal and Control* (ed. by A.T. Peacock and D.J. Robertson), pp. 111–127. Edinburgh, Oliver and Boyd

VICKREY, W. (1939). Averaging of Income for Income Tax Purposes. *Journal of Political Economy* **47**, 379–397

VICKREY, W.S. (1947). *Agenda for Progressive Taxation*. New York, Ronald Press

VICKREY, W. (1957). Expenditure, Capital Gains and the Basis of Progressive Taxation. *The Manchester School* **25**, 1–13. Repr. 1970 in *Public Finance* (ed. by R.W. Houghton), pp. 117–128. Harmondsworth, Penguin

VICKREY, W.S. (1960). Utility, Strategy and Social Decision Rules. *Quarterly Journal of Economics* **74**, 507–535

VICKREY, W.S. (1961a). Counterspeculation, Auctions and Competitive Sealed Tenders. *Journal of Finance* **16**, 8–37

VICKREY, W.S. (1961b). Risk, Utility and Social Policy. *Social Research*, Repr. in *Economic Justice* (ed. by E.S. Phelps), 1973, pp. 286–297. Harmondsworth, Penguin

VINER, J. (1927). Adam Smith and *laisser-faire*. *Journal of Political Economy* **35**, 198–232

WALD, H.P. (1945). The Classical Indictment of Indirect Taxation. *Quarterly Journal of Economics* **59**, 577–596

WALKER, D. (1955). The Direct–Indirect Tax Problem: Fifteen Years of Controversy. *Public Finance* **10**, 153–176

WAGNER, R.E. (1976). Revenue Structure, Fiscal Illusion, and Budgetary Choice. *Public Choice* **25**, 45–61

WEST, E.G. (1976). Adam Smith's Economics of Politics. *History of Political Economy* **8**, 515–539

WILLIS, J.R.M. and HARDWICK, P.J.W. (1978). *Tax Expenditures in the United Kingdom.* London, Heinemann

WILSON, T. (1976). Sympathy and Self-interest. In *The Market and the State, Essays in Honour of Adam Smith* (ed. by T. Wilson and A.S. Skinner), pp. 73–99. Oxford, The Clarendon Press

Chapter Five

Oligopoly and the Theory of the Firm

A.S. Skinner and M.C. MacLennan

5.1 Introduction

This chapter falls into two distinct parts. The first is essentially historical, and is intended to set the scene for the more analytical approach to the study of oligopoly which follows. In section 5.2 an attempt is made to recall some familiar features of Marshall's work before going on to consider a number of contributions to particular topics, such as the theories of perfect competition, duopoly and monopoly. Section 5.3 is concerned with competition and monopoly, with particular reference to the work of Edward Chamberlin.

The purpose of the second part is to review the various routes which economic theory has followed since Chamberlin. Section 5.4 considers developments which are broadly associated with the content and limitations of Chamberlinian analysis. These include the problems posed by the existence of a kinked demand curve, barriers to entry and the existence of potential competition, the departure from the objective of profit maximization based on marginalist rules in favour of normal cost, entry-deterring pricing, and the various methods of collusion and co-operation which firms may adopt to deal with the uncertainty created by their awareness of interdependence. The problems of oligopolistic interdependence are then re-considered in terms of the 'new' theories which treat the firm as a complex, multi-product, multi-plant organization where ownership and management are vested in separate groups; where short-run profit maximization is replaced by other objectives; and the growth of the firm is explicitly considered.

Section 5.5 then identifies the main points of difficulty in oligopoly theory, to which the work reviewed has drawn attention, and considers how these might be dealt with. This involves an examination of current and projected work on oligopoly, and a reconsideration of some earlier work which has important 117 implications for oligopoly analysis but which has tended to be overlooked or given insufficient emphasis.

It should be made clear at the outset that this chapter is not a complete survey of the literature: nor is it a systematic attempt to examine the origin and nature of the theory of the firm in its contemporary setting. Both parts of the chapter are highly thematic, although the argument as a whole is an attempt to bring the perspectives of the historian and the applied economist to the study of a single problem—oligopoly. Both perspectives help to confirm that the development of the model, and subsequent research in the area, have been associated with a return to the broader vision of Alfred Marshall, but following a path which was only opened up by the revolution of the 1930s.

5.2 Historical background

5.2.1 MARSHALL

It was from Cournot, and to a lesser extent von Thunen, that Marshall had come to appreciate the importance of the *margin*. Yet at the same time it should be recalled that if the *form* of Marshall's work owed much to Cournot, its *substance* was more profoundly affected by contemporary work on biology, history and philosophy, where the authorities cited were those of Spencer and Hegel. The perspectives thus supplied gave Marshall (1890) a distinctive grasp of the inherent complexity of economic phenomena, which in turn caused him 'to banish his mathematics from the surface of his argument' (Schumpeter, 1954). The same considerations may help to explain his preference for diagrammatic representations (themselves confined to footnotes) over mathematical symbols and his contention that the 'chief use of pure mathematics in economic questions seems to be in helping a person to write down quickly, shortly and exactly, some of his thoughts for his own use' (1890, p. x). In Marshall's case, the result of this concern with reality was not so much imprecision as a higher degree of complexity.

It is not hard to see how this result came about, even looking only at the restricted field of the present chapter. One obvious area of difficulty emerges when considering that Marshall's main attention was focused on the *industry*, which was assumed in turn to be made up of a number of firms all at different stages of their life-cycle. As he noted, 'At any particular moment some businesses will be rising and others falling' (p. 378).

Similar problems affect Marshall's treatment of competition, which is never stated to be 'perfect' but rather as 'open' or 'free'—a term which 'neither seeks nor affords much precision in definition' (Hutchison, 1953). Monopoly, too, presents its own problems even if

Marshall did isolate the extreme case (p. 477) and comment on the phenomenon of 'a severely monopolistic price policy' (1919, p. 396). But Marshall (1890) also observed that 'there is much to be learnt from a study of the relations in which the interests of the monopolist stand to those of the rest of society' (p. 477) before going on to consider the importance of long-run pricing policy and situations where the monopolist may be sensitive to the benefits which accrue to himself *and* to the consumer (pp. 486ff.). Equally, he was alive to the problems of pricing policy in the light of 'sources of possible competition', noting that even where 'large and strong', the monopolist 'will not make full use of his power but will adjust his prices to obtaining a firm hold on the market before he can be caught by competitive supply' (1919, pp. 396–397). Elsewhere, Marshall was to note, that 'though monopoly and free competition are ideally wide apart, yet in practice they shade into one another by imperceptible degrees' (p. 397).

Into this rather loose set of classifications, Marshall was to fit the problems presented by time, risk and information; the role of innovation, advertising and the structure and management of the firm (O'Brien, 1981, 1982). It is hardly surprising that Schumpeter (1954) should have referred to 'Marshall's broad and deep comprehension of the monopolistic and quasi monopolistic phenomena of his age' as one of the major features of his work.

Yet it is also understandable that complexity bred its own problems, leading to Samuelson's (1967) exaggerated claim that 'much of the work from 1920 to 1933 was merely the negative task of getting Marshall out of the way'.

The material which immediately follows is in a sense a commentary on Samuelson's claim. It also confirms that much of the work done in the post-Marshallian period reflected the application of 'more rigorous academic standards of logical and terminological tidiness and precision' (Hutchison, 1953) in a series of developments which culminate in the treatment of Chamberlin's *Monopolistic Competition* (1933, all references are to the 5th edition, 1946). Three broad developments, involving the theories of duopoly, perfect competition and monopoly deserve some attention.

5.2.2 DUOPOLY

One major development was the restatement of a duopoly model which also dates back to Cournot (1838) and Edgeworth (1897). In Cournot's now familiar example, two producers offer an identical product with no costs of production. The model suggests that there will be a determinate outcome (depending on the number of sellers) where mutual dependence is ignored and where each seller determines his policy on the assumption that the *output* of his rival will remain constant. A second example of this kind of approach was associated with Bertrand (1883) and Pareto (1896), where policy is decided on the assumption that rival sellers will maintain a constant *price*, leading to an outcome where the latter will ultimately settle at a level similar to that expected under conditions of competition[1].

Edgeworth (1897), on the other hand, while using a similar approach, was critical of Cournot, arguing that the solution is indeterminate where the number of competitors is small. Edgeworth's argument was that there could be a range of outcomes between the monopoly and competitive solutions[2].

Hotelling (1929) later explored the implications of a situation where groups of buyers deal with a seller in spite of differences in price, explaining this phenomenon by reference to space, and concluding, in criticism of Cournot, Edgeworth and Amoroso, that the independent actions of two competitors not in collusion can lead to a type of equilibrium much less fragile than had been supposed[3].

A more typical reaction to the literature was that of Pigou (1924), who drew attention to the lack of determinacy in the case of 'multiple monopoly', making the point that in real life it is unlikely that each 'seller will hold any consistent view about his rivals' state of mind':

As in a game of chess each player will act on some forecast of the other's reply, but the forecast he acts on may, according to his mood and his reading of that opponent's psychology, be one thing or another thing (p. 267).

The chess analogy had already been noted by Edgeworth and by Irving Fisher (Hutchison, 1953; see also Rothschild, 1947). Chamberlin (1957) himself later made use of the same analogy in contrasting the case of collusion with the recognition of mutual dependence (p. 39).

The point is an important one, since Chamberlin (1946) was moved to observe that his own case of mutual dependence which he described as 'a new phase of the problem' (p. 46) had been anticipated by Fisher (1898) and Moore (1906). Where dependence is recognized, Chamberlin argued that the most likely solution was akin to that of monopoly[4]. But while observing that many of his own results had been developed independently by Kahn, Chamberlin (1946) drew attention not only to the case of dependence but also to the problem of uncertainty, arguing that it is this condition, which, 'where present... renders the outcome indeterminate (pp. 51–53). Chamberlin's original thesis that 'Duopoly is not one problem but several... The solution varies, depending on the conditions assumed' (p. 53) has been properly cited as his most important contribution to the contemporary debate (Steiner, 1964).

5.2.3 PERFECT COMPETITION

The move from the study of competition in the Marshallian manner to that of perfect competition involved a further attempt to recapture the precision of Edgeworth (1897), perhaps the 'first to attempt a systematic and rigorous definition' of the model (Stigler, 1965; Shackle, 1967). Stigler (1965) attributed the initial reformulation to J.B. Clark (1899), while it is also well known that H.L. Moore, fittingly a commentator on Cournot, also complained of the 'bewildering vagueness of a fundamental term' (see Hutchison, 1953). But perhaps the classic statement of the assumptions needed to define the case occurs in Knight (1921), where it is noted, significantly, that these assumptions must include the now-familiar reference to rationality, perfect knowledge, large numbers, product homogeneity, costless intercommunication and perfect mobility in all economic adjustments, moving Stigler (1965) to remark:

> It was the meticulous discussion in this work that did most to drive home to economists generally the austere nature of the rigorously defined concept and so prepare the way for the widespread reaction to it in the 1930's (p. 256).

It is no accident that one of the most sophisticated modern statements should occur in Joan Robinson (1933). In the same vein Chamberlin (1946) devoted a separate chapter to the less restrictive concept of 'pure competition'; a term 'chosen deliberately to describe competition unalloyed with monopoly elements' (p. 6).

But greater precision not only involved giving attention to the necessary conditions of the model; it also featured a technical advance in the shape of the concept of marginal revenue now added to marginal cost, which, for the Cambridge (England) economists, constituted the 'clue and catalyst that transformed everything' (Shackle, 1967), thus lending a further degree of precision to the models of perfect competition *and* of monopoly. Something of the flavour of the period is to be gained from Joan Robinson's (1933) introductory remarks, where she cited some eight people (including a research student) who in discovering marginal revenue had arrived almost simultaneously at the same 'Pole'. Chamberlin, whose original thesis was filed in 1927, developed the concept independently while pointing out that:

> I must confess that I found it in Marshall's Mathematical Appendix. Marshall does not draw a diagram, but he gives and discusses at some length the algebraic formula (1961, p. 524).

This helps to explain Samuelson's (1967) complaint:

> That grown men argued seriously in 1930 about who had first used or named
> the curve that we now call 'marginal revenue' is a joke. Cournot had settled all
> that a century earlier... (p. 110).

This is the reaction of an economist preoccupied with the mathematics of the case. The significant development seems to have been that the marginal curves were *drawn* in this period (Boulding, 1942) as, for example, in Harrod's 1930 article which deployed both revenue and cost *curves* in the discussion of equilibrium. The most remarkable example however is surely Viner (1931), who had been presenting 'fundamental charts' (drawn by Y.K. Wong) long before the date of publication.

As Andrews (1964) has noted, these developments marked a major change of emphasis which witnessed not only the translation of diagrammatic representations from the notes to the main text, but also a renewed preoccupation with the firm as a producing, as distinct from an organizational, unit.

Equally important was the emergence of a new orthodoxy; an established image of the economic process which, in Shackle's (1967) words,

> showed a smooth sea of perfectly competitive firms in equilibrium, interrupted
> here and there by a few monopolist whirlpools obeying a different law... In a
> perfectly competitive world the laws of value would have approached the
> universal validity and beautiful simplicity of the law of gravity (p. 43).

Once again the Newtonian analogy had triumphed, in a manner which would have been readily understood by Jevons, and indeed by Adam Smith.

5.2.4 MONOPOLY AND IMPERFECT COMPETITION

A third element in the 'equation', which was to some extent a consequence of the contemporary definition of perfect competition, was the discussion concerning the laws of return. While this discussion may have been initiated by J.H. Clapham (1922) it was given added impetus by Sraffa (1926). Two major points should be noted. First, Sraffa argued that

> Everyday experience shows that a very large number of undertakings—and the
> majority of those which produce manufactured goods—work under conditions
> of individual diminishing costs (p. 189).

In these circumstances, the outcome is indeterminate under conditions of free competition, from which it follows that

---

It is necessary, therefore, to abandon the path of free competition and turn in the opposite direction, namely, towards monopoly (p. 187).

But monopoly was now defined in a new and particular way; as relating to a situation where the buyers of goods were not indifferent as between producers of similar, but not identical commodities[6].

In short, Sraffa was drawing attention, in an article critical of Marshall, to the 'intermediate zone' between perfect competition and monopoly, narrowly defined, thus giving a considerable stimulus to the study of monopoly in the broadest sense[7].

The work which most explicitly built on the Sraffa thesis was Joan Robinson's *Economics of Imperfect Competition* (1933), where it is argued that 'We have only to take the word monopoly in its literal sense, a single seller, and the analysis of monopoly immediately swallows up the analysis of competition' (p. 5). Mrs Robinson's concern was with the intermediate case, and something of the quality of her analysis can be seen in her treatment of consumer preferences for the output of different producers in the Sraffian manner (pp. 89–90) and of the elasticity of the revenue curves, where the latter are affected by the number of competing monopolists and the substitutability of their products. As is now well known, the analysis embraces a discussion of competitive equilibrium wherein the 'tangency solution' is developed, yielding a case where a state of equilibrium is attained under conditions of decreasing cost. Further technical advances included the isolation of an average revenue curve with a varying slope (as distinct from a kink), together with the attendant discontinuities in marginal revenue (p. 37). To this must be added the introduction of monopsony (p. 215) and the important attempt to explore the properties of monopoly and monopsony treated as the two sides of a single coin.

While the book considers the case of small numbers, the difficulties involved are largely side-stepped by incorporating reactions into the average revenue (AR) curve. It also neglects the complications presented by time (p. 16) and by advertising costs (p. 21) together with the case of bilateral monopoly (as developed by Edgeworth and Marshall), with its attendant implications for the issue of determinancy (Schumpeter, 1954). Yet it is remarkable not merely for its exploration of monopoly in the broad sense, but also for its technical content. It is to Mrs Robinson that we owe much of the geometry of modern price theory (developed in Part I), elaborated in a book which was 'presented to the analytical economist as a box of tools. It is an essay in the technique of economic analysis and can make only an indirect contribution to our knowledge of the actual world' (p. 1). The result was a reaffirmation of the mathematical (and geometrical) approach; a perspective which was in sharp contrast to that adopted by Marshall and by Marshallians such as Robertson and Shove (O'Brien, 1982) who had sought to rehabilitate the representative firm in the face of Sraffa's criticism[8].

5.3 Monopolistic competition

5.3.1 ORIGINS OF THE THEORY

Chamberlin's work, *The Theory of Monopolistic Competition*, published in the same year, shows striking parallels with *Imperfect Competition*; parallels of such an extent as to justify Shackle's (1967) claim that 'in describing the structure and mechanism of equilibrium in firms and groups of firms where oligopoly and selling expenditure are absent, the two books present identical theories'. However, there are equally noteworthy differences of emphasis which reflect the specific origins of *Monopolistic Competition*. As Chamberlin (1961) himself stated, his thesis was not connected with Joan Robinson's macro-economic interests nor with the Sraffa article: nor indeed 'did the book itself attack Marshall...on any of the issues there involved' (p. 532). Chamberlin insisted that his work 'was an attack, not on Marshall, but on the theory of perfect competition' (p. 540). Rather the book emerged from a more institutional background which included the 'Taussig–Pigou controversy as to whether charging what the market will bear in railway rates was to be explained in terms of monopolistic discrimination or in terms of joint costs' (p. 517). To this Chamberlin added his early interest in business economics, with special reference to advertising and retail markets, acknowledging in this connection the influence of Pigou (p. 529). But perhaps the most important stimulus was provided by 'the literature of business' (p. 525; 1948, ch. 4) and especially by Allyn Young's (1925) treatment of trade marks and patents, which were shown to confer a monopoly element while being consistent with competition. For Chamberlin (1961), this perspective 'became the key to the whole analysis' (p. 526). The book is also informed by Chamberlin's early interest in duopoly, or competition with small numbers, and served to bring what had once been a theoretical curiosity into the mainstream of the subject.

Chamberlin's interest in the actual (Georgescu-Roegen, 1967) and his 'attempt to interpret more fully the world Marshall discussed' (Robinson, 1971) have often been noted. It is also relevant to observe another general feature, namely, that while successfully formulating the marginal curves Chamberlin made relatively little use of them, leading to Shackle's (1967) surmise that 'he originally worked out his whole book with no such tool in mind (p. 62):

> I have no doubt that the lack of realism in the marginal revenue technique
> played a large and important part in leading me to use it hardly at all and to
> explain everything in terms of the average curves, where the graphics do not
> seem to get in the way of what really happens (Chamberlin, 1957, p. 276).

But Chamberlin's 'hybrid' theory (like that of Mrs Robinson) was very much a reaction to the 'established image' which Shackle (1967) described (p. 47); a point which is made plain in the preface to the first edition (p. xi). Almost twenty-five years later, Chamberlin (1957) was to repeat the point in suggesting that the purpose of the original book was 'to do a better job of explanation by presenting a continuum between two extremes' (p. 5). The main purpose of the theory was to examine a situation where a number of firms manufactured products which while physically similar were also differentiated, thus explaining the relevance of the 'monopoly' and 'competitive' elements in a single market. At the same time, Chamberlin (1946) was equally concerned with the sources of disequilibrium, emphasizing that the essence of monopolistic competition was not to be found in the reaction of a number of firms to exogenously determined signals (such as price), but rather in their continuing attempts to create situations of advantage for themselves (pp. 10, 213)[9]. While a competitive situation will normally ensure that positions of advantage are eliminated by virtue of the reaction of rivals, Chamberlin's point was that change in the monopolistic situation is likely to be continuous for reasons which are inherent in its nature. It was in this connection that he chose to emphasize the importance of product variation and of selling costs. Indeed Chamberlin (1946) contended that the distinction which he drew between selling and production costs was a novel one, and that economic literature in general had neglected the problem of competitive demand creation at the time of writing (p. 126).

5.3.2 THE SMALL GROUP

Differentiation of the product, and all that this implies with regard to the nature of competitive activity, were to become the key feature of the two cases which Chamberlin isolated. But by 1957 he had reached the conclusion that:

> In the real world that most common case is certainly 'differentiated oligopoly',
> or small numbers *plus* a differentiated product; and it would seem that this
> would be monopolistic competition *par excellence* (p. 33).

The two applications of the basic model have a number of common features. Both employ cost curves modified by selling costs, and both

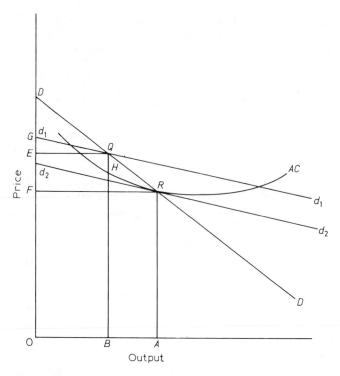

Figure 5.1 Chamberlin's two average cost curves

'proceed under the heroic assumption that...demand and cost curves for all the "products" are uniform throughout the group' (1948, p. 82). But the most striking feature of the model arises from Chamberlin's introduction of the two average revenue curves; curves which reflect the fact that the group is defined as being composed of a number of firms manufacturing physically similar, but differentiated products. These are shown in *Figure 5.1*. The curves d_1, d_2 are defined by Chamberlin (1946) as showing the increase in sales which an individual seller 'could realize by cutting his price, *provided* others did not also cut theirs; and conversely, it shows the falling off in sales which would attend an increase in price, *provided* other prices did not also increase' (p. 90). The *DD* curve, on the other hand, emerges as the 'fractional part of the demand curve for the general class of product, and will be of the same elasticity' (p. 90). The two curves are then stated to be related in that a decision by one seller to move along a *dd* curve with a view to increasing sales could be matched by his competitors, thus causing it to 'slide' down *DD*.

Interestingly enough, Chamberlin used both curves in illustrating the large group case. In terms of *Figure 5.1*, he takes a case where a firm is selling *OB* units at the price *BQ*. In such a situation:

profits may be increased for any individual seller by moving to the right along *dd*; and he may do this without fear of ultimately reducing his gains through forcing others to follow him because his competitors are so numerous that the market of each of them is inappreciably affected by his move (pp. 90, 91).

However, the consequence of each seller, acting in the same way when confronted by the same information is to generate a movement down the fractional part of the market demand curve, so that if *dd* shows expected sales, '*DD* shows his actual sales as the *general* downward movement takes place' (p. 91) with the lower limit reached where *dd* is tangent to *AC*. In fact, Chamberlin also used another case to illustrate the possibilities involved, where starting from a point such as *Q*, 'additional sellers are attracted by the high profits, and intrench themselves in the field before the price-cutting corrective takes place' (p. 92). Here the limiting case would be one where *DD* was forced to the left, until a position of tangency was reached with *AC* (see 1957, p. 281).

In the 'small group' case the *dd* and *DD* curves acquire an added significance which reflects the number of assumptions which may be made with regard to the behaviour of firms. In this connection Chamberlin was to point out that one solution might be established at *Q* in *Figure 5.1*; a solution akin to that expected under monopoly and which will remain stable so long as no member firm seeks to move along *dd*. At the other extreme, persistent attempts to move along *dd* could result in arrival at the point *R*, that is the solution which might 'normally' be expected in the large group case (as a consequence of new entry). Yet again, Chamberlin seems to suggest that the actual solution would probably be found at a point intermediate between the two extremes; the case where mutual dependence is ultimately recognized as distinct from that previously considered, where mutual dependence was consistently ignored.

It is to be noted that the range *RQ* in *Figure 5.1* can be extended to include the impact of new entry (1946, p. 92) and that a competitive pricing policy may 'arise out of an attempt to secure a final victory in the struggle and eliminate all rivals' (1957, p. 60). This type of conflict suggests that the structure of a firm's assets will be an important key to survival, although Chamberlin did not develop the theme (Silberston, 1970).

5.3.3 TECHNICAL IMPLICATIONS

Three broadly technical aspects of the argument may be emphasized at this point. First, while it seems a short step from the analysis just considered to the 'kinked demand' curve model, Andrews (1951) only found in the *Monopolistic Competition* 'an ingenious piece of analysis' which should 'now be recognised as a general background to the theory'. On the other hand, Hall and Hitch (1939) acknowledged that Chamberlin's 'two demand curves' were based on the same assumptions as their own 'illustrative curves'. In noting the point, Chamberlin (1957) was to argue, quite correctly, that the version associated with Hall and Hitch was 'merely a combination of my own d and D curves, with the more elastic d portion lying above the ruling price' (p. 288). But Chamberlin (1946) did not develop the kinked demand curve model in its now familiar form, and may well have believed that under most circumstances, the more elastic section of dd which lay above the ruling price was irrelevant:

> business men may set their prices with reference to costs rather than to demand, aiming at ordinary rather than at maximum profits, and more or less taking it for granted that they will continue to enjoy about their usual share of the total business... In this case, since the prices of all move roughly together, ...the curve dd is of no significance (p. 105)[10].

This would suggest that the Chamberlinian 'kink' would be expressed by a line such as EQD in the figure rather than the more typical GQR—thus widening the range of discontinuity when the marginal curves are added, and yielding an example similar in form to the case of limit pricing discussed below.

Second, some attention should be given to the heroic assumption on which the analysis was based and to Chamberlin's (1961) equally heroic attempt to escape from its consequences. He recognized the problems of aggregation (p. 527) in making the point that the cost and demand functions facing each producer in the group must vary in terms of their position and shape (1946, p. 110). From one point of view the problem was not a serious one (p. 111); it merely means that to 'picture the situation adequately, a separate figure should be drawn' for each producer (1946, p. 110; 1957, p. 302). The 'tangency solution' was not a necessary feature of his treatment of the large group case, where it was noted that 'some (or all) of the curves may lie at various distances to the right of the point of tangency, leaving monopoly profits scattered throughout the group' (1946, p. 113). In the same way it should be noted that the identification of the range RQ in the small group situation depends upon the 'heroic' assumption, and that the identification of this particular range is not a necessary feature of the model.

Third, it is interesting that Chamberlin (1946), while sticking closely to his role of positive economist, had perceived (like Joan Robinson) the need to develop the analysis of input markets in the light of his treatment of output, exploring the situation where 'even a slight element of monopoly necessarily reduces the remuneration of all factors employed in a given firm below the value of their marginal products (p. 181). As a result, Chamberlin (1957) emphasized the distinction between marginal product and marginal *revenue* product; a distinction which he considered to be 'one of the truly revolutionary features of the new analysis' (p. 7). The case is an important one since it means that the revenue product curves will have shapes determined by the *DD* and *dd* curves, while in addition there must be a 'kink' in the revenue product curve which is the counterpart of that found on the output side in all its versions (Skinner, 1981). Chamberlin (1946) did not develop this case, but he did explore the implications of a positively sloped supply curve for the factor (p. 84). Later (1957) he was to develop the argument that in the context of monopolistic competition, broadly defined, the relevant model is that of bilateral monopoly 'more or less restricted by competitive elements on both sides' (pp. 255, 260)[11]. The following statement gives some idea of the novelty of the thought and its attendant implications:

> Economists as well as the public are fooled by the fact that the adjective 'monopoly' is always attached to the noun 'profit' and never to the noun 'cost'. But economists at least should not be fooled in a matter as straightforwardly technical as this appears to be (1931, p. 266).

Looked at in one way, all of this can be seen as the result of a long process of refinement, drawing upon elements from most of the areas of analysis mentioned above. Yet at the same time, the features of the models just considered were quickly associated with acute difficulties in analysis, profoundly damaging to the 'new' price theory. For example, if the positively sloped factor supply curve alters the *shape* of *AC*, a situation of bilateral monopoly makes both the wage rate and the *position* of the cost curve indeterminate. The problems are further exacerbated by the fact that the factor supply curve may be kinked (see Reid, 1981).

Chamberlin (1961) himself drew attention to the problems presented by spatial and temporal product differentiation (p. 522) and to the fact that differentiation affects the capacity to construct an industry demand curve and hence to visualize the shape of the fractional part of the curve facing the firm. He concluded that 'to a very considerable extent the scheme of prices is the result of conditions unique to each product and to its market—it defies comprehensive description as a 'group' problem' (1946, p. 82). The implications of this point were to be elaborated by Triffin (1956).

While the 'dependence recognized' case remains one of Chamberlin's most important contributions, in a context (oligopoly) where the group is more readily identifiable, the model does not yield a determinate result. This condition is further aggravated by the problem of uncertainty which he had already considered in the discussion of duopoly (1946, p. 101). Strictly speaking, Chamberlin's *DD* and *dd* curves mark the limits of an area of uncertainty. Sweezy (1939) later raised a related point. The two curves are essentially 'imagined' curves, thus forming fluid boundaries which are liable to change in consequence of the experience of price cutting and non-price competition, where the latter also renders the cost and revenue functions interdependent in respect of position and shape. Thus there is no clearly definable path to equilibrium under such circumstances; indeed, 'in this fog of ignorance, there is no equilibrium' (Loasby, 1976).

Although one might argue about the extent to which such lessons have been learned, exploration of the 'monopoly' model served to expose the fragility of the elegant geometrical constructions on which it relied and which had been so painfully formulated in the post-Marshallian period. As Shackle (1967) has emphasized, Hicks was among the first to perceive that the general development involved the wreckage of the greater part of economic theory, including such fundamental concepts as demand and supply.

One reaction to the situation outlined is largely to ignore it, a position imputed to the Chicago School[12]. Another has been stimulated, not perhaps by the logical implications of the situation so much as by the perception that oligopoly is in fact one of the most important market forms[13], together with a growing awareness of the limitations of the Chamberlinian theory.

5.4 Post-Chamberlinian developments

Oligopoly theory is a complicated business. It lends itself reluctantly to tidy or to elegant treatment. Indeed,

> Oligopoly theory provides one of the clearest examples for the malaise in micro-economics. It is here that the contrast between institution-free and detail-rich approaches is the most striking. Furthermore dynamic problems appear in their starkest form.
>
> There is no oligopoly theory. There are bits and pieces of models: some reasonably well analyzed, some scarcely investigated. Our so-called theories are based upon a mixture of common sense, uncommon sense, a few observations, a great amount of casual empiricism, and a certain amount of mathematics and logic (Shubik, 1970, p. 415).

However, Shubik has not lapsed into passive pessimism. Oligopoly is now the dominant type of industrial structure, and he provides an order of the day which may be taken as a text for what follows:

...the time is ripe not merely for a new institutional economics, but for the development of a *mathematical institutional economics* which if anything must be simultaneously more abstract than most of received microtheory, that is, it must deal in abstractions such as flexibility, viability, strategic advantage, information state, and so forth. Yet when applied, the mapping from the abstract concepts to the specific variables must be far more detailed, process oriented, and institutional than is the case with current microeconomic theory. Questions such as what is a transaction or what is a market are key questions. They can be investigated at a high level of abstraction but the application of these investigations requires a considerable level of concretion (1980, p. 29).

Chamberlin's work on oligopoly, or more precisely duopoly, is one of a family of theories based on the work of Cournot, which seek to establish a determinate price and output equilibrium on the basis of firms' reaction patterns. These theories have attracted heavy criticism. The unrealistic myopia of Cournot's duopolists and the restrictive assumptions of Chamberlin's joint-profit maximizing solution have already been referred to. The theories suffer from the weakness of squeezing an essentially dynamic problem of sequential reactions into a comparative static framework.

The timing of reactions, survival, and the learning from wrong guesses about rivals' reactions are central to the theory and are not mere technical, institutional details. A more realistic and detailed model of the firm is clearly required to take these factors into account.

5.4.1 THE KINKED DEMAND CURVE

One particular conjectural variation has attracted wide attention— the kinked demand curve hypothesis. This postulates a discontinuity in firms' conjectural variations: a zero reaction for a price rise; a positive reaction for a price cut. Prices, therefore, will tend to be rigid in the face of moderate changes in an individual firm's costs and estimated demand conditions.

This hypothesis has proved a sturdy survivor, despite criticism on theoretical and empirical grounds (Stigler, 1947; Reid, 1981). Paradoxically, this widely cited construction is a rather special case in the analysis of oligopoly. The 'standard' kinked demand curve may be ironed out or even reversed if, as demand expands and capacity limits are reached, or a price leader emerges, firms lose their fear of raising prices (Efroymson, 1955). If account is taken of the capacity constraints, inventory costs, the degree and speed of rivals' reactions and consumer loyalties and addictions (Scitovsky, 1978), then the kinked demand curve becomes a simplified case of a more general theory of *contingent* demand curves[14]. Contingent demand curves will have kinks, gaps and discontinuities which reflect the limitations imposed on rivals' responses by capacity, transport costs and the varying degrees of substitutability of firms' differentiated products. This simplification may, however, draw attention to the fact that oligopolists are human, operating, as Williamson would put it, under conditions of 'bounded rationality' (Williamson, 1975). In other words, they do not possess the capacity, even if they had all relevant information on the above constraints, to process and use it.

The kinked demand curve analysis is limited in another sense. In its standard form, it allows only two options: that all firms maintain prices or all cut prices. But if firms are aware of all the combinations of price cutting and price maintenance open to themselves and their rivals, and have a knowledge of their profit pay-offs or outcomes, the decision to alter prices becomes a game theoretic situation in which the rational firm will cut price rather than maintain it: a mini–max solution.

If it cuts price and its rivals follow suit it will lose profits; if they do not follow suit its profits will increase; if it maintains price and its rivals cut theirs it will lose even more profits than if it cut its price along with them—the 'prisoner's dilemma' case[15]. A superior profit outcome would, of course, be a zero profit change with unchanged prices. But without communication or collusion the 'loyalty' required to achieve this outcome cannot be assumed.

In an oligopolistic industry, however, without overt collusion, firms can, by testing their market with price changes or limited price experiments, learn about the timing and probability of their rivals' reactions in a manner denied the prisoners. If one firm, as a result of its experience, comes to believe that the probability of a swift reaction is high then it will assume that not only will a unilateral price cut be unprofitable but that all other firms will have reached the same conclusion. Price will then tend to stick in this atmosphere of pessimism about the profit consequences of price changes, and the mutually unfavourable mini–max outcome will be avoided (Hay and Morris, 1979). While this restores the kinked demand curve predictions for a price cut the reasoning involves more complex assumptions about timing, probabilities and learning than the standard version.

The kinked demand curve is a relatively unsophisticated version of a number of game theoretic models which have been developed to analyse oligopoly (Shubik, 1980). Simulation techniques using computers have been developed to play more complex duopoly and oligopoly games. These experiments cannot lead to a general theory, although they give some support for collusion as the most effective route to joint profit maximization. They do, however, highlight the need to be precise about the timing of reactions, the means by which firms learn about the probable reaction patterns of their rivals, the financial strength of the firm and the aspirations and motives of its owners and managers. But, at the same time, the business of pricing becomes much more sophisticated and cannot be handled by the standard textbook models. A game theoretic approach to oligopoly thus requires both techniques of modelling and much more detailed institutional knowledge of firms' structures and objectives.

At the same time the relationship between firms in an industry needs to be examined in a different way. They can no longer be seen as entities interacting solely through the market. They must be seen as a group, in which each is aware of the others as individual rivals, with varying degrees of adherence to group goals formed by quasi-agreements or quasi-bargaining arrangements (Fellner, 1949). Group adherence will, of course, be related to the performance which is achieved as a result of it, and will change as demand conditions change, as product differentiation and the introduction of new processes takes place, and with the level of barriers to entry. This emphasis on the 'social relations' of oligopolistic industries clearly implies considerable knowledge of particular industrial situations which may make generalization difficult (Phillips, 1960; Williamson, 1975).

The kinked demand curve is a hypothesis about changes in published prices under oligopoly: the level of price, that is, the position of the kink, is not explained. Nor does it explain how price will settle down after industry-wide changes in costs or demand have induced 'safe' price changes. Hall and Hitch (1939) combine their discussion of the kinked demand curve with their formulation of the full-cost pricing principle to explain how prices are calculated in manufacturing industry. But they do not claim that the latter is a theory of oligopoly price. The 'reasonable' profit margin established by 'full-costers' on the basis of convention or a community of outlook has no necessary links with the kinked demand curve hypothesis; it may support it or conflict with it (Reid, 1981). The linking of the two is the work of Andrews (1949, 1975) which will be considered later.

The kinked demand curve is associated with another widely accepted dictum, namely, that price competition is not present under oligopoly. This is a sweeping claim with far-reaching implications, which will be discussed below. But at this stage a number of points may be made. Empirical work by Stigler and others indicates that prices under monopoly are more stable than under oligopoly (Stigler, 1947; Primeau and Bomball, 1974), suggesting that there are other reasons for price stability. Second, it is necessary to consider 'off-list' or 'transactions' prices in testing for price flexibility. And finally, doubts may reasonably be expressed about conclusions about price competition in the absence of a theory of how oligopoly prices are determined.

5.4.2 ENTRY AND POTENTIAL COMPETITION

The discussion so far has been cast in terms of the relationships between firms within an established industry. The extension of the analysis of oligopoly to include the problems of entry where the entrants operate on a scale sufficiently large to affect post-entry output and price is associated with the work of Bain (1956), Sylos-Labini (1962) and Modigliani (1958).

Bain (1956) introduced a systematic analysis of barriers to entry and potential competition. With these influences present, the firm's maximand is the present value of a stream of future profits which will be affected both by successful entry and by entry-deterring price and output policies. Price will settle at a limit, or entry-deterring, level which will be less than monopoly price but greater than a perfectly competitive price by an amount equal to the premium which barriers to entry allow firms in an existing industry to charge.

Entry barrier models may be seen as an extension of the conjectural variations theories to encompass a double form of recognized interdependence: between firms already established in the industry and between this group of firms and potential entrants. In fact, the weight of entry-barrier analysis concentrates on the second of these interdependencies and, with some ambivalence, assumes it to be the major problem. Bain assumes that existing firms will collude in face of the entrants, price being set at a level equal to the long-run average cost (including normal profit) of the most efficient firm, plus a premium or margin dependent on conditions of entry. Sylos-Labini (1962) assumes price leadership by the largest firm, which is assumed to have the lowest costs, the price set, however, being acceptable to the smaller firms in the industry. Modigliani assumes that all firms will be operating at a minimum optimal scale, the price being set at an entry-deterring level by the largest firm.

Having got the existing firms together in some kind of alliance against the outsiders, the next question concerns the conjectures which this alliance and potential entrants will make about the other's intentions. Sylos-Labini and Modigliani argue that maintenance of pre-entry levels of output is the most likely behaviour. (It also helps the attainment of a determinate equilibrium.) For existing firms it will keep unit costs down and leave no room for new entrants; for new entrants, engaged in the uncertain business of entering a new industry, it represents a realistically pessimistic assumption. If they do press ahead, they may, depending on the elasticity of the industry demand curve, their scale of output and the shape of their cost curves, confront a post-entry price which may be highly unprofitable (Scherer, 1980).

But if entry does occur on a large scale, existing firms will also suffer from the lower prices which will prevail, and the alliance against the outsider may break up in a price war, unless output is reduced by existing firms to offer partial accommodation to entrants, and price is allowed to fall, but not to the levels consistent with output maintenance. Bain thinks this is the more realistic response. Certainly, it may be a more effective deterrent to a large entrant who knows that, once he enters, output maintenance by existing firms will be destructively irrational. On the other hand, the threat, or the actual implementation of 'irrational' responses, may be what really deters a potential entrant (Scherer, 1980), in which case, a deliberate price war against a selected entrant may serve as a short, sharp lesson to others. Alternatively, firms may charge a profit-maximizing price, but retain reserve or excess capacity to expand output and reduce price to an entry-deterring or competitive level if and when entrants appear. There is also the probability of entry to consider; too many potential entrants may deter all entrants (Shepherd, 1979). These variants on the original Bain–Sylos postulates indicate that between existing firms and potential entrants there are many possible strategies; they are, in fact, in the same game theoretic situation as actual competitors (Marris, 1971; Caves and Porter, 1977).

In their analysis of limit-pricing Sylos-Labini and Modigliani assume that firms produce a homogeneous product. Bain's work, on the other hand, established product differentiation as a major barrier to entry. This raises the 'Chamberlinian' question of the definition of the industry, or group, being entered. Following Hicks (1946) and Samuelson (1967), the industry may be defined as a group of differentiated products for which a stable price-quality pattern emerges (Koutsoyiannis, 1979). A more fruitful approach (Hay and Morris, 1979; Scherer, 1980) is to use the 'product characteristics' approach to consumer theory developed by Lancaster (1966). This enables an industry to be defined in terms of characteristics space, which existing firms and entrants will seek to fill by means of product proliferation.

Once the notion of product competition and product proliferation is brought into the picture so, naturally, is the multi-product firm. The entry barrier analysis discussed above assumes that potential competition comes from new firms which have to create new capacity of minimal optimal scale to effect entry. But the more typical entrant may be a profitable, established, multi-plant, multi-product firm. This type of cross-entry competition which has been emphasized by Andrews (e.g. Andrews and Brunner, 1975) raises, if it does not resolve, the question of how prices are determined in multi-product firms with joint costs using product development and life cycle pricing as a means of competition and entry deterrence or entry retardation. It focuses attention, too, on the nature of the industry when such firms are taken to be the typical unit. In all the foregoing discussion it has been assumed that the industry is given, or exogenously determined. But how it came into being and how it came to have the number of firms it has is not explained.

5.4.3 COLLUSION

In the discussion so far it has been assumed that neither collusion nor co-operation occurs. But it has been observed also that the uncertainty arising from recognized interdependence both within an industry and between existing firms and potential competitors may lead firms towards some form of formal collusion on pricing. Although collusion has been declared illegal in many countries there is ample evidence that not all its forms are effectively suppressed, and that the desire to enter this form of contract is endemic in market economies— a point trenchantly noted by Adam Smith and Marshall. If this is so, then collusion deserves a theory rather than dismissive remarks about conspiratorial businessmen (Dewey, 1969, 1979, 1982). Dewey's thesis is that more attention should be paid to the profit-sharing cartel with optimally rationalized plants operating under the threat of entry as a model of oligopoly where firms are seeking to avoid the costs of uncertainty.

An immediate problem is the establishment of collusion, say, in the form of a cartel. Although all firms know they will gain by joining, they will wish to possess full information about market conditions and each other's market shares, costs and product qualities. If this is not the case, some firms may gain at the expense of others by giving false initial information about their costs and profits. This requirement can be a stringent one if the market environment and costs and technology are changing rapidly, and if there is more than a small number of firms involved.

Collusion can take a number of forms, but a formal cartel rather than a tacit agreement, or 'conscious parallelism', offers significant advantages. The pooling of information reduces the costs of monitoring and makes it easier to detect secret price-cutters. It provides a framework for administering the profit-pooling and side-payments needed to ensure that, where firms have different costs and demands, all firms will gain from the price and output policy— whether joint profit-maximizing or entry-deterring—of the cartel as a whole[17].

If collusive agreements are an attractive way of escape from oligopolistic uncertainty, they are nonetheless highly unstable. If certain firms are required to accept a relatively small share of the market or even retrenchment, they must, to find this acceptable, have a view of their future prospects, appropriately discounted, which is different from other more favoured firms. Conflict over such intrinsically uncertain matters is much more likely than not (Fellner, 1949). For such firms are putting themselves at risk if, whatever their view of their own future prospects, they accept a weak share of the market. They will then lay themselves open to pressures from larger firms to renegotiate less advantageous terms. Should the agreement break down, they will find themselves at a disadvantage in the competition which ensues.

Even if firms arrange to charge an agreed price they may retain the freedom to pursue intensive non-price competition to increase their market share. This may lead to what might be termed a 'non-price war', with a consequent reduction in profits for all firms as a result of the costs of aggressive marketing policies which cancel themselves out. This may place such a strain on the agreement that firms losing out will try to cheat by making secret price cuts or by provoking an open price war. The alternative is the extension of the agreement to cover non-price competition. But this is likely to be costly and very difficult to arrange and monitor.

Another source of instability arises out of firms' attempts to increase their market shares by increasing capacity. This will create excess capacity in the industry and firms will come under pressure to reduce prices in order to increase capacity utilization. Similar pressures arise if demand for the industry's product falls. They will be particularly acute where additions to capacity have to be undertaken in large, indivisible lumps. In such cases, fixed costs will be proportionately high, and firms will be tempted to cut prices, perhaps deeply, down to near the level of average variable costs, in order to keep their plant in operation. If demand comes in large, discrete orders, failure to get a particular order may be so serious that profitless competition may seem the only alternative to shut-down. The outcome here is either a price war and the emergence of a smaller industry with a probable tendency to chronic undercapacity, or the formation of some form of investment agreement which would arrange a system of bidding for contracts which would simulate competitive bidding but would, in fact, ensure that the order and the consequent increase in capacity would be assigned to a particular firm offering the agreed industry price. This spreading of lumpy demand and capacity creation is an attractive option, but it is likely to be feasible only in a settled, highly concentrated, industry with high entry barriers and good 'social relations' which allows tight agreement on output and capacity shares[18].

A perennial threat to price agreements is 'cheating' or 'chiselling' through secret price cuts. This problem has been examined by Stigler (1968). The reaction of an oligopolistic industry to cheating is another 'prisoner's dilemma' problem where, if cheating can be done successfully, all firms will match the secret price cuts with consequent losses. To maintain the agreement and avoid such losses a method of detecting cheaters has to be found, and penalties or sanctions imposed to make cheating unprofitable. Since detection will depend on information 'leaks' from buyers, or inferences from sales, and involve the setting of critical levels of sales switching which will denote the probability of cheating, it is likely that some cheating will take place.

The financial strength of the firms in the industry and the size structure of firms within it has to be known before predictions can be made.

The analysis of collusive oligopoly draws attention to the need to study the non-market links which firms establish with each other. In some recent work Williamson presents this problem as one of contracting, or the making of transactions under conditions of bounded rationality and unequally distributed information (Williamson, 1975). In particular, he compares the much greater difficulties which oligopolists face in arranging and maintaining complex agreements than multi-plant monopolists. The work of Richardson raises issues of greater generality (Richardson, 1960). His analysis of the problem of information and investment in all market structures and the need to include non-market arrangements between firms in any solution suggests that some of the problems discussed in terms of oligopoly above are, in fact, completely general ones present in all market economies. This highly significant point will be discussed further below.

5.4.4 OLIGOPOLY AND MANAGERIAL THEORIES

In much of the foregoing discussion the model of the firm has been that of standard, static microeconomics: a single, profit-maximizing owner–manager producing a single product, which may be differentiated. It has been shown that this model fails to capture the dynamic, uncertain organizationally complex world of multi-product oligopolists. The last two decades, however, have seen the emergence of 'new' managerial theories of the firm which seek to incorporate many of these factors[19].

It may seem, then, that oligopoly theory and theories of the firm are fruitfully converging. Indeed, in some cases such as Baumol's sales-maximization hypothesis, it is the very presence of oligopoly which has stimulated new thinking about the firm. It is, however, a striking fact that the new work on the firm has addressed itself hardly at all to the problems of oligopolistic interdependence, although the models of the firm which it has produced are along the lines required to deal with them. The firms are assumed to operate in a 'negotiated environment' in which some form of collusion allows them to neglect the threat of competitors' reactions. The theories' essential business is to analyse the workings of firms where ownership and control are vested in different groups and where goals other than profit-maximization are pursued. The theories are theories of the firm rather than the industry.

It is perhaps unreasonable to expect theories breaking new ground in analyses of the internal structure of modern firms to deal extensively with the interrelations of these entities at the same time

(Wood, 1971). But the problems posed by them remain. The objectives of the firms involve achieving particular growth rates of sales, output and assets, and the use of advertising and diversification of products and processes to achieve this. Such activities are bound to invoke a response by rivals; it is implausible to assume that demand can expand sufficiently to accommodate them all. The incorporation of oligopolistic reactions into the theory of the growing, 'real world', firm is one of the next steps for oligopoly theory.

5.5 Some problems in the analysis of oligopoly

5.5.1 OLIGOPOLY, PERFECT COMPETITION AND INFORMATION

The analysis of oligopoly, treated as a dynamic problem of interdependence and indeterminacy, usually assumes an 'ideal' perfectly competitive market structure where the problem does not exist, thus confirming the powers of survival of this model. In a seriously neglected work Richardson (1960) supports the view that this is a post-Marshallian simplification which is wrong and badly misleading (see also O'Brien, 1982). While the presence of many sellers eliminates the need for an individual producer to make specific assumptions about his rivals' reactions to any price, output or investment decisions he may take, he still needs to predict what his numerous competitors will do, since he will be affected by their response. All firms are affected by the response to common stimuli, e.g. an increase or decline in demand signalled by higher or lower 'given' prices. If a firm cannot obtain such information then indeterminacy exists, even in the presence of many sellers. It may be thought that the assumption of perfect knowledge will save the day. But, as Richardson points out, an individual firm can make a fully informed decision only after all his fellows have made theirs; and this is the situation for all of them.

The problem is simply illustrated. Assume that there is an increase in demand for the industry's product which is deemed to persist. The market signal to each producer is to expand capacity. But by how much? If all firms expand simultaneously and entrants flood into the industry, then, even if each firm faces decreasing returns to scale, the total increase in capacity may be excessive. Each producer needs to know what the total increase in capacity will be to find out whether there is room for him to expand profitably.

A general profit opportunity which is both known to everyone and equally capable of being exploited by everyone, is, in an important sense, a profit opportunity for no-one in particular (Richardson, 1960, p. 57).

Richardson's attack is quite remarkably destructive, more so even than that of Sraffa discussed above. As he puts it:

> The maximum potential volume of competitive supply is unlimited, not because of the possibility of indefinite expansion by each individual firm, but of the indefinitely large number of firms which might expand (p. 34).

He demonstrates that the model of perfect competition is logically inconsistent. The fault lies in a misplaced reliance on the assumption of perfect knowledge and inattention to the fact that the process by which equilibrium is reached is in reality a problem akin to that of oligopoly and, indeed, more formidable, since so many other firms are involved. The problem of oligopolistic interdependence and how firms cope with this shifts once more to the centre of the stage.

Having wreaked destruction Richardson proceeds to analyse ways in which his 'problem of knowledge' might be resolved. The implications for oligopoly theory are significant. If firms are hopelessly adrift in a sea of market uncertainty, then it may be that the way towards reducing this uncertainty lies in an admixture of ignorance and what are called, with deeply embedded value implications, 'imperfections in the market'. As Richardson puts it: 'Ignorance, by checking the response of some, may be a necessary condition for the response of others.'

Here is a reinstatement of Schumpeter's entrepreneur, and Shackle's concept of profit arising from the differential valuation by the imaginative, audacious, lucky or more knowledgeable few (Loasby, 1977; Chamberlin, 1957, Essay 10). The solution is tantamount to a renunciation of equilibrium economics in favour of the 'Austrian' perspective of the market as a process which throws up prices which are sure to be disequilibrium prices at any given time (Hayek, 1949, Kirzner, 1981; Loasby, 1976).

Having floated this solution, Richardson turns to another which is only slightly less heretical and to an extent at odds with the first. He argues that imperfections in the market are, in fact, necessary for it to work at all. Thus, limits on the growth of firms and barriers to entry set the necessary constraints and impose the delays on the scale and timing of firms' supply responses, which they require to make any commitment at all. Similarly, agreements to fix prices and to share markets and investment plans constitute a necessary form of co-ordinating machinery which gives firms some guarantee of profit from any expansion they undertake. The complex web of contracts that firms make with customers, retail outlets, suppliers and producers of complementary products may be seen as efforts to render more stable the parameters of their decision-making (Richardson, 1972).

The organization of industries along these lines may, of course, produce economic rents, wasteful restriction of output, X-inefficiency and a smothering of the most efficient and dynamic firms. The optimum strength of the imperfections is not, however, zero; they are required to some extent if markets are theoretically to work. What this optimum level is, is likely to vary according to particular industrial circumstances. There is no longer an 'ideal', Paretian allocational norm. It is swept away along with perfect competition. Competition is now a dynamic process no longer identified with one particular and rather odd market structure, but one which must be rendered effective, or 'workable' in all markets (Clark, 1940; Sosnick, 1958; Swann et al., 1974; Reekie, 1979).

Richardson recognizes the possible conflict between stability and market discipline but sees it as inherent in any system of decentralized decision-making. It should be recalled here that, apart from legal obstacles, cartels are not easy to establish or maintain, particularly if competition involves cross-entry by established concerns. Nor will they always be dominated by the most inefficient firms. The nature of the competitive pressures which exist under oligopoly must now be examined.

5.5.2 PRICE COMPETITION AND OLIGOPOLY

The view that oligopoly, even in the absence of collusion, will greatly reduce the extent of price competition is so widely held as to amount to conventional wisdom (Galbraith, 1967). It has sweeping implications. If there is no price competition under oligopoly then it must be concluded that there will be next to none at all, given the oligopolistic nature of most markets. Under perfect competition, if this flawed construction is accepted, all firms take price as given. The only possibility if Chamberlin's monopolistic competition of the large group type, which its creator more or less abandoned. This conclusion is especially bizarre, since oligopoly is the main market form where firms are price-makers and in which competition in the sense of active rivalry, in which firms really are at war with each other with their very survival at stake, exists.

Clearly, the nature of price competition needs closer examination. One positive approach to this problem has been offered by Wilson and Brown (1969), developing earlier work by Wilson (1962; see also Swann et al., 1974). The authors draw a distinction between price competition of 'Type A' which involves cutting published prices and 'Type B', which is the operation of market pressures to keep prices sufficiently low to prevent firms from earning abnormally high long-term profits and to force down the level of costs. Competition is thus no longer identified with price instability, which, it may be noted, is absent from perfect competition as well as from successful cartels. A similar notion is present in Richardson's (1967) distinction between short-run and long-run price competition.

Wilson and Brown argue that their 'Type B' competition is present under oligopoly, including collusive oligopoly, and that its pressures impinge on firms at the time when they are fixing prices. The model of price-fixing they adopt is essentially the normal cost principle developed by Andrews (Andrews, 1949; Wilson and Andrews, 1952). Price is set on the basis of the costs of a reasonably efficient firm, with competitors' costs frequently used as a guide, given a normal utilization of the capacity required to meet estimated demand, with a profit margin set at a safe and sustainable level having regard both to actual competitors (the producers of known close substitutes) and potential competitors.

It is, of course, well established that this model lacks formal precision. There is uncertainty about costs, which are not uniform, and about the fixing of 'normal' capacity utilization levels. There are the problems of attributing joint costs in a multi-product firm and the dynamic problems of life-cycle pricing of products. There is also the difficulty of knowing where a potential entrant may spring from, and reckoning precisely the conditions of entry (Stigler, 1968). But, as Wilson and Brown point out, all of these uncertainties confirm that oligopolists are subject to competitive pressures every time they fix or adjust the price of existing or new products.

Emphasis on the price-fixing process allows discussion about how firms use price as a competitive weapon to proceed in more realistic terms. Even if firms agree to hold to a fixed price, through fear of retaliation or as a co-ordinating device, this does not mean that they abandon all flexibility. As Rothschild (1947) points out, 'oligopolistic circumstances lead to a multitude of conditions surrounding the quoted price'.

Some examples may be given. In a period of inflation firms may increase product prices by less than factor prices by improving their efficiency. Many oligopolistic industries produce on a contract basis where the trimming of the price bid, in the absence of rigged or collusive bidding, may involve quite intense and finely tuned price competition. Discounts may also involve active price competition, if reductions from published prices for certain customers are greater than the economies of large-scale orders alone would justify.

There is, finally, the important matter of new product lines. The floating of a new product may be a moment when firms seek to incorporate new cost-saving techniques and increase profit margins or, in setting the product price, cut margins as low as possible as part of marketing policy. Price and non-price competition here go naturally together; they are complementary and not clearly separated alternative strategies.

The presence of potential cross-entry competition is an extremely important element in the theory of competitive oligopoly (Andrews and Brunner, 1975). It imposes on firms the need to consider not simply their familiar, well-known competitors but to be aware that outside this group there are widening circles of potential competitors who may as yet produce no close substitute product but who possess the capacity to do so quickly and on a considerable scale. The potential entrant may also possess the financial reserves to mount a powerful advertising campaign in its 'new' market. It may be a well-known name in its own markets, and this brand loyalty may be easily carried over to its new product. If the product is an intermediate product, or a consumer good sold through knowledgeable business buyers or wholesalers, the new entrant's pedigree will be known. Entry barriers may, therefore, crumble considerably and quickly in the face of such an assault. They may indeed be a means of facilitating entry to a new market (Demsetz, 1982). In this situation existing firms may, in fixing price, be very wary about attributing a low elasticity to their demand curve, and take considerable pains over its estimation. If their costs are relatively constant over a large volume of their output, and price set with a close eye on the cost schedules of an efficient competitor, they may end up very close to the price and output position of the marginalist profit-maximizer, and with costs pressed down under the threat of competition to a level consistent with little X-inefficiency or 'slack' (Wilson, 1952).

This outcome may, of course, be impeded by factors other than collusion. Conditions of exit will be unpropitious if loss-making, inefficient firms can hang on with average variable costs less than the total costs of a potential entrant. Subsidies and protective labour market legislation may create further barriers to exit.

Andrews and Brunner (1975) define the industry in terms of firms with similar production processes capable in any given time period of producing a range of products, rather than in terms of product markets and consumer preferences. Since oligopoly is concerned with producer competition this is distinctly helpful. Their analysis of the industry is also realistically dynamic. The boundaries of the industry will be constantly changing, as will its member-firms' positions in individual product markets, as potential competition exerts its pressure. Firms will both supply and compete with each other, and small firms will be potential competitors with units or divisions of large firms. There will not, however, be continual price changes. Competition will work through the fixing of entry-deterring, normal-cost pricing, embellished by a complex mixture of product competition and price adjustment.

5.5.3 OLIGOPOLY, MANAGERIAL THEORIES AND THE GROWTH OF THE FIRM

Cross-entry competition implies a model of the firm much closer to the 'new' theories of the firm than the standard textbook exhibit. The price-fixing process of an entry-deterring, normal cost oligopolist will surely bear a close resemblance to Baumol's profit-constrained sales revenue-maximizer, if the threat of potential competition, which a sales maximizer is bound to encounter, is built into the profit constraint. If entry-deterrence is taken into account the scope for discretionary expenditures by managers may be significantly reduced (Williamson, 1964). Williamson himself has recognized the constrained nature of these expenditures in his work on the U- and M-form firm[20]. The latter, with its multi-divisional profit centres, strips away much of the slack of the U-form and simulates many of the features of the profit-maximizing models. This still, however, assumes away oligopolistic interdependence. But it may be argued that an entry-deterring, multi-product oligopolist will be forced towards an M-form organization under the pressure of potential competition (Williamson, 1975; Wildsmith, 1975).

A significant feature of the new theories of the firm for oligopoly analysis is their treatment of the growth of the firm. This is conducted largely in terms of a steady-state growth model, where the profits, assets and sales of a multi-product firm grow at the same rate as output, which is sold at a constant price somehow agreed in the industry. The firm's demand curve now becomes a relationship between total profit and total capacity. Assuming that the firm has chosen an optimal mix of outputs from a fixed range of products, this demand curve will define a maximum profits point for every level of assets. Growth then becomes a process of shifting the demand curve, as defined above, outwards by product diversification, so that the revenue accruing enables the firm to earn sufficient profits to sustain the required growth indefinitely.

The nature of this total demand growth has been examined in detail by Marris (1964), but the treatment of interdependence leaves some unanswered questions. Interdependence is an omnipresent and powerful force in Marris's model. The essence of the firm's growth is an aggressive campaign of product development to capture a large share of a growing market. A new form of indeterminacy appears.

The financing of diversification joins with the satisfaction of shareholders' requirements (to avoid takeover) as a constraint on the firm's growth–profit trade-off. But if firms are all engaged in active diversification, then no firm can be certain of the pay-off in terms of profits. The growth–profit relationship thus becomes indeterminate.

Marris' treatment of this problem is to assume that firms operate in two environments: an immediate environment, comprising demand curves, entry barriers, product preferences, etc. which they seek to manipulate; and a super-environment, which the firm cannot influence and which limits its capacity to change its immediate environment. This comprises consumer tastes, wants and resistance to firms' diversification efforts, and the diminishing returns to which expenditures on R and D, product development and product differentiation are subject. Marris argues that firms will tend to collude or form truces in their campaigns to alter their immediate environments, and on the basis of such agreements, which are assumed to include prices, firms will form a view of their growth –profits trade-off.

The trouble with this approach is that the super-environment will be affected by firms' uncertainty about this trade-off. The super-environment then becomes endogenous. It is affected by what firms do (Hay and Morris, 1979). Determinacy, therefore, has to be imposed by collusion. But such collusion is by its nature a much more wide-ranging, costly and imprecise operation than price agreements, and consequently a rather weak platform on which to build a solution to a problem of intricate interdependence.

5.5.4 CONTESTABLE MARKETS

Some of the most recent work on oligopoly by Baumol and others has produced an impressive attempt to formalize and generalize many of the points this section has covered (Baumol, 1982; Baumol et al., 1982). Its essence is the replacement of perfect competition as an ideal market type by a construction which Baumol terms a perfectly contestable market. This is a market where entry is absolutely free and exit is absolutely costless. The contestable market is constantly under the threat of what Baumol calls the hit-and-run potential entrant. If profits are super-normal, an entrant may undercut an incumbent's prices slightly, steal his share of the market and depart with his temporary and still super-normal profits. In a perfectly contestable market, therefore, profits must be normal regardless of its structure. By the same token, any X-inefficiency will leave an inviting loophole for the transient entrant.

The concept of the contestable market enables the structure of an industry to be determined endogenously. If neither allocational nor X-inefficiency can exist, then the industry must be organized on an optimal scale; it might be a single-firm monopoly, or contain thousands of firms. The only requirement is that unit costs are minimized for a given output (Baumol deals in detail with the problem of multi-product firms). In the case of oligopoly this allows prices, outputs and profits to be determined without worrying about conjectural variations or reaction functions, or as Baumol puts it, 'the other paraphernalia of standard oligopoly analysis'. Moreover, if the modern theory of L-shaped costs is followed, the contestable market price, which must yield only normal profits, will coincide with long-run marginal cost if firms are operating plants of minimum optimal scale where long-run average costs and marginal cost are equal. The welfare implications of contestable oligopoly are thus favourable.

This summary of the contestable market theory is unjustly abbreviated. Its framework is, however, the really important matter. It represents a formal theory which gives hope of a more general order which may be interestingly compared with Shubik's approach quoted earlier.

First, it replaces perfect competition as an alternative ideal market structure which can subsume all the traditional market types. It allows an analysis of the competitive features of oligopolistic industries where competition is not identified simply with a price instability or its absence by the observation of steady prices. Potential competition is the major transmission mechanism of competitive forces. Its central requirement of free entry and costless exit does not rule out the possibility that some limitations on both may exist which may blunt competitive pressures and injure consumers or confer benefits by reducing uncertainty. It provides a theoretical explanation of differences in industrial structures which has been lacking in much previous work. It offers a demonstration that entry-deterring average cost pricing may produce the welfare benefits of competition hitherto expressed in terms of unoperational, marginalist, static Paretian terms. It does not quite pull clear of conjectural variations; entry and entry-deterrence may still involve game-playing. Finally, it restores analysis of the industry in terms of multi-product firms into which the insights of the new theories of the firms can be inserted.

While these developments lead well beyond the theoretical and empirical framework which was established by Chamberlin, they also confirm the importance of the general perspective supplied by Marshall's *Industry and Trade*.

Notes

1. Both theories were reviewed by Chamberlin (1929). For discussion of and further references to Edgeworth's analysis, see Creedy (1981).
2. Chamberlin (1946, pp. 40–41) concentrated on the suggestion that the price may oscillate between the limits.
3. For discussion see Hutchison (1953, p. 469). Chamberlin (1946) excluded Hotelling from his chapter on duopoly. Schneider (1967, pp. 141–142) suggests that Hotelling's results were anticipated by Launhardt (1885).
4. Chamberlin (1946, pp. 47–49) associated this result with Young (1925), Schumpeter (1928), and J.M. Clark (1940).
5. Chamberlin's interest in the uncertainties surrounding price competition is recalled by Machlup's distinction between short- and long-run demand curves (1937).
6. In Sraffa's words: 'Long custom, personal acquaintance, confidence in the quality of the product, proximity, knowledge of particular requirements...the reputation of a trade mark, or sign, ...such special features of modelling or design in the product as...have for their principal purpose that of distinguishing it from the products of other firms' (1926, repr. 1953, pp. 190–191).
7. See Galbraith (1948, p. 99). Examples of precedents include Cassell (1923), J.M. Clark (1923), Bowley (1924), and this approach was developed by Pigou (1928), Shove (1928) and Stackelberg (1952).

8. 'They examined the existing world in a spirit of respect, they brought as much of it intact into their discourse as they could, they valued the contours and features of the landscape they beheld and tried to mould their argument upon them rather than cut a path direct to rigorous conclusions. Mrs Robinson did the opposite. Clear and definitive questions cannot be asked about a vague, richly detailed, fluid and living world. This world must therefore be exchanged for a *model*, a set of precise assumptions collecively simple enough to allow the play of logic and mathematics... The model is a work of art, freely composed within the constraints of a particular art-form, namely the logical binding together of propositions' (Shackle, 1967, p. 47).

9. Chamberlin believed that 'the theory of monopolistic competition permits us to pass over to the study of dynamics, and in particular to the problems of development and growth' (1957, p. 62). He also drew a parallel between his own work and Schumpeter's emphasis on innovation, concurring with the latter's belief that 'the bulk of what we call economic progress is incompatible with...perfect competition' (1957, p. 64). See also 'The Impact of Recent Monopoly Theory on the Schumpeterian System' (Chamberlin, 1957, Essay 10).

10. It is this point which explains Chamberlin's contention that he had anticipated the 'full cost' principle normally associated with Andrews, and his view that this principle was fully consistent with his original analysis (1957, p. 272). Machlup (1946) provides an interesting point of comparison.

11. This view is more commonly associated with Galbraith (1952). See Silberston (1970, p. 528) and Papandreou (1952, p. 200). Bilateral monopoly, as developed by Edgeworth, was examined in the survey by Haley (1948), albeit without reference to *Monopolistic Competition*.

12. See Robinson (1971, p. 53), Samuelson (1967, p. 108), Chamberlin (1957).

13. See Galbraith (1948, p. 107), Bain (1964, p. 29; 1967, p. 164).

14. See Reid (1981, pp. 53–57), Shubik and Shapley (1969, pp. 30–44), and Scitovsky (1978, pp. 277–237).

15. See Shubik (1959), Scherer (1980, pp. 160–164), and Marris (1971, pp. 283–304).

16. This had, however, been raised earlier by Kaldor (1935, pp. 33–50), Hicks (1954, pp. 41–54) and Harrod (1952, pp. 139–174). Hicks drew a distinction between 'snatchers', who maximize short-run profits, regardless of entry risks, and then leave the industry, and 'stickers', whose concern is with long-run profits, even if this means accepting lower short-run profits to deter entry. The need to consider entry had also been stressed by Stigler (1950), who saw in the formulation of conditions of entry a more manageable problem with testable hypotheses than the discussions about conjectural variations.

17. A similar argument applies to such things as market-sharing agreements and basing point pricing schemes.

18. See Richardson (1965, pp. 432–439; 1966, pp. 73–92), Hay and Marris (1979, pp. 167–179).

19. See Baumol (1958, pp. 187–198), Williamson (1964), Marris (1964), Simon (1955, pp. 99–118), Cyert and March (1963), Koutsoyiannis (1979).

20. The U-firm is a unitary organization with functional divisions, e.g. sales and production. The M-firm is organized into semi-autonomous divisions on a product or geographical basis. In the M-form, divisions compete with each other and have to justify their claims on company resources, thus leading to behaviour more closely associated with profit-maximization. The managers of the U-firm divisions will be more likely to pursue non-profit-maximizing goals.

References

ANDREWS, P.W.S. (1949). *Manufacturing Business*. London, Macmillan

ANDREWS, P.W.S. (1951). Industrial Analysis in Economics. In *Oxford Studies in the Price Mechanism* (ed. by T. Wilson and P.W.S. Andrews), pp. 139–172. Oxford, Oxford University Press

ANDREWS, P.W.S. and BRUNNER, E. (1975). *Studies in Pricing*, pp. 35–46. London, Macmillan

BAIN, J.S. (1956). *Barriers to New Competition*. Cambridge, Mass., Harvard University Press

BAIN, J.S. (1964). The Impact on Industrial Organisation. *American Economic Association Papers and Proceedings* **74**, 28–32

BAIN, J.S. (1967). Chamberlin's Impact on Microeconomic Theory. In *Monopolistic Competition Theory: Studies in Impact* (ed. by R.E. Keunne), pp. 147–176. London, John Wiley

BAUMOL, W.J. (1958). On the Theory of Oligopoly. *Economica* **25**, 187–198

BAUMOL, W.J. (1967). *Business Behavior, Value and Growth*, Rev. edn. New York, Harcourt, Brace and World

BAUMOL, W.J. (1982). Contestable Markets: an Uprising on the Theory of Industry Structure. *American Economic Review* **72**, 1–15

BAUMOL, W.J., PAYZOV, J.C. and WILLIG, R.D. (1982). *Contestable Markets and the Theory of Industry Structure*, San Diego, Harcourt Brace Jovanovich

BERTRAND, J. (1883). Review of Cournot. *Journal des Savants* 503

BOULDING, K.E. (1942). The Theory of the Firm in the last Ten Years. *American Economic Review* **32**, 791–802

BOWLEY, A.L. (1924). *The Mathematical Groundwork of Economics*. Oxford, Oxford University Press

CASSEL, G. (1923). *The Theory of Social Economy*. London, T. Fisher Unwin

CAVES, R.E. and PORTER, M.E. (1977). From Entry Barriers to Mobility Barriers. Conjectural Decisions and Contrived Deterrence to New Competition. *Quarterly Journal of Economics* **41**, 241–261

CHAMBERLIN, E.H. (1946). *The Theory of Monopolistic Competition*, 5th edn. Cambridge, Mass., Harvard University Press

CHAMBERLIN, E.H. (1957). *Towards a More General Theory of Value*. Oxford, Oxford University Press

CHAMBERLIN, E.H. (1961). The Origin and Early Development of Monopolistic Competition Theory. *Quarterly Journal of Economics* **75**, 515–543

CLAPHAM, J.H. (1922). Of Empty Economic Boxes. *Economic Journal* **32**, 305–314

CLARK, C. (1899). *The Distribution of Wealth*. New York, Macmillan

CLARK, J.M. (1923). *Studies in the Economics of Overhead Cost*. Chicago, University of Chicago Press

CLARK, J.M. (1940). Towards a Concept of Workable Competition. *American Economic Review* **30**, 241–256

COURNOT, A. (1838). *Recherches sur les Principes Mathématiques de la Theorie des Richesses*, Paris

CREEDY, J. (1981). F.Y. Edgeworth 1845–1926. In *Pioneers of Modern Economics in Britain* (ed. by D.P. O'Brien and J.R. Presley), pp. 72–104. London, Macmillan

CYERT, R.M. and MARCH, J.G. (1963). *A Behavioural Theory of the Firm*. Englewood Cliffs, NJ, Prentice-Hall

DEMSETZ, H. (1982). Barriers to Entry. *American Economic Review* **72**, 47–57

DEWEY, D. (1969). *The Theory of Imperfect Competition*. New York, Columbia University Press

DEWEY, D. (1979). Information, Entry and Welfare: the Case for Collusion. *American Economic Review* **69**, 587–594

DEWEY, D. (1982). Welfare and Collusion: Reply. *American Economic Review* **72**, 276–281

EDGEWORTH, F.Y. (1897). La Teoria Pura del Monopolio, trans. in *Papers Relating to Political Economy*, Vol. I, pp. 111–142. London, Macmillan, 1925

EFROYMSON, C. (1955). The Kinked Demand Curve Reconsidered. *Quarterly Journal of Economics* **69**, 110–136

FELLNER, W. (1949). *Competition among the Few*. New York, Alfred Knopf

FISHER, I. (1898). Cournot and Mathematical Economics. *Quarterly Journal of Economics* **12**, 126–127

GALBRAITH, J.K. (1948). Monopoly and the Concentration of Economic Power, In *A*

Survey of Contemporary Economics (ed. by H.S. Ellis), pp. 99–128. Homewood, Ill., R.D. Irwin

GALBRAITH, J.K. (1952). *American Capitalism; the Concept of Countervailing Power.* Boston, Houghton Mifflin

GALBRAITH, J.K. (1967). *The New Industrial State.* London, Hamish Hamilton

GEORGESCU-ROEGEN, N. (1967). Chamberlin's New Economics and the Unit of Production. In *Monopolistic Competition Theory: Studies in Impact* (ed. by R.E. Keune), pp. 31–62. London, John Wiley

HALEY, B.F. (1948). Value and Distribution. In *A Survey of Contemporary Economics* (ed. by H.S. Ellis), pp. 1–48. Homewood, Ill., R.D. Irwin

HALL, R.L. and HITCH, C.J. (1939). Price Theory and Business Behaviour. *Oxford Economic Papers* **2**, 12–45

HARROD, R. (1952). *Economic Essays.* London, Macmillan

HAY, D. and MARRIS, D. (1979). *Industrial Economics. Theory and Evidence*, pp. 147–160, 194–198, 289–299. Oxford, Oxford University Press

HAYEK, F.A. (1945). The Use of Knowledge in Society. *American Economic Review* **35**, 519–530

HAYEK, F.A. (1949). *Individualism and Economic Order.* London, Routledge and Kegan Paul

HICKS, J.R. (1946). *Value and Capital*, pp. 311–312. Oxford, Oxford University Press

HICKS, J.R. (1954). The Process of Imperfect Competition. *Oxford Economic Papers* **6**, 41–54

HOTELLING, H. (1929). Stability in Competition. *Economic Journal* **39**, 41–57. Reprinted in *Readings in Price Theory* (ed. by K. Boulding and G.J. Stigler), pp. 467–484. London, George Allen and Unwin, 1953

HUTCHISON, T.W. (1953). *A Review of Economic Doctrines 1870–1929*, pp. 76, 309, 313, 315. Oxford, Oxford University Press

KALDOR, N. (1935). Market Imperfection and Excess Capacity. *Economica* **2**, 33–50

KIRZNER, I.M. (1981). The 'Austrian' Perspective on the Crisis. In *The Crisis in Economic Theory* (ed. by D. Bell and I. Kristol), pp. 111–122. New York, Basic Books

KNIGHT, F.H. (1921). *Risk, Uncertainty and Profit.* New York, Houghton Mifflin

KOUTSOYIANNIS, A. (1979). *Modern Microeconomics*, 2nd edn, pp. 301–304. London, Macmillan

LANCASTER, K.J. (1966). A New Approach to Consumer Theory. *Journal of Political Economy* **74**, 132–157

LAUNHARDT, W. (1885). *Mathematische Begründung der Volkswirtschaftslehre.* Leipzig, Wilhelm Engelmann

LOASBY, B.J. (1976). *Choice, Complexity and Ignorance*, p. 189. Cambridge, Cambridge University Press

LOASBY, B.J. (1977). Imperfections and Adjustments. *University of Stirling Discussion Papers in Economics, Finance and Investment, No. 50*

MACHLUP, F. (1937). Monopoly and Competition: A Classification. *Ameican Economic Review* **27**, 445–451

MACHLUP, F. (1946). Marginal Analysis and Empirical Research. *American Economic Review* **36**, 519–554

MARRIS, R. (1964). *The Economic Theory of Managerial Capitalism.* London, Macmillan

MARRIS, R. (1971). The Modern Corporation and Economic Theory. In *The Corporate Economy* (ed. by R. Marris and A. Wood), pp. 270–317. London, Macmillan

MARSHALL, A. (1890). *Principles of Economics*, 9th (Variorum) edn (ed. by C.W. Guillebaud). London, Macmillan, 1963

MARSHALL, A. (1919). *Industry and Trade*, 3rd edn, 1920. London, Macmillan

MODIGLIANI, F. (1958). New Developments on the Oligopoly Front. *Journal of Political Economy* **66**, 215–232

MOORE, H.L. (1906). Paradoxes of Competition. *Quarterly Journal of Economics* **20**, 211

O'BRIEN, D.P. (1981). A. Marshall, 1842–1924. In *Pioneers of Modern Economics in Britain* (ed. by D.P. O'Brien and J.R. Presley), pp. 36–71. London, Macmillan

O'BRIEN, D.P. (1982). The Evolution of the Theory of the Firm. *University of Durham Working Paper, No. 46*

PAPANDREOU, A.S. (1952). Some Basic Problems in the Theory of the Firm. In *A Survey of Contemporary Economics* (ed. by B.F. Haley), pp. 183–219. Homewood, Ill., R.D. Irwin

PARETO, V. (1896). *Cours d'Economie Politique*, I. Lausanne, F. Rouge

PHILLIPS, A. (1960). A Theory of Interfirm Organisation. *Quarterly Journal of Economics* **74**, 602–613

PIGOU, A.C. (1924). *The Economics of Welfare*, p. 267. London, Macmillan

PIGOU, A.C. (1928). An Analysis of Supply. *Economic Journal* **38**, 238–257

PRIMEAU, W.J. and BOMBALL, M.R. (1974). A Re-examination of the Kinky Oligopoly Demand Curve. *Journal of Political Economy* **82**, 851–862

REEKIE, W.D. (1979). *Industry, Prices and Markets*, Oxford, Philip Allan

REID, G. (1981). *The Kinked Demand Curve Model of Oligopoly*, pp. 33–34. Edinburgh, Edinburgh University Press

RICHARDSON, G.B. (1960). *Information and Investment*, pp. 3, 57. Oxford, Oxford University Press

RICHARDSON, G.B. (1965). The Theory of Restrictive Practices. *Oxford Economic Papers* **17**, 432–449

RICHARDSON, G.B. (1966). The Pricing of Heavy Electrical Equipment: Competition or Agreement? *Bulletin of Oxford Institute of Statistics* **28**, 73–92

RICHARDSON, G.B. (1967). Price Notification Schemes. *Oxford Economic Papers* **19**, 359–369

RICHARDSON, G.B. (1972). The Organisation of Industry. *Economic Journal* **82**, 883–896

ROBINSON, J.V. (1933). *The Economics of Imperfect Competition*, pp. vi–vii, 5, 26. London, Macmillan

ROBINSON, R. (1971). *Edward H. Chamberlin*, p. 10. New York, Columbia University Press

ROTHSCHILD, K. (1947). Price Theory and Oligopoly. *Economic Journal* **57**, 299–320

SAMUELSON, P.A. (1967). The Monopolistic Competition Revolution. In *Monopolistic Competition Theory: Studies in Impact* (ed. by R.E. Kuenne), pp. 105–138. London, John Wiley

SCHERER, F.M. (1980). *Industrial Market Structure and Economic Performance*, 2nd edn, pp. 243–248, 259–260. Chicago, Rand–McNally

SCHNEIDER, E. (1967). Milestones on the Way to the Theory of Monopolistic Competition. In *Monopolistic Competition Theory: Studies in Impact* (ed. by R.E. Kuenne), pp. 139–144. London, John Wiley

SCHUMPETER, J.A. (1928). The Instability of Capitalism. *Economic Journal* **38**, 361–386

SCHUMPETER, J.A. (1954). *History of Economic Analysis*, pp. 956, 978n., 983–984. London. George Allen and Unwin

SCITOVSKY, T. (1978). Asymmetrics in Economics. *Scottish Journal of Political Economy* **25**, 227–237

SHACKLE, G.L.S. (1967). *The Years of High Theory*, pp. 26, 27, 43, 47, 62, 64. Cambridge, Cambridge University Press

SHEPHERD, W.G. (1979). *The Economics of Industrial Organization*, pp. 288–294. London, Prentice-Hall International

SHOVE, G.F. (1928). Varying costs and Marginal Net Products. *Economic Journal* **38**, 258–266

SHUBIK, M. (1959). *Strategy and Market Structure*. New York, John Wiley

SHUBIK, M. (1970). A Curmudgeon's Guide to Microeconomics. *Journal of Economic Literature* **8**, 405–434

SHUBIK, M. and SHAPLEY, L. (1969). Price Strategy Oligopoly with Product Variation. *Kyklos* **20**, 30–44

SHUBIK, M. with LEVITAN, R. (1980). *Market Structure and Behaviour*, p. 29. Cambridge, Mass., Harvard University Press

SILBERSTON, A. (1970). Price Behaviour of Firms. *Economic Journal* **80**, 511–582

SIMON, H.A. (1955). A Behavioural Model of Rational Choice. *Quarterly Journal of Economics* **69**, 99–118

SKINNER, A.S. (1981). Of Factor and Commodity Markets: A Note on E.H. Chamberlin. *Oxford Economic Papers* **33**, 122–134

SOSNICK, S.H. (1958). A Critique of Concepts of Workable Competition. *Quarterly Journal of Economics* **72**, 380–423

SRAFFA, P. (1926). The Laws of Returns under Competitive Conditions. *Economic Journal* **36**, 535–550. Repr. in *Readings in Price Theory* (ed. by K. Boulding and G.J. Stigler), 1953, pp. 180–197. London, George Allen and Unwin

STACKELBERG, H.v. (1952). *The Theory of the Market Economy*, trans. by A.J. Peacock, London, William Hodge. Originally published as *Grundlagen der Theoretischen Volkswirtschaftlehre*, 1948

STEINER, P.O. (1964). The Theory of Monopolistic Competition after Thirty Years: Discussion. *American Economic Association, Papers and Proceedings* **54**, 55–57

STIGLER, G.J. (1947). The Kinky Oligopoly Curve and Rigid Prices. *Journal of Political Economy* **55**, 432–449

STIGLER, G.J. (1950). Capitalism and Monopolistic Competition. *American Economic Review Papers and Proceedings* **40**, 63

STIGLER, G.J. (1965). Perfect Competition Historically Considered. In *Essays on the History of Economics*, pp. 234–267. Chicago, Chicago University Press

STIGLER, G.J. (1968). *The Organisation of Industry*, pp. 5–22. Homewood, Ill., R.D. Irwin

SWANN, D., O'BRIEN, D., MAUNDER, W.P.J. and HOWE, W.S. (1974). *Competition in British Industry*, pp. 124–129. London, George Allen and Unwin

SWEEZY, P.M. (1939). Demand Under Conditions of Oligopoly. *Journal of Political Economy* **47**, 568–573

SYLOS-LABINI, P. (1962). *Oligopoly and Technical Progress*. Cambridge, Mass., Harvard University Press

TRIFFIN, R. (1956). *Monopolistic Competition and General Equilibrium Theory*, p. 88ff. Cambridge, Mass., Harvard University Press

VINER, J. (1931). Cost Curves and Supply Curves. *Zeitschrift fur Nationalokonomie*, 23–46. Reprinted in *Readings in Price Theory* (ed. by K. Boulding and G.J. Stigler), 1953, pp. 198–232. London, John Wiley

WILDSMITH, J.B. (1975). *Managerial Theories of the Firm*. London, Martin Robertson

WILLIAMSON, O.E. (1964). *The Economics of Discretionary Behavior: Managerial Objectives in a Theory of the Firm*. Englewood Cliffs, NJ, Prentice-Hall

WILLIAMSON, O.E. (1975). *Markets and Hierarchies: Analysis and Antitrust Implications*. New York, The Free Press

WILSON, T. (1952). The Inadequacy of the Theory of the Firm as a Branch of Welfare Economics. *Oxford Economic Papers* **4**, 18–44

WILSON, T. (1962). Restrictive Practices. In *Competition, Cartels and their Regulation* (ed. by J.P. Miller), pp. 114–168. Amsterdam, North-Holland

WILSON, T. and ANDREWS, P.W.S. (1951). *Oxford Studies in the Price Mechanism*. Oxford, Oxford University Press

WILSON, T. and BROWN, C.V. (1969). Price Competition under Oligopoly. Unpublished Ms.

WOOD, A. (1971). Economic Analysis of the Corporate Economy: A Survey and Critique. In *The Corporate Economy* (ed. by R. Marris and A. Wood), pp. 37–67. London, Macmillan

YOUNG, A. (1925). Review of Bowley's Mathematical Groundwork. *Journal of the American Statistical Association* **20**, 134

Chapter Six

Economic Statistics and Econometrics

A.C. Darnell

6.1 Introduction

Econometrics as a specialized discipline is a recent development but, representing as it does the combination of the mathematical formulation of economics and those developments of mathematical statistics relevant to economic data, its roots lie in the historical development of these two specialisms[1]. This chapter begins by examining the need for quantitative information, the rise of 'Political Arithmetic', and subsequent nineteenth-century developments. At a later point the development of inferential procedures and the formal methods of statistics is examined, and this leads to the union of the two strands of development in econometrics proper.

6.1.1 THE NEED FOR QUANTITATIVE INFORMATION

As soon as people became grouped into large units it became necessary to answer quantitative questions by 'enumerations, classifications and statistical summarisations' (Lundberg, 1971, p. 111). The motivation for such questions was invariably problems of war or public finance. For example, a census was taken in Egypt around 3000 BC as a preliminary step to the building of the pyramids, and the ancient Greeks and Romans carried out many investigations to determine their military strength. The enumerations of Charlemagne in 807, of William the Conqueror in 1066, of Edward III in 1377 and of Frederic II of Prussia in 1741 are well documented. In such cases the purpose of the exercise concerned taxation, land distribution or military might.

They did not, however, form a part of a continuous study of society and they were not founded upon any methodological or scientific considerations. Indeed, it might be argued by a modern statistician that, because such studies did not have a sound basis in statistical method, and paid little or no attention to scientific principles, they are not deserving of the adjective 'statistical'[2].

6.1.2 STATISTICS: DATA AND METHODS

The earliest studies which may be unambiguously labelled as statistical were those of the seventeenth century conducted by the founders of 'Political Arithmetic', John Graunt and William Petty. Both were concerned with the investigation of questions using numerical methods; and the work of both men involved the interpretation for one purpose of data which had been collected with other purposes in mind. Indeed, a characteristic of modern social analyses is that investigators use data which have been collected for other purposes. Graunt analysed birth and death figures which had been acquired through the process of religious registrations, and, similarly, applied econometricians today analyse data which, because they were not collected primarily for their analysis, are imperfect. That social scientists' empirical investigations are limited in this way gives rise to the development of two sorts of model, theoretical and empirical. The crucial difference between them is that in the latter, modifications in order to bring together theoretical concepts and their observable counterparts have been attempted. Thus social scientists have, by necessity, developed particular methods of empirical analysis in two important ways: on the one hand, theoretical concepts are constructed so as to have empirical analogues; on the other, statistical theory is extended so as to allow probabilistic interpretation of the non-experimental data of the social sciences.

The beginnings of these important developments are to be found in the work of the Political Arithmeticians.

In 1662 Graunt's *Natural and Political Observations on the London Bills of Mortality* was published. This was the first treatise on vital statistics and attempted to apply theoretical considerations to a statistical problem. Its true authorship has been the subject of some debate, and it is unclear precisely what role Graunt's close friend Sir William Petty (1623–1687) played in its writing. What is certainly clear is that between them, Petty and Graunt founded the British School of Political Arithmetic.

The ideas of the political arithmeticians were taken up by the mathematicians Halley and de Moivre and, through Bernoulli, Euler and others, the work spread to other Continental mathematicians. The work of Poisson and Laplace is especially important, for it introduced the calculus of probability into the subject[3].

6.1.3 MATHEMATICS, STATISTICS AND ECONOMETRICS

Economic theory frequently provides a 'qualitative calculus' which predicts the *direction* in which an endogenous variable will respond to a change in an exogenous variable. In order to provide a 'quantitative calculus' in which the magnitude of the change is predicted it is first necessary to write the hypothesized economic relationship in mathematical form, with known variables and unknown fixed parameters. Given suitable observations on the variables, the application of statistical methods will result in estimates of the parameters and will provide a test of the hypothesis. This combination of deductive economics (using the symbolism of mathematics) with the methods of statistics is the basis for modern econometrics. Econometric theory is concerned with the tools of inference as required by analysts of non-experimental data (notably economic data), and applied econometrics uses these tools on economic data both to test economic theory and to provide a quantitative calculus.

Econometrics is employed in particular in conjunction with the hypothetico–deductive method, which deduces predictions from a set of axioms, tests the predictions against appropriate data and modifies the model accordingly. An alternative approach involves the formation of hypotheses by inferential analysis of a set of data testing them against another set of data. This approach, which may be labelled inductivist, has been attacked as 'measurement without theory' (Koopmans, 1947). In criticizing *Measuring Business Cycles* by Burns and Mitchell, Koopmans (1947) argued that 'utilization of the concepts and hypotheses of economic theory as a part of the process of observation and measurement promises to be a shorter road...to the understanding [of economic phenomena]' (p. 162). Vining (1949a,b) defended the work of Burns and Mitchell as representing an exercise in taxonomy and hypothesis-formation, but Koopmans's (1949a) view was that

> If hypothesis-seeking means just looking for hypotheses which find some support in the data (without specifying what alternative hypotheses find less support) it will be hard to prove that tools as formal and elaborate as those employed by Burns and Mitchell are better than, as good as, or not greatly inferior to other possible measures or test criteria (p. 91).

Today economists tend, like Koopmans, to look to the method of physics, with its emphasis on hypothesis formation, development and testing. But earlier generations, perhaps partly under the influence of what was believed to be a 'Baconian' methodology, deriving from the work of Sir Francis Bacon, tended to attempt induction of generalized hypotheses from a mass of data. Indeed the aims and methods of Political Arithmetic seem to show Bacon's influence.

6.2 Data collection and description

6.2.1 THE FOUNDATIONS OF POLITICAL ARITHMETIC

Graunt and Petty pioneered the use of numerical methods in the social sciences. Graunt's *Observations* were based upon data, covering more than sixty years, on the numbers of christenings and deaths in London. The deaths were categorized according to sixty causes, and, despite a lack of much information, Graunt succeeded in constructing a life table indicating what proportion of a given cohort may be expected to live to specified ages[4]. Halley recognized the possibilities for the management of life assurances which were opened by the construction of such a table, but Graunt himself did not explore this aspect to any extent in his *Observations*. He did consider the question of different rates of mortality to be found in rural and urban environments, and was the first investigator to test whether the rates differed to any clear extent[5]. His book represents a landmark in the study of society, being the first published investigation to use a thoroughly numerical method.

However, it was Petty who coined the expression 'Political Arithmetic' and who may be regarded as the 'father' of social statistics. He quite possibly inspired the writing of Graunt's *Observations*; he had in the 1650s given serious thought to social statistics and he wrote many pamphlets and essays on the subject (Hull, 1899). Moreover it was Petty who, in the seventeenth century, proposed that a Central Statistical Office be set up. He suggested that its scope should encompass the registration of births, deaths and marriages; age, sex and occupational distributions of the population; and figures relating to government revenues, education and trade. He even drew up a census form which was broader than that used in the first official censuses of 1801 and 1811.

Petty summarized his approach as follows:

> I have taken the course (as a specimen of the *Political Arithmetick* I have long aimed at) to express myself in terms of number, weight or measure; to use only arguments of sense; and to consider only such causes as have visible foundations in nature, leaving those that depend on the mutable minds, opinions, appetites and passions of particular men to the consideration of others (reprinted in Hull, 1899, Vol. I, p. 244).

It is clear, then, that Petty's vision of 'Political Arithmetic' was the objective study of society by the numerical method, and that its success would depend upon the improvement of the available data. He began writing his *Political Arithmetic* in 1671 and did so primarily to disprove the suggestion that England was suffering a decline of trade and to demonstrate that, in fact, the country was richer than ever before[6]. His method, like that of Graunt, was Baconian in spirit.

6.2.2 THE EIGHTEENTH CENTURY

Although political arithmetic had had a vigorous beginning in the seventeenth century, interest in it declined in the first half of the eighteenth[7], and the study of social statistics became almost synonomous with the study of vital and demographic data. Of those who imitated Petty's work, Davenant (1657–1714) and King (1648 –1712) are amongst the most important. Of those who followed Graunt in constructing life tables, Halley (1656–1742), an English astronomer, and Neumann (1648–1715) of Breslau stand out[8]. De Moivre (1667–1754) improved the concept of a life table by proposing a simple formula for death rates, but he is best remembered for some highly significant contributions to the calculus of probabilities, which will be discussed below.

6.2.3 THE NINETEENTH-CENTURY STATISTICAL MOVEMENT

The statistical economic investigations of the nineteenth century were mainly studies in which economic concepts were given quantitative measure. Because the techniques of inference which then existed had been developed by mathematicians and were not generally known to the economic statisticians, statistical work concentrated on reporting figures and also, especially in the work of J.R. McCulloch, in providing economic commentary upon the raw data (O'Brien, 1970). Estimates obtained from samples were treated, for practical purposes, as accurately reflecting their population counterparts, and techniques of inference were not employed. Indeed, it was not until the second half of the nineteenth century that practising statisticians began to be concerned with such questions of accuracy. Nevertheless the nineteenth century was a period marked by considerable development in the treatment of economic statistics, particularly in Britain. In 1833 the Board of Trade expanded to include a Statistical Department, with G.R. Porter at its head. The Board had previously been a repository for some of the statistics acquired through returns made to Parliament, but under Porter's guidance it was hoped that it would be possible to gather statistics relating to proposed reforms. The high hopes were not realized, but the Department published annual tables which reproduced, in an orderly fashion, official data from other departments. Also important to the statistical movement was the establishment, in 1837, of civil registration of vital statistics in England and Wales (later extended to Ireland and Scotland). Farr (1807–1883), renowned for his work on medical statistics, was an influential member of the Registrar-General's staff. The published reports bear testimony to his remarkable ability[9].

The nineteenth century is thus important for the development of systematic collection of data. But because statistics occasionally used probability, statisticians came into contact with the work of those mathematicians who were developing the theory of errors. In the work of the Belgian Quetelet, applications of social statistics, economic statistics, and probability are to be found.

Quetelet's contributions were wide-ranging. He urged the improvement of census-taking and promoted international uniformity and comparability of data; he was especially interested in the collection and analysis of statistics of crime; he also developed Graunt's work on demographic statistics and, following Halley, produced life tables for Belgium. At a theoretical level he advanced the use of the normal curve of error and introduced the concept of 'average man' whom he conceived as

a fictious being for whom all things proceed conformably to the average results obtained for society. If we wish to establish the basis of a social mechanics, it is he whom we should consider, without stopping to examine particular or anomalous cases (quoted by Lundberg, 1971, p. 122).

In Britain, Quetelet influenced the establishment of the Statistical Society, the roots of which are to be found in the 1833 meeting of the British Association for the Advancement of Science held at Cambridge. The Association itself dates from 1831, and was modelled upon European examples existing to bring scientists in provincial cities together annually to discuss their work. After a shaky start, due to the reluctance of British scientists to join a provincial body[10], a third meeting was held at Cambridge, where the sciences were dominated by men like William Whewel. It was Whewel who invited Quetelet to attend the meeting.

On his arrival at Cambridge Quetelet was met by Richard Jones, Professor of Political Economy at King's College, London. He had arranged a small meeting, separate from the official meetings, to give those interested in statistics the opportunity of hearing the great European statistician present his most recent work on suicide and crime. Charles Babbage, the mathematician, was invited to the meeting, and he decided to approach those members who had an interest in statistical research with a view to forming a statistical section of the Association. From this section developed the Statistical Society of London[11].

6.2.4 THE STATISTICAL SOCIETY OF LONDON

The prospectus of the Society stated that the objectives were to procure, arrange and publish, 'facts calculated to illustrate the condition and prospects of society' and emphasized that 'the first and most important rule of its conduct [is] to exclude all opinions'. Thus to the founders of the Society, 'statistics' meant the materials of a science rather than a science in its own right. The Society would appear to have intended to confine members to collecting data and presenting them. Indeed, the emblem of the Society, a sheaf of wheat signifying that the members were to gather data but not thresh conclusions, served to reinforce the view. However, although the emblem still remains, the narrow view of statistical researches was repudiated by many of the leading nineteenth-century members. Thus Sir Rawson Rawson (1885) told the Jubilee meeting of the Society:

> I am not prepared to make statistics the handmaiden of social science, to degrade the parent into the position of a hewer of wood and drawer of water in the service of its own offspring (p. 9).

Thus, fifty years after the Society was formed, its original prospectus had been implicitly amended and it had enlarged its scope.

The Statistical Section of the British Association became Section F, The Economic and Statistical Section, in 1856. But in 1877 Francis Galton proposed its abolition on the grounds that the papers presented had too small a scientific content. Galton, however, had overstated his case, and the opposition, led by William Farr and the Council of the Statistical Society, was successful. The following year the President of Section F, Ingram, took the opportunity to defend the Section's activities and to propose that the method of economic study should be historical (Ingram, 1878). The historical method holds that history evolves according to discernible patterns, and that the economist should assemble the raw data and discover those patterns.

However, nineteenth-century economists did not collect data for their own sake. The quantitative analysis of economic questions was a legitimate branch of economic enquiry, as witnessed by the monumental work of Tooke and Newmarch (1838–1857). They were followed by Jevons, whose work shows a major advance in scientific analysis of data (Jevons, 1884).

Jevons (1871) attached considerable importance to quantitative analysis and believed that 'the want of [a perfect system of statistics] is the only insuperable obstacle in the way of making Political Economy an exact science' (p. 14). Marshall, too, attached importance to the development of quantitative analysis (Marshall, 1897); and his pupil A.L. Bowley applied himself to the problem of providing a quantitative analogue to Marshall's qualitative economic system. Bowley's work on wages led him to consider the problem of measuring the national income. His highly successful collaboration with Stamp culminated in their pioneering publication *The National Income* (1927).

The use of statistics by nineteenth-century economists, as described by J.N. Keynes (1890), was to determine the areas for which particular theoretical conclusions were valid, i.e. the areas in which their truth was 'verified':

> Comparison with observed facts provides a test for conclusions deductively obtained, and enables the limits of their application to be determined (p. 17).

Keynes emphasized this aspect of economics. He believed that 'political economy, whether having recourse to the deductive method or not, must both begin with observation and end with observation' (p. 227). Again

> The functions of statistics in economic enquiry are, first, to suggest empirical laws, which may or may not be capable of subsequent deductive explanation; and, secondly, to supplement deductive reasoning by checking its results (pp. 343–344).

Thus in the view of Keynes (and others) observation and statistical work also had a role to play in the formation of hypotheses which could serve as the basis for deductive reasoning.

In this discussion Keynes, in conformity with the custom of his time, treats 'statistics' as synonomous with data. Appreciation of the possibility of the use of statistical *method* to test economic theories was limited. Such a development was based upon the integration of the calculus of probabilities into statistics and it is to this subject that attention is now turned.

6.3 Statistics and probability

6.3.1 THE CALCULUS OF PROBABILITIES

The calculus of probabilities has its origin in the study of games of chance[12]. In the sixteenth century the gambler Cardan wrote on the subject, and during the next century Galileo took up similar problems. Two questions in particular were addressed. First, given the probabilities of all possible events, what is the likely result in a particular trial? Second, if the probabilities were unknown, how might information from actual trials be used to infer the true probabilities? It must be stressed that although these questions occupied the attention of some of the greatest mathematicians, the 'statisticians' (of whom there were very few) were little troubled by them. For example, while mathematicians might ask what could be inferred of the true death rate from a single observation, the vital statisticians treated the sample rate as if it were the true figure. However, practising statisticians could do little else until an appropriate method had been developed. The political arithmeticians were pragmatists; the mathematicians, while occasionally prompted by practical questions of gambling, were, in the main, abstract thinkers.

The calculus of probabilities was founded in Italy, but French mathematicians, notably Pascal (1623–1662) and Fermat (1601 –1665), worked on gaming problems. Huygens also took up such problems, but the most important of the seventeenth-century contributions came from Jacob (also known as James) Bernouilli (1654–1705). Bernouilli's unfinished work *Ars Conjectandi* was published in 1713, the same year that de Moivre's *Doctrine of Chances* appeared. It contains a reprint of Huygen's treatise *De Ratiociniis in Ludo Aleae*, presents a theory of permutations and combinations, and develops further theories concerning games of chance. The final unfinished section, in which it was Bernouilli's intention to apply this body of theory to questions of morals and economics, described the experiment now known as Bernouilli Trials and outlined a theory of inference within a Binomial distribution. Had his work been continued by his immediate followers, the ability of investigators to determine the appropriate sample size to achieve a desired degree of accuracy in a proportion would have been available in the seventeenth century, rather than remaining undiscovered, as it did, until the early twentieth century.

The work on the Binomial distribution was developed by de Moivre in his *Doctrine of Chances*. He examined the terms of the Binomial expansion, assisted by Stirling's formula for evaluating factorials. The most important consequence of this was that de Moivre (1667–1754) examined the limit of the binomial expansion and came to the formula now recognized as that of the normal distribution. This is some forty years prior to Laplace, who has been credited with the discovery of the normal form[13].

Although the work of Bernouilli and de Moivre did not inspire their contemporaries to develop the analysis of the accuracy of an observed proportion, the next major developments in this field, made by mathematicians such as Laplace (1749–1827), Legendre (1752–1833) and Gauss (1777–1855) have their direct precursors in the work of these two men.

6.3.2 THE THEORY OF ERRORS

From very early times people have sought appropriate techniques for choosing one single value to summarize many items of information. For example, in 1632 Galileo (1564–1642) examined the question of determining the true distance of a star from the earth, given seventy-eight different measurements. Astronomers, when faced with this problem, usually took the arithmetic mean as the best estimate, but it was not uncommon to find one particular observation, chosen with due care, used as the best estimate. In 1756 Simpson (1710–1761) examined this practice theoretically, demonstrating that the probability of being in error by a specified amount was lower in the case of the average than in the case of a particular observation. In 1778 Daniel Bernouilli (1700–1782) assumed a particular form of distribution and advocated the adoption of that estimate whose value ensured that the probability of observing the given data was a maximum. Thus the principle of maximum likelihood estimation can be traced to the eighteenth century[14].

Laplace (1786) considered the problem of fitting a straight line to three or more non-collinear points. He suggested two criteria of fit: minimization of the maximum residual, or minimization of the sum of absolute residuals, constraining both procedures to have a zero mean residual. The first known published exposition of the method of least squares is due to Legendre (1805), although Gauss (1806) claimed priority in its use. In a later work Gauss (1809) demonstrated that, given the normal law of error, the method of least squares yields results identical to those yielded by the principle of maximum likelihood. This justification for the method of least squares has proved to be most persuasive, although the equivalence of least squares and maximum likelihood rests upon the underlying distribution being normal.

6.3.3 THE BAYESIAN APPROACH

A pragmatic approach, using the simple technique of ordinary least squares or maximum likelihood, is frequently adopted. A less pragmatic approach stems from the work of Bayes (1702–1761), whose name is associated both with a branch of statistical enquiry and with a particular theorem. The theorem concerns the determination of the probability of a specified event and is not questioned; the issue which has caused a great deal of controversy is whether it is a suitable foundation upon which to build inferential statistics. Opinion has fluctuated markedly, and at the moment Bayesian techniques are enjoying a period of resurgence[15].

Suppose an investigator wishes to know the true value of a parameter. It is presumed that the population is described by a probability distribution characterized by the parameter of interest. Thus, given the value of the parameter, the form of the probability density function enables the investigator to determine the density associated with any hypothetical data set. However, it is the converse of this which is required, i.e. the value of the parameter is required and the data set is known. There are ways of using the sample information to obtain inferences about the unknown parameter, one of which is based on Bayes's Theorem. Sampling theory is an alternative which will be examined below. The use of Bayes's Theorem for making inferences has a continuous history of well over a hundred years; non-Bayesian sampling approaches are much younger. The Bayesian approach consists of introducing a *prior* distribution which expresses the investigator's prior beliefs about the true parameter, θ. Given the information contained in the sample data, the prior distribution is modified according to the rules laid down by Bayes's Theorem, which results in a distribution known as the *posterior* distribution. It is from this distribution that inferences are made.

Given the data, x, the conditional distribution of x given θ, as a function of θ, is usually called the likelihood function. The actual distribution of θ is never known, but a particular form is presumed; this distribution is the prior. The conditional distribution $p(\theta|x)$ is the posterior distribution. Bayes's Theorem relates these distributions and is nothing more than a statement of conditional probabilities.

The debate concerns the appropriateness of basing inferences upon this statement of probability. The two areas of debate are, first, the nature and meaning of probability, and, second, the choice and necessity of the prior. In Bayes's Theorem the parameters are considered as random variables. This follows from their being assigned a probability distribution. However, it is not necessary to interpret probability in the classical sense of limiting frequencies; an alternative is to regard probability as indicating a degree of belief. Thus to say that an investigator holds a prior probability of one half that some event will occur means that the investigator has as much faith in the specified event occurring as he does in a 'fair' coin revealing a head on being tossed.

Throughout the nineteenth century, Bayes's Theorem formed the basis of inferential statistics. It was not until a fairly tumultuous period in the 1930s that the dominance of Bayesian statistics was severely called into question. However, nineteenth-century statistical studies were of a quite different flavour from those of today, and the use of *any* inferential procedure was, in the vast majority of studies, not seen to be required. This was because the investigators were, in the main, not asking questions about the accuracy of the estimates, and any inference from a sample estimate to its population counterpart was direct.

6.4 Inference and hypothesis testing

It has been said that at the beginning of the twentieth century 'statistics in the sense of methods of estimation and inference were comparatively new and not well understood by most economists' (Stone, 1980, p. 724). There is much truth in this, although, as noted above, mathematicians had succeeded in developing a sophisticated body of statistical methods applicable to experimental data. What economics required was a body of statistical techniques appropriate to the analysis of economic (that is, non-experimental) data, and it is to the development of these that this section is devoted.

6.4.1 USE OF THE THEORY OF ERRORS IN ECONOMICS

The theory of errors, described briefly above, was well developed by the latter half of the nineteenth century. However, the application of such techniques, routine in astronomy and geodesy, was virtually non-existent in economics. In 1883 Edgeworth published the first of a sequence of papers devoted to the role of statistical methods in the social sciences[16]. As S.M. Stigler (1978) has indicated:

> Edgeworth's plan...was to do at last what had been talked about and assumed possible for over a century, but had never been accomplished: adapt the statistical methods of the theory of errors to the quantification of uncertainty in the social, particularly economic, sciences (p. 295).

Edgeworth's methodology was Bayesian, but in applying inverse probability (a label used to describe a part of the Bayesian technique) he was not entirely consistent: when testing a hypothesis concerned with the difference between two means he reverted to the more 'classical' approach of analysing sampling distributions rather than posterior distributions. Nevertheless, for social scientists, these papers by Edgeworth provided the reference source of such material, at least until the appearance of Bowley's *Elements of Statistics* in 1901.

It is interesting to note that the period in which Edgeworth wrote was remarkable for the number of major advances made in pure statistical theory; yet, with the exception of his contributions, major developments were not presented to the Royal Statistical Society. The inventive theoretical work was produced by biometricians (although the label was not invented until later).

6.4.2 RESEARCH IN BIOMETRICS

The men primarily responsible for this work were Francis Galton (1822–1911), Walter Weldon (1860–1906) and Karl Pearson (1857–1936). Galton's achievements were immense in many fields, and he is particularly noteworthy for having recognized the importance of the concepts of correlation and regression in relation to heredity[17]. The theoretical developments made by Galton are more important than the uses to which he put them, however, for his ideas have found almost universal applicability.

The normal curve of error and the binomial distribution, from which it had been originally derived, were the two leading concepts of statistical thinking in the 1890s. Galton, and the school of biometricians, extended the range of concepts available to include regression and correlation. However, the approach to correlation and regression was not through the theory of errors[18]. Rather, Galton had collected data on parental and offspring characteristics, arranging them in a two-way table. He observed that the measurements, taken individually, were approximately normal within each population. But he also noted that the array means fell on a straight line, and he further noted that the variation within the arrays was nearly constant. From this observation he developed regression. The same arrangement of data allowed him to draw contour lines of equal probability density, which he found were nearly elliptical, and was led in 1886 to the equation of the bivariate normal surface[19]. Two years later he conceived the correlation coefficient, a development which had a marked influence upon Edgeworth but an even more immediate influence upon Weldon, who recognized its potential for examining the Darwinian theories of natural selection. In 1891 Weldon and Pearson began a fruitful partnership which was cut short by the former's death at the early age of forty-six. Pearson's work, notably on his system of frequency curves and the use of multiple correlation and regression, was of great importance. Furthermore, the biometricians had research assistants and a school of followers which ensured the dissemination of their results, something which Edgeworth's work—highly sophisticated and written in very difficult language—never enjoyed.

However, there was productive correspondence between Edgeworth on the one hand and Pearson and Weldon on the other. For example, during the 1890s the method of statistics lacked a measure of goodness-of-fit, though it was recognized that such a test was necessary. Edgeworth had attacked the problem in a paper of 1887, in which he proposed a test for normality. His test, though equivalent to a Chi-squared test, was of only limited power. But thirteen years later his correspondence with Pearson contributed to the publication of Pearson's χ^2 test.

6.4.3 SAMPLING THEORY

The next major innovation in the theory of statistics was made by William Gosset, remembered by his pseudonym, 'Student' and by the distribution which bears that name[20]. Gosset's attention was focused upon a small-sample problem, an area of statistical theory which had been virtually ignored to that date by the biometricians, because they were able to obtain large samples by experiment[21]. Using small samples he sought to assess the quality of raw materials and its relationship to the quality of the final product. Of the inadequacy of existing techniques for such enquiries Gosset (1908a) wrote:

> it is sometimes necessary to judge of the certainty of the results from a very small sample, which itself affords the only indication of variability. Some chemical, many biological, and most agricultural and large scale experiments belong to this class, which has hitherto been almost outside the range of statistical enquiry (p. 1).

Gosset spent a year with Pearson and his colleagues at the Biometric Laboratory, and out of this study came three crucial papers. In Gosset (1907) there is a rediscovery of Poisson's limit to the binomial; in Gosset (1908a) there is the derivation of the *t*-distribution; and in (1908b) there is an inspired guess at the distribution of the sample correlation coefficient in normal populations when the true population value is zero. Of the second paper, Hotelling (1930) concluded that it opened 'the way for escape from the haze of hypothetical standard errors and inverse probability which have obfuscated the theory of statistics' (p. 189).

6.4.4 SAMPLING TECHNIQUE

The social scientist is unable to replicate the conditions which give rise to the data and thus requires a method of drawing a sample and then forming inferences from that sample. The basic tool of inference which was originally available was Bayes's Theorem, and this was generally applied to large samples so that the form of the posterior was dominated by the likelihood of the data, thus minimizing the role of the prior. At the turn of the nineteenth century survey design was an emerging subject, and the scientific community, especially the International Statistical Institute (ISI), debated the merits of the representative method of sampling. Kiaer was one of the main proponents of sampling, and in 1901 he demonstrated that stratified sampling was capable of generating good estimates of finite population parameters (see Kiaer, 1903). The ISI recommended, in 1903, that stratified sampling be regarded as an acceptable scientific method of data collection. Bowley contributed significantly to this work in 1906 when, in his Presidential Address to Section F of the British Association, he integrated the existing theory of survey sampling from finite populations with inferential statistics based on Edgeworth's version of the Central Limit Theorem. Bowley demonstrated that the accuracy of estimates drawn from random samples could be assessed and also examined stratified sampling[22].

Bowley used the sampling technique with great success. His *Livelihood and Poverty* (1905) discussed the theoretical issues of representativeness, accuracy, measurement error and sampling error and also provides an exemplary application of the method. Kruskal and Mosteller (1980) have concluded that the most influential developments in the understanding of the representative method of sampling in the period 1903–1925 stemmed from Bowley's work. 1925 is chosen as the end of the period considered by Kruskal and Mosteller, for it was in that year that the ISI met in Rome to discuss the issues concerned with representative sampling. Jensen and Bowley were the major contributors, and their report was given a sound mathematical foundation by a separate report written by Bowley (1926)[23]. This report and discussion spurred Jerzy Neyman (1934) to examine the basis of sampling from finite populations.

6.4.5 THE CONFIDENCE INTERVAL

Neyman (1934) discussed the logic of inference based upon his newly developed concept of the confidence interval. His statement of the confidence interval was the first exposition in English, and it is interesting to note the reception given to the paper. His approach was non-Bayesian; he treated population parameters as fixed numbers; and his statement of the confidence interval, while set in terms of probability, was a statement of probability as frequency rather than as a Bayesian measure of belief. Bowley, in proposing the vote of thanks to Neyman, said that he was 'not at all sure that the "confidence" is not a "confidence trick"' and asked: 'Does it really lead us towards what we need—the chance that in the universe we are sampling the proportion is within these certain limits?' (1934, p. 609). Bowley was trying to associate probability with the true proportion, whereas in Neyman's confidence interval the probability is associated with the *limits of the interval* which, with specified probability, encompassed the true parameter. Neyman (1934) was fully aware of this crucial difference in approach and pointed out that Bowley's remarks contained

> the statement of the problem of estimation in the form of Bayes. Simple algebra shows that the solution of this problem *must* depend upon the probability law *a priori*...The present progress is concerned with...solving some other mathematical problem...which (i) has a solution independent of...the probability law *a priori*, and (ii) may form a basis for the practical work of a statistician concerned with problems of estimation. Both [approaches] are dealing with probabilities, but these probabilities apply to different events (pp. 623–624).

A similar non-Bayesian stance was taken by R.A. Fisher. Although he publicly associated himself with some of Neyman's work, there is no doubt that even between these two writers there was a wide gulf[24].

Fisher's work on 'fiducial probability', once seen as having a close relationship to the Neyman frequency interpretation of confidence intervals, was, in fact, quite distinct from Neyman's. The possible differences between the two theories caused much debate in the 1930s, a debate which recalls the earlier debate over the Bayesian and non-Bayesian approaches. The two debates influenced statistical thinking for the next half-century. Even today the issues, especially those concerning the Bayesian approach, are far from settled[25].

In both debates, Fisher played a leading role. His 1912 paper contains his original presentation of the method of maximum likelihood and his 1921 paper the original definition of likelihood *per se*. His 1922 paper has the exposition of maximum likelihood as a method of point estimation. In this paper he repudiated Bayes's postulate, but the exposition is a little unclear, for he introduced the concept of the 'fiducial probability density function' (pdf). This was a source of immediate confusion. Fisher treated the fiducial pdf as if it were a proper pdf, an approach inconsistent with non-Bayesian beliefs. The concept was not generally adopted by the statisticians of the day, but Fisher's other contribution—maximum likelihood—was readily adopted, and the demise of the use of Bayes's Theorem as a basis for inference had begun in earnest.

It is important to realize that this debate was conducted within the confines of the statistical community. Economists (with a few exceptions, especially Bowley) did not enter the debate. In fact, the concerns of quantitative economists during the 1920s were at a much more mechanical level, and the debates among statisticians would, in the main, have been beyond them. By the time the econometric movement began to gain momentum during the early 1930s, the predominant flavour of mathematical statistics was non-Bayesian, and the dearth of Bayesian techniques in early econometrics is partly attributable to this. It is also true that in order to answer the questions posed by econometricians it was, and still is, much easier to manipulate the algebra of a non-Bayesian approach. Indeed, the reliance upon least-squares techniques, which persists to this day, may have more to do with mathematical and numerical tractability than with any philosophical considerations about the nature of probability or of the interpretation of Bayes's Theorem.

Another reason for the present dearth of Bayesian techniques in econometrics stems from joint work by Neyman and Egon Pearson published in the early 1930s. The 'Neyman–Pearson revolution' was the culmination of their research begun in 1926[27]. In 1933 they produced a now-celebrated theorem concerning a test of one simple hypothesis against another. Their procedure relied upon the concept of likelihood rather than Bayes's Theorem. This sort of procedure was precisely what was required for many of the questions then being attacked by econometricians.

Many of the leading econometricians were, in any case, trained in non-Bayesian institutions. The two main centres for the teaching of statistics at this time were the Biometric Laboratory in London, where Pearson and Neyman worked, and the Rothamstead Agricultural station headed by Fisher. Both units attracted graduates from England and the United States—Henry Schultz, Henry Moore and Harold Hotelling were students in London, while Hotelling also spent six months with Fisher.

6.5 Early econometric studies

The Econometric Society was formed in 1930, and its journal, *Econometrica*, was first published in 1933[28]. From then on, 'econometrics' began to be known as a separate discipline within economics. However, there had been econometric studies prior to this, especially demand studies[29]. The earliest empirical demand schedule was published in 1699 by Davenant, using data attributed to King. Notable work on demand curves and budget studies was carried out in the nineteenth century by Ernst Engel. However, it was the development of statistical technique during the 1880s and 1890s which gave the immediate stimulus to the modern era of demand studies.

6.5.1 THE IDENTIFICATION PROBLEM

The applied demand work carried out in the early twentieth century is characterized by the lack of a stochastically specified model and consequently by the use of a variety of fitting techniques. The work also presumed that the observed relationship between price and quantity was the demand curve. This line of inquiry well illustrates the need for the interaction of theoretical analysis and data analysis. Lenoir (1913) explained that, if the supply curve shifts over time and the demand curve is relatively static, the observed price/quantity pairs will lie approximately on the demand curve. If it is the supply curve which is relatively static and the demand curve which shifts through time, then the data will identify the supply curve. This exposition of the identification problem was, unfortunately, not widely noticed.

However, significant early econometric work which did attract attention was carried out by Moore (1869–1958). In 1908 he described some of the statistical techniques available to economists and emphasized the existence of empirical regularity which required *ex post* theoretical rationalization. Three years later, in his *Laws of Wages*, his full research programme appeared. He argued that the pure theory of economics had reached a sufficiently sophisticated form to be amenable to empirical analysis: the use of symbolic mathematics to describe economic relationships was sufficiently developed; and, as a by-product of the State's increasing activities in the economic world, the data required for the 'concrete treatment of economic questions' were available. Two other developments which were central to his programme had also taken place—the 'invention of a calculus of mass phenomena' (that is, statistical theory) and the 'perfection of mechanical devices for performing mathematical computations'. Together these four strands of development supported the research programme and involved three distinct sorts of study: the testing of theories, the estimation of economic parameters and the discovery of empirical laws[30].

Moore's *Laws of Wages* attempted the testing of theories and the discovery of 'laws' and was generally well received. Edgeworth (1912) wrote in a favourable review that it was 'the first time...that the higher statistics, which are founded on the calculus of Probabilities, have been used on a large scale as a buttress of economic theory' (p. 67). The work was, however, marred by a spurious level of numerical accuracy combined with grossly oversimplified theoretical statements[31].

Moore's first work on demand curves appeared in his *Economic Cycles* of 1914, a discussion which is famous for his 'discovery' of a positively sloping demand curve for pig-iron (which Moore used as a 'representative producers' good'). Lehfeldt (1915), who had himself published material on demand elasticities in 1914, was highly critical of this which was, in his view,

---

not a demand curve at all, but much more nearly a supply curve. It is arrived at by the intersection of irregularly fluctuating demands on supply conditions, that, on the whole, may be regarded as steady (p. 411).

Lehfeldt contrasted this situation with the demand curves Moore had constructed for agricultural products which were 'based on considering the intersection of irregular supply (due to fluctuations of weather) with a steady demand' (p. 411). Nevertheless Moore's investigation was extremely influential, and served to popularize statistical demand analysis, although, as G.J. Stigler (1954) emphasizes, the influence was 'not attributable to priority or to excellence, for in both respects Moore must bow to Lenoir' (p. 112).

Moore's demand function for iron exemplifies the identification problem which arises in economic models with simultaneous equations. In the analysis of price and quantity data the variables are subject to more than one behavioural equation. Even presuming that the data represent equilibrium values, they are the outcome of the interaction of demand and supply.

In addition to the identification problem, the joint determination raises a problem of estimation. The regression model was designed to analyse simple relationships in which one variable, labelled the dependent variable (the regressand), is determined by a set of independent variables (regressors). In a simple market model neither price nor quantity can be viewed as an independent variable and so the technique of simple regression is inapplicable.

Although the identification problem was discussed in the context of demand analysis from 1914, perhaps the most significant early contributions were made by Working (1927) and Frisch (1933). This laid the foundation for the more systematic studies of identification and estimation in simultaneous systems which were made after the Second World War by members of the Cowles Commission. The classic papers from this later period are by Haavelmo (1943) and Koopmans (1949b).

At the beginning of this century econometricians had adopted tools of data analysis developed by natural scientists. That they chose demand analysis as the area to study first reflects the important position of the demand curve in economic theory; but of the possible areas of empirical economics few could have presented so many pitfalls, and few could have been so ill-suited to a simple application of the regression technique.

The regression model postulates a cause and effect relationship between the regressor and the regressand. However, in many economic situations it is more reasonable to think of a two-way causality with variables jointly determined[32]. This is the situation in a simple market model, and it is one for which regression was not designed. The choice of dependent variable was seen by the early empirical economists as either a matter of *a priori* theory regarding the direction of causality, or as an *a priori* decision based on which of the two variables suffered the greater measurement errors. This issue relates to the use of regression in the absence of an explicit stochastic specification.

6.5.2 ERROR SPECIFICATION

Least-squares theory developed initially as an answer to a measurement error problem; and it was an obvious interpretation of the regression model to view the 'disturbance term' (which was, up to 1940, only implicit) as representing the measurement errors in observations of the dependent variable and to view the independent variable as measured without error. This, however, is only one of many possible interpretations of the disturbance term.

Alternatively the disturbance term may be viewed as representing the combined effects of all the variables other than the regressor which together determine the value of the regressand. Thus the error term relates to 'error in equation' rather than 'errors in variables'[33]. Under both interpretations it is, however, presumed that the average effect of error is zero.

The interpretation placed upon the error term affects the choice of dependent variable and the appropriate criterion of fit. These problems were clearly recognized by Schultz (1925, 1928, 1938) who viewed the 'errors in variables' model as a general model within which the 'errors of equation' model is a special case. His favoured criterion was to minimize a weighted sum of the squares of errors in the two variables, producing as a special case orthogonal regression. This has, however, one serious drawback. Unlike ordinary least squares regression, orthogonal regression is sensitive to the units in which the variables are measured. The problem was recognized in the 1920s and in response to it Frisch proposed 'diagonal mean regression', where the slope estimator is the geometric mean of the two OLS slope estimators.

Thus, without a well-specified stochastic model of the underlying economic behaviour there is ambiguity over the appropriate fitting technique. A stochastic model of the process under consideration is therefore required *prior* to the analysis of data.

Schultz viewed data as generated by a deterministic process plagued by measurement errors—hence his extensive use of orthogonal regression. The use of diagonal mean regression to estimate economic relationships was not uncommon, and it implied no assumption about causality. However, these techniques are uncommon today. The method of Ordinary Least Squares takes precedence partly because, under certain conditions, it produces estimators which have desirable statistical properties (at least within a particular class of stochastically specified models), and partly because it is computationally simple.

6.5.3 ORDINARY LEAST SQUARES

The optimal nature of ordinary least-squares estimators is established by the Gauss–Markov Theorem, which dates from the early nineteenth century[34]. The theorem states that, within the class of linear unbiased estimators, the ordinary least squares estimators have the smallest sampling variances. A major landmark in the history of the linear model was reached in 1934, when an important work synthesizing least squares theory, and providing the first matrix presentation of the linear model, was published by Aitken[35]. In Aitken's general model the observations of the dependent variable were presumed to be 'not uncorrelated' with each other and to have unequal weights (that is, they were presumed autocorrelated and heteroscedastic). Thus Aitken's analysis of a general model with a non-scalar variance–covariance matrix led him to derive the generalized least squares (GLS) estimator. It is interesting to note that his presentation of the general linear model describes the determination of a dependent variable measured with error, and that even in his work the error term itself is not given a symbol.

Aitken was a mathematician, so the fact that he viewed the model as applicable to an errors-in-variables problem is not surprising. However, the reluctance exhibited by economists to make explicit the stochastic model within which they used regression techniques requires comment. Schultz (1938) had stressed the almost cavalier way in which applied econometricians simply adopted regression without properly specifying their stochastic model[36]. Furthermore, the early workers (who were usually not statisticians and had little mathematical training) were perhaps influenced by the immediate attractions of a method developed by natural scientists which seemed to facilitate the quantification of the social sciences. Since the mechanical application of regression yielded 'satisfactory' results, the need for a better specification was not appreciated.

The idea that regression yielded satisfactory results requires explanation. The early empirical investigators, working before the 1930s, tended to use the tools of correlation and regression simply to give empirical content to economic theory, rather than to test the theory. Thus results which accorded with their *a priori* expectations were immediately acceptable. Moore's positively sloped demand curve suited his theory of the cycle and it was therefore adopted by him as a demand curve. His opponents concentrated on the fact that the result was to them implausible and due to inappropriate data used for its estimation. The use of formal statistical criteria for judging the quality of results is a development of relatively recent origin.

6.5.4 THE PROBABILITY APPROACH

In stressing the necessity for a stochastic model as a prerequisite for the application of regression techniques, the contribution of Haavelmo (1944) is very important. His study is one of the most fundamental contributions to econometrics and provides the foundation of much of the modern formulation of empirical economic models. His explicit intention was to develop the stochastic specification of economic models and thus make them amenable to the techniques of statistical inference. His use of probability theory gives his monograph a unique flavour and position in the history of econometric theory. Prior to it a probabilistic approach was not taken, yet it is the foundation of probability theory which enables the econometrician to make statistical inferences. According to Haavelmo (1944), his work represents an attempt to supply a theoretical foundation for the analysis of inter-relations between economic variables. It is based upon modern theory of probability and statistical inference... So far, the common procedure has been, first to construct an economic theory involving exact functional relationships, then to compare this theory with some actual measurements, and finally, 'to judge' whether the correspondence is 'good' or 'bad'...if we want to apply statistical inference to testing the hypotheses of economic theory, it *implies* such a formulation of economic theories that they represent *statistical* hypotheses... The belief that we can make use of statistical inference without this link can only be based upon lack of precision in formulating the problems (pp. iii, iv).

Haavelmo addressed many of the fundamental questions of econometrics, in particular the connection between abstract models and reality, the stability of economic relationships, the role of stochastic models within economics, identification, multicollinearity and prediction. His section on identification is notable for its use of the 'reduced form' and the application of least squares to the reduced form[37]. He pointed out that the most salient feature distinguishing economic data from that of the natural sciences was its non-experimental nature. The non-repeatable characteristic of economic data, the simultaneity of economic relationships and the dynamics of economic processes required a new approach to their analysis; simply adopting the tools used by natural scientists was inadequate. Haavelmo succeeded in describing how, within a properly defined stochastic model, it is possible to adapt statistical tools to enable investigators to make statistical inferences from non-experimental economic data.

6.6 Development of econometric theory

6.6.1 SINGLE-EQUATION MODELS

The adoption of a single-equation model of an economic relationship (in which a stochastic dependent variable is deemed to be determined linearly by a set of independent variables and a well-specified stochastic variable) gives rise to a number of questions. In particular it must be asked whether the assumptions of the distributional nature of the model are met in practice and whether the model is properly specified in linear form. It is also necessary to ask questions about measurement error, aggregation, stability and multicollinearity. Indeed, the econometric theory of a single-equation model may be characterized by the examination of the validity of the underlying assumptions and by the consequent modifications necessary in order to obtain unbiased and efficient estimators.

In OLS it is assumed, among other things, that the disturbance terms are statistically independent of one another (a lack of autocorrelation) and that they all have the same variance (homoscedasticity). The use of time series data and the dynamic nature of many economic relationships suggests, however, that successive disturbances may be interdependent while the use of cross-section data often suggests that the variances may be unequal. When either assumption breaks down, the use of OLS will not yield 'Best Linear Unbiased Estimators' (BLUE)—a result following from the Gauss–Markov Theorem. Although the linear and unbiased qualities of the parameter estimators are retained, their sampling variances are not minimal within that class, and, moreover, the simple mechanical application of the least-squares formulae for variances will actually lead to biased variance estimators.

The Generalized Least Squares (GLS) developed by Aitken (1934) produces Best Linear Unbiased Estimators when the exact nature of the breakdown of the original assumption is known. Even if the nature of the breakdown is unknown, and has to be estimated, the technique offers an improvement over OLS.

Because GLS provides a remedy for violation of the underlying assumptions of OLS, much research energy has been devoted to the testing of the assumptions and to estimation of the precise form of violation where it occurs. One of the earliest tests for autocorrelation used the regression residuals to make inferences about the true disturbances; assuming that if the latter are not autocorrelated the same will be true of their observed counterparts[38]. This, however, was invalid. A related, but valid, test was devised by Durbin and Watson (1950, 1951). It is applicable where the regressors are non-stochastic and the alternative hypothesis to zero autocorrelation is first-order autocorrelation. Unfortunately the calculated statistic has a distribution which depends partially upon the configuration of the regressors. For this reason upper and lower critical values of the statistic are given and an observed value lying between the two is inconclusive. There have been many attempts to refine the test in order to eliminate the inconclusive region[39].

In 1957 Durbin modified the test to enable it to be used in simultaneous systems, and in 1970 he derived an alternative test statistic for cases where the regressors included lagged dependent variables. This test, Durbin's h, is widely used. These later developments apply to first-order autocorrelation; to extend the use of the test to higher orders Durbin (1969) recommends the use of the periodogram[40].

The problem of heteroscedasticity is more commonly associated with cross-section than with time series data. Formal tests of its presence are more recent than those used for autocorrelation. One of the earliest tests, devised by Goldfeld and Quandt (1965), is applicable when heteroscedasticity takes the form of monotonic change in the variance with respect to one of the regressors, but more general tests have been designed, notably by Glejser (1969). However, measures to remedy heteroscedasticity have a very long history; that of weighting observations according to their estimated precision dates from the work of Hauber (1830)[41].

In the presence of either autocorrelation or heteroscedasticity, GLS will provide an improvement over OLS. However, alternatives to GLS have been developed for both problems. With the widespread availability of computers, the use of maximum likelihood techniques is a feasible solution. Their application generally requires the solution of a set of non-linear equations using iterative techniques.

As noted above, violation of the assumptions of the regression model with regard to autocorrelation or heteroscedasticity results in unbiased estimators when OLS is applied, except in the case of autocorrelation with a lagged dependent variable. However, there are violations which result in the much more serious problem of biased estimators. Of particular importance is the problem of stochastic regressors which are not independent of the disturbance term. Within this class is the case of errors-in-variables. Ironically, as noted above, the existence of measurement errors was one of the original *justifications* for the use of classical least squares techniques with economic data. Wald (1940)[42] recognized that OLS would yield inconsistent estimators in the presence of errors in the measurement of independent variables; his solution is a special case of the use of Instrumental Variables Estimation, although the label was not invented until 1945. The technique of Instrumental Variables, which is a very general approach to solving the problem of stochastic regressors, is attributed to Reiersøl (1945) and was developed by Geary (1949) (see Leser (1968)). Although errors in variables imply stochastic regressors, a more general class of problems also characterized by stochastic regressors is that of simultaneous equations systems, which will now be considered[43].

6.6.2 SIMULTANEOUS-EQUATION MODELS

The major advance in the analysis of a simultaneous system of stochastic linear equations was achieved by Haavelmo (1943, 1944, 1947). Use of OLS on one structural equation of a simultaneous system leads to biased and inconsistent estimators. Koopmans *et al.* (1950) developed the technique known as Full Information Maximum Likelihood (FIML), in which the likelihood function of all the endogenous variables, conditional upon the predetermined (exogenous and lagged endogenous) variables, is expressed as a function of the structural coefficients and the variance/covariance matrix of the contemporaneous disturbances. The numerical difficulties in computing FIML estimates are considerable (Chernoff and Divinsky, 1953) and special cases of simultaneous systems have been analysed to avoid the necessity of employing FIML. For example, if the matrix of structural coefficients on the endogenous variables is triangular, the system is 'recursive'. There is a chain of stepwise causality from one variable to another. If the contemporaneous disturbances in such a model are independent of each other then FIML and OLS estimators are identical. This result, due to Bentzel and Wold (1946), was further developed by Wold (1959, 1960). The concept of 'recursive' systems has been extended to the case of 'block-recursive' systems in which different sectors of an economic model are recursive.

As a development of the theoretical works by Girshik and Haavelmo (1947), Anderson and Rubin (1949, 1950) maximized the likelihood of the observations subject only to the exclusion restrictions on the equation in question. This technique, known as Limited Information Maximum Likelihood, does not examine the system as a whole but individual equations. The same estimator was derived later by Koopmans and Hood (1953) using the principle of least variance. Yet another approach to the estimation of a single equation of a simultaneous system was derived independently by Theil (1953a,b) and Basmann (1957). This technique, known as Two Stage Least Squares (TSLS), produces an estimator by the application of ordinary least squares *twice*. It has therefore the advantage of computational simplicity compared with any of the likelihood techniques. However, the techniques of OLS, TSLS and LIML are, in fact, intimately related, as demonstrated by Theil (1958) in his work on 'k-class' estimators.

To estimate a whole system of equations under more general conditions than permitted by FIML, Zellner and Theil (1962) derived the 'three stage least squares estimator' in which the techniques of TSLS and Aitken's GLS are both utilized in order to obtain more efficient estimators. But it becomes natural to question what gains are achieved by the use of such sophisticated techniques. Under fairly innocuous assumptions about the underlying model, each of the techniques mentioned above, with the exception of OLS, yields consistent estimators of the model's parameters, given that they are identifiable. A consistent estimator is one such that, were the sample size to increase, the estimator would produce, in the limit, an estimate identical with the true parameter; that is, the estimator converges in probability to the population value. Consistency is thus desirable. However, sample sizes are not unlimited in practice, and although there are good reasons for preferring an estimator which has the most desirable asymptotic (large sample) properties, it is important to know something of the small (finite) sample properties of such techniques.

The small sample properties of estimators may be examined theoretically or by the use of 'Monte Carlo' studies. The latter proceed by generating samples of data from known populations and then applying particular estimating techniques to the data in order to compare the resultant estimates with the known population parameters. However, the theoretical analysis of simultaneous equation estimators, pioneered by the work of Nagar (1959, 1962) and Basmann (1961, 1963), showed that, in a number of special cases, the sampling distributions of TSLS estimators do not have a finite variance. This precludes the use of mean squared error criteria to judge such estimators in the context of Monte Carlo studies. Nevertheless Monte Carlo analysis has been used extensively to investigate the small sample properties of estimators.

The various methods of estimating the parameters of a simultaneous set of stochastic economic equations have been applied not only in the analysis of small models of individual sectors of an economy, but also in the estimation and analysis of large scale models of whole economies. One of the earliest attempts to model an economy was by Tinbergen (1935), who constructed a macro-dynamic model of Holland in order to investigate the policy options available to a small country existing in an environment of world depression. Tinbergen followed this with his studies for the League of Nations (1939a,b) and his 1951 model of the British economy[44].

Of those who followed his example, Klein is one of the most notable. He constructed a model of the American economy (1950) and, with Goldberger (1955), further developed this model. In collaboration with members of the Oxford Institute of Economics and Statistics he published, in 1961, an econometric model of the British economy.

The construction of large-scale models has been pursued particularly in the United States partly, perhaps, because of the availability of data for the US economy and partly because of the proliferation of research institutes which ensured that an essentially labour-intensive programme could be undertaken. In England such work has been associated with the Department of Applied Economics at Cambridge under the direction of Stone.

6.7 Conclusions

Econometrics is the culmination of many years of development, beginning with Political Arithmetic in the seventeenth century. Following the nineteenth-century development of statistical theory in relation to the empirical study of social phenomena, econometrics has emerged in this century as the union of economic theory and inferential statistical methods. The Econometric Society, formed in 1930, exhibited in its constitution a clear desire to place economics on a footing similar to that of the natural sciences. The econometric movement thus represents a coherent attempt to utilize the scientific method of hypothesis construction by deduction from a set of assumptions followed by testing the predictions of such theory against data. In order to carry out such a programme it is thus necessary to collect data and to make decisions regarding the acceptability of hypotheses. Econometric theory concerns itself with providing the theoretical basis on which such decisions may be made while applied econometrics concerns itself with the task of choosing that structure (the economic model with its equations and parameters numerically specified) which best serves the intended purpose. The econometrician has, then, a three-fold task: the formulation of an econometric model of the economic relationships under consideration; the estimation and statistical testing of that model using appropriate techniques and appropriate data; and, finally, the use of that model in the interpretation of economic behaviour. A model is a simplified characterization of real world phenomena, and the use of a model to analyse complex phenomena invites criticism. Moreover, econometric models are, of necessity, at a much lower level of generality than that employed by abstract economic theory. As Malinvaud (1970) has remarked:

> The choice of the model conditions every econometric investigation and in fact raises a delicate problem. The model condenses all *a priori* information, which, together with the analysed data, makes statistical inference possible. This information is generally vague and badly formulated. It often appears fairly subjective. The art of the econometrician consists as much in defining a good model as in finding an efficient statistical procedure. Indeed this is why he cannot be purely a statistician, but must have a solid grounding in economics. Only if this is so, he will be aware of the mass of accumulated knowledge which relates to the particular question under study and must find expression in the model. Finally, we must never forget that our progress in understanding economic laws depends strictly on the quality and abundance of statistical data. Nothing can take the place of the painstaking work of objective observation of the facts. All improvements in methodology would be in vain if they had to be applied to mediocre data (p. 723).

Notes

1. For overviews of the history of statistics and econometrics, see Pearson and Kendall (1970), Kendall and Plackett (1977), Kruskall (1968), Kendall (1968) and Strotz (1968) and the references cited therein. On econometrics, see also Schumpeter (1933), Klein (1957) and the survey by Leser (1968). On method and the role of statistics and econometrics in economics, see, for example, Stewart (1979) and Blaug (1980). For details of modern techniques of statistical investigators of economic phenomena, see, for example, Goldberger (1964), Christ (1966), Malinvaud (1970), Maddala (1977), Harvey (1981) and the references cited therein.
2. The word 'statistics' has undergone many changes in meaning over the last three hundred years. For details of its etymology see the Introduction to Pearson (1978), Westergaard (1932) and Cullen (1975).

3. For details of the early use of the calculus of probabilities, see Pearson (1978) and Westergaard (1932).
4. For further details of Graunt's work and of investigations following from it, see Greenwood (1941, 1942. 1943).
5. Graunt could only compare the estimates. The concept of, for example, a statistically significant difference was not developed until the nineteenth century.
6. For further details of Petty's work, see Greenwood (1941) and Letwin (1963).
7. Smith remarked: 'I have no great faith in Political Arithmetic' (1776, p. 111 of the 1976 reprint of the Cannan edition).
8. For details of Halley and Neumann, see Pearson (1978).
9. For further details, see Cullen (1975).
10. The Royal Society was London-based and the British Association was designed to fill the gap left in the provinces.
11. For further details, see Cullen (1975) and *Annals of the Royal Statistical Society 1834–1934.*
12. Indeed, it is common to introduce students to concepts of probability through games of chance.
13. Gauss has been associated with the invention of the normal curve but Laplace's work predates Gauss and in turn Laplace is predated by de Moivre.
14. For details of the history of likelihood, see Edwards (1974).
15. See Box and Tiao (1973), for example.
16. An important economic statistician prior to Edgeworth was W.S. Jevons. See Stigler (1978, pp. 287–288).
17. Galton presented 'regression' in a bivariate model to the British Association meeting in Aberdeen, 1885.
18. Correlation had been observed by Scholls (1875) who noted the correlation between the vertical and horizontal errors in shots fired at a target, but no numerical measure was available until Galton's work. See also Pearson (1920).
19. Galton's equations were derived with the help of the Cambridge mathematician Dickson.
20. Gosset used a pseudonym at the insistence of his employers, Guinness, who normally forbade their research workers from publishing any results.
21. The problem with Bayesian techniques in small samples was that the posterior distribution became very sensitive to the choice of prior.
22. Bowley preferred simple random samples for their simplicity and found that the gains from stratified sampling were not large.
23. The 1925 ISI discussion was the outcome of a committee set up by the 1924 meeting. See Kruskal and Mosteller (1980).
24. See, for example, the remark by Fisher (1935) in reply to discussion of his 1935 paper where he associated himself with Neyman's work. However, this association was due to the fact that Fisher believed 'Neyman to have taken his ideas—and spoilt them' (Kendall, 1963, p. 3). The two statisticians feuded for over twenty five years. In fact, Fisher had many feuds, especially with members of Karl Pearson's school.
25. See the assessment of Bayesianism by de Finetti (1974).
26. See especially Neyman (1941).
27. For details of this collaboration, see Pearson (1966).
28. There had been an abortive attempt to form an econometric society as early as 1912 by Fisher but there were too few interested. See Christ (1952).
29. For a useful discussion of identification and model choice problems in early econometric work on demand, see Morgan (1981). There were also early econometric studies of production, notably by Cobb and Douglas (1928).
30. See especially Moore (1911).
31. Some simplifications were necessary in order to make any progress at all but Moore's work used many unnecessary oversimplifications, to the detriment of this pioneering monograph.
32. On identifying cause and effect, see, for example, Grainger (1969) and Sims (1972).
33. This model may be expanded to allow for errors in both variables.
34. For details of the historical development of the linear model, see Seal (1967), and for an account of the development of least squares, see Harter (1974–1975).
35. Aitken (1945) popularized the use of matrices, but it is to be noted that his use was prompted by that of Frisch (1928).
36. See Schultz (1938, p. 147): 'The empirical statistician is hardly aware of this question.'
37. The derivation of the reduced form from the structural form dates at least from the work of Tinbergen (1930).

38. This test is due to von Neumann (1941).
39. See, for example, Maddala (1977).
40. The analysis of economic time series has become increasingly popular recently. See Hannan (1960), Box and Jenkins (1970) and Harvey (1981).
41. For details of tests for heteroscedasticity, see, for example, Maddala (1977).
42. See also Madansky (1959) and Sargan (1958).
43. Space prohibits any discussion of other single-equation problems but on multicollinearity, see, for example, Frisch (1934), Farrar and Glauber (1967), Haitovsky (1969) and Toro-Vizcarrondo and Wallace (1968); on aggregation, see, for example, Theil (1954) and Green (1964); on linearity, see Zarembka (1968); on stability, see Suits (1957) and Chow (1960); on specification and model selection, see Harvey (1981).
44. The work on business cycles by Tinbergen (1939a) was heavily criticized in a review by Keynes (1939), whose conclusions were later described as being those of 'a sadly misinformed and misguided man' (Vining, 1949a, p. 93).

References

AITKEN, A.C. (1934). On Least Squares and Linear Combinations of Observations. *Proceedings of the Royal Society of Edinburgh* **60**, 42–48

AITKEN, A.C. (1945). Studies in Practical Mathematics. IV On Linear Approximation by Least Squares. *Proceedings of the Royal Society of Edinburgh* **62**, 138–146

ANDERSON, T.W. and RUBIN, H. (1949). Estimation of the Parameters of a Single Equation in a Complete System of Stochastic Equations. *Annals of Mathematical Statistics* **20**, 46–63

ANDERSON, T.W. and RUBIN, H. (1950). The Asymptotic Properties of Estimates of the Parameters of a Single Equation in a Complete System of Stochastic Equations. *Annals of Mathematical Statistics* **21**, 570–582

BASMANN, R.L. (1957). A Generalised Classical Method of Linear Estimation of Coefficients in a Structural Equation. *Econometrica* **25**, 77–83

BASMANN, R.L. (1961). A Note on the Exact Finite Sample Frequency Functions of Generalised Classical Linear Estimators in Two Leading Overidentified Cases. *Journal of the American Statistical Association* **56**, 619–636

BASMANN, R.L. (1963). A Note on the Exact Finite Sample Frequency Functions of Generalised Classical Linear Estimators in a Leading Three Equation Case. *Journal of the American Statistical Association* **58**, 161–171

BENTZEL, R. and WOLD, H. (1946). On Statistical Demand Analysis from the Viewpoint of Simultaneous Equations. *Skandinavisk Aktuarietidskrift* **29**, 95–114

BERNOUILLI, D. (1778). Dijudicatio maxime probabilis plurium observationum discrepantium atque verisimillima inductio inde formanda. *Acta Academiae Scientiorum Petropolitanae* 1, 3–23 (English trans. in G.C. Allen (1961). The most probable Choice between several discrepant Observations and the Formation therefrom of the most likely Induction (with an introductory note by M.G. Kendall and observations by L. Euler). *Biometrika* **48**, 1–18

BLAUG, M. (1980). *The Methodology of Economics*. Cambridge, Cambridge University Press

BOWLEY, A.L. (1901). *Elements of Statistics*. London, P.S. King

BOWLEY, A.L. (1906). Presidential address to Section F of the British Association. *Journal of the Royal Statistical Society* **69**, 540–558

BOWLEY, A.L. (1926). Measurement of the Precision Attained in Sampling. *Bulletin of the International Statistical Institute* **22** (Supplement), 6–62

BOWLEY, A.L. and BURNETT-HURST, A.R. (1905). *Livelihood and Poverty*. London, Bell

BOWLEY, A.L. and STAMP, J. (1927). *The National Income*. Oxford, The Clarendon Press

BOX, G.E.P. and JENKINS, G.M. (1970). *Time Series Analysis: Forecasting and Control*. San Francisco, Holden-Day

BOX, G.E.P. and TIAO, G.C. (1973). *Bayesian Inference in Statistical Analysis*. Reading, Mass., Addison-Wesley

BURNS, A.F. and MITCHELL, W.C. (1946). *Measuring Business Cycles*. New York, National Bureau of Economic Research

CHERNOFF, H. and DIVINSKY, N. (1953). The Computation of Maximum Likelihood Estimates of Linear Structural Equations. In *Studies in Econometric Method* (ed. by W.C. Hood and T.C. Koopmans), pp. 236–302. Cowles Commission Monograph 14, New York, John Wiley

CHOW, G.C. (1960). Tests of Equality between Sets of Coefficients in Two Linear Regressions. *Econometrica* **28**, 591–605

CHRIST, C.F. (1952). History of the Cowles Commission, 1932–1952. In *Economic Theory and Measurement: A Twenty Year Research Report, 1932–1952*. Chicago, Cowles Commission for Research in Economics

CHRIST, C.F. (1966). *Econometric Models and Methods*. New York, John Wiley

COBB, C.W. and DOUGLAS, P.H. (1928). A Theory of Production. *American Economic Review* **18** (Supplement), 139–165

CULLEN, M.J. (1975). *The Statistical Movement in Early Victorian Britain*. Bristol, Harvester

DURBIN, J. (1969). Testing for Serial Correlation in Regression Analysis based on the Periodogram of Least Squares Residuals. *Biometrika* **56**, 1–15

DURBIN, J. (1970). Testing for Serial Correlation in Least Squares Regression when some of the Regressors are Lagged Dependent Variables. *Econometrica* **38**, 410–421

DURBIN, J. and WATSON, G.S. (1950). Testing for Serial Correlation in Least Squares Regression. *Biometrika* **37**, 409–428

DURBIN, J. and WATSON, G.S. (1951). Testing for Serial Correlation in Least Squares Regression. *Biometrika* **38**, 159–178

EDGEWORTH, F.Y. (1883). The Law of Error. *Philosophical Magazine (Fifth Series)* **16**, 300–309

EDGEWORTH, F.Y. (1887). The Empirical Proof of the Law of Error. *Philosophical Magazine (Fifth Series)* **24**, 330–342

EDGEWORTH, F.Y. (1912). Review of Moore's *Laws of Wages*. *Economic Journal* **22**, 66–71

EDWARDS, A.W.F. (1974). The History of Likelihood. *International Statistical Review* **42**, 915

FARRER, D. and GLAUBER, T. (1967). Multicollinearity in Regression Analysis: the Problem Revisited. *Review of Economics and Statistics* **49**, 92–107

DE FINETTI, B. (1974). Bayesianism: its Unifying Role for both the Formulation and Applications of Statistics. *International Statistical Review* **42**, 117–130

FISHER, R.A. (1912). On an Absolute Criterion for Fitting Frequency Curves. *The Messenger of Mathematics* **41**, 155–160

FISHER, R.A. (1912). On the 'Probable Error' of a Coefficient of Correlation Deduced from a Small Sample. *Metron* **1**, 3–32

FISHER, R.A. (1922). On the Mathematical Foundations of Theoretical Statistics. *Philosophical Transactions of the Royal Society Series A* **222**, 309–368

FISHER, R.A. (1935). The Logic of Inductive Inference (with discussion). *Journal of the Royal Statistical Society* **98**, 39–82

FRISCH, R. (1928). Correlation and Scatter in Statistical Variables. *Nordic Statistical Journal* **8**, 36–102

FRISCH, R. (1933). *Pitfalls in the Statistical Construction of Demand and Supply Curves*. Leipzig, Hans Buske

FRISCH, R. (1934). *Statistical Confluence Analysis by means of Complete Regression Systems*. Oslo, University Institute of Economics

GALILEO, G. (1632). *Dialogo sopra i due massimi sistemi del mondo: Tolemaico e copernicano*. Florence, Landini. (English trans. in Drake, S. (1953).) *Dialogue concerning the two chief world systems, Ptolemaic and Copernican*, Berkeley, University of California Press

GALTON, F. (1877). Considerations Adverse to the Maintainance of Section F. *Journal of the Statistical Society of London* **40**, 468–473

GAUSS, C.F. (1806). II Comet vom Jahr 1805. *Monatliche Correspondenz zur Beforderung der Erd- und Himmels-Kunde* **14**, 181–186

GAUSS, C.F. (1809). *Theoria Motus Corporum Coelestium in Sectionibus Conicus Solem Ambientium.* Hamborg's Besser

GEARY, R.C. (1949). Determination of Linear Relations between Systematic Parts of Variables with Errors of Observations, the Variances of which are Unknown. *Econometrica* **17**, 30–58

GREEN, H.A.J. (1964). *Aggregation in Economic Analysis: An Introductory Survey.* Princeton, Princeton University Press

GIRSHICK, M.A. and HAAVELMO, T. (1947). Statistical Analysis of the Demand for Food: Examples of Simultaneous Estimation of Structural Equations. *Econometrica* **15**, 79–110

GLEJSER, H. (1969). A New Test for Heteroscedasticity. *Journal of the American Statistical Society* **64**, 316–323

GOLDBERGER, A.S. (1964). *Econometric Theory.* New York, John Wiley

GOLDFELD, S.M. and QUANDT, R.E. (1965). Some Tests for Homoscedasticity. *Journal of the American Statistical Society* **60**, 539–547

GOSSET, W.S. (1907). On the Error of Counting with a Haemarctometer. *Biometrika* **5**, 351–364

GOSSET, W.S. (1908a). The Probable Error of a Mean. *Biometrika* **6**, 1–25

GOSSET, W.S. (1908b). Probable Error of a Correlation Coefficient. *Biometrika* **6**, 302–310

GRAINGER, C.W.J. (1969). Investigating Causal Relations by Econometric Models and Cross-spectral Methods. *Econometrica* **37**, 424–438

GREEN, H.A.J. (1964). *Aggregation in Economic Analysis.* Princeton, Princeton University Press

GREENWOOD, M. (1941). Medical Statistics from Graunt to Farr, Introduction, *Biometrika* **32**, 101–127

GREENWOOD, M. (1942). Medical Statistics from Graunt to Farr, Continuation. *Biometrika* **32**, 203–225

GREENWOOD, M. (1943). Medical Statistics from Graunt to Farr, Conclusion. *Biometrika* **33**, 1–24

HAAVELMO, T. (1943). The Statistical Implications of a System of Simultaneous Equations. *Econometrica* **11**, 1–12

HAAVELMO, T. (1944). The Probability Approach in Econometrics. *Econometrica* **12** (Supplement), 1–118

HAAVELMO, T. (1947). Methods of Measuring the Marginal Propensity to Consume. *Journal of the American Statistical Association* **42**, 105–122

HAITOVSKY, Y. (1969). Multicollinearity in Regression Analysis. *Review of Economics and Statistics* **51**, 486–489

HANNAN, E.J. (1960). *Time Series Analysis.* London, Methuen

HARTER, H.L. (1974–1975). The method of Least Squares and some Alternatives. Parts I, II, III, IV, V. *International Statistical Review* **43**, 147–174; 235–264; 1–44; 125–190; 269–278

HARVEY, A.C. (1981) *The Econometric Analysis of Time Series.* Oxford, Philip Allan

HAUBER, C.F. (1830). Über die Bestimmung der Genauigkeit der Beobachtungen. *Zeitschrift für Physik und Mathematik* **7**, 286–314

HOTELLING, H. (1930). British Statistics and British Statisticians Today. *Journal of the American Statistical Association* **25**, 186–190

HULL, C.H. (ed.). (1889). *The Economic Writings of Sir William Petty together with the observations upon the Bills of Mortality more probably by Captain John Graunt,* 2 vols. Cambridge, Cambridge University Press

INGRAM, J.K. (1878). Economic Science and Statistics. *Journal of the Statistical Society of London* **41**, 602–629

JEVONS, W.S. (1871). *The Theory of Political Economy*. London, Macmillan

JEVONS, W.S. (1884). *Investigations in Currency and Finance*. London, Macmillan

KENDALL, M.G. (1963). Ronald Aylmer Fisher, 1890–1962. *Biometrika* **50**, 1–15

KENDALL, M.G. (1968). Statistics: the History of Statistical Method. *International Encyclopaedia of the Social Sciences* **15**, 224–232

KENDALL, M.G. and PLACKETT, R.L. (1977). *Studies in the History of Probability and Statistics*, Vol. II. London, Griffin

KEYNES, J.M. (1939). Professor Tinbergen's Method. *Economic Journal* **49**, 558–570

KEYNES, J.N. (1890). *The Scope and Method of Political Economy*. London, Macmillan (4th edn, 1917)

KIAER, A.N. (1903). Sur les méthodes représentative on typologiques (with discussion). *Bulletin of the International Statistical Institute* **13**, 66–78

KLEIN, L.R. (1950). *Economic Fluctuations in the United States, 1921–1941*. New York, John Wiley

KLEIN, L.R. (1957). The Scope and Limitations of Econometrics. *Applied Statistics* **6**, 1–17

KLEIN, L.R. and GOLDBERGER, A.S. (1955). *An Econometric Model of the United States, 1929–1952*. Amsterdam, North-Holland

KLEIN, L.R. *et al.* (1961). *An Econometric Model of the United Kingdom*. Oxford, Basil Blackwell

KOOPMANS, T.C. (1947). Measurement without Theory. *Review of Economics and Statistics* **29**, 161–72

KOOPMANS, T.C. (1949a). A Reply. *Review of Economics and Statistics* **31**, 86–91

KOOPMANS, T.C. (1949b). Identification Problems in Economic Model Construction. *Econometrica* **17**, 125–144

KOOPMANS, T.C. and HOOD, W.C. (1953). The Estimation of Simultaneous Linear Relationships. In *Studies in Econometric Method* (ed. by W.C. Hood and T.C. Koopmans), pp. 112–199. Cowles Commission Monograph 14, New York, John Wiley

KOOPMANS, T.C., RUBIN, H. and LEIPNIK, R.B. (1950). Measuring the Equation Systems of Dynamic Economics. In *Statistical Inference in Dynamic Economics* (ed. by T.C. Koopmans), pp. 53–237, Cowles Commission Monograph 10, New York, John Wiley

KRUSKAL, W.H. (1968). Statistics: the Field. *International Encyclopaedia of the Social Sciences* **15**, 206–224

KRUSKAL, W.H. and MOSTELLER, F. (1980). Representative Sampling IV: the History of the Concept in Statistics, 1895–1939. *International Statistical Review* **48**, 169–195

LAPLACE, P.S. (1786). Mémoire sur la figure de la terre. *Mémoires de l'Académie Royale des Sciences de Paris* 17–46

LEGENDRE, A.M. (1805). *Nouvelles Méthodes pour la Détermination des Orbites des Comètes*. Paris, Courcier

LEHFELDT, R.A. (1914). The Elasticity of Demand for Wheat. *Economic Journal* **24**, 212–217

LEHFELDT, R.A. (1915). Review of Moore's *Economic Cycles*. *Economic Journal* **25**, 409–411

LENOIR, M. (1913). *Etudes sur la formation et le mouvement des prix*. Paris

LESER, C.E.V. (1968). A Survey of Econometrics. *Journal of the Royal Statistical Society Series A* **131**, 530–566

LETWIN, W. (1963). *The Origins of Scientific Economics*. London, Methuen

LUNDBERG, G.A. (1971). Statistics in Modern Social Thought. In *Contemporary Social Theory* (ed. by H.E. Barnes, H. Becker and F.B. Becker), pp. 110–40. New York, Russell and Russell

MADANSKY, A. (1959). The Fitting of Straight Lines when both Variables are Subject to Error. *Journal of the American Statistical Association* **54**, 173–205

MADDALA, G.S. (1977). *Econometrics*. New York, McGraw-Hill

MALINVAUD, E. (1970). *Statistical Methods of Econometrics*, 2nd edn. Amsterdam, North-Holland

MARSHALL, A. (1897). The Old Generation of Economists and the New. *Quarterly Journal of Economics* **11**, 115–135

MOORE, H.L. (1908). The Statistical Complement of Pure Economics. *Quarterly Journal of Economics* **23**, 1–33

MOORE, H.L. (1911). *Laws of Wages*. New York, Macmillan

MOORE, H.L. (1914). *Economic Cycles—Their Law and Cause*. New York, Macmillan

MORGAN, M.S. (1981). Identification and Model Choice Problems in Early Econometric Work on Demand. Unpublished paper, London School of Economics

NAGAR, A.L. (1959). The Bias and Moment Matrix of the General k-class Estimators of the Parameters in Simultaneous Equations. *Econometrica* **27**, 575–595

NAGAR, A.L. (1962). Double k-class Estimators of Parameters in Simultaneous Equations and their Small Sample Properties.*International Economic Review* **3**,168–188

NEUMANN, J. VON (1941). Distribution of the Ratio of the Mean Successive Differences to the Variance. *Annals of Mathematical Statistics* **12**, 367–395

NEYMAN, J. (1934). On Two Different Aspects of the Representative Method (with discussion). *Journal of the Royal Statistical Society* **97**, 558–625

NEYMAN, J. (1941). Fiducial Argument and the Theory of Confidence Intervals. *Biometrika* **32**, 128–150

NEYMAN, J. and PEARSON, E.S. (1933). On the Problem of the Most Efficient Tests of Statistical Hypotheses. *Philosophical Transactions of the Royal Society of London Series A* **231**, 289–337

O'BRIEN, D.P. (1970). *J.R. McCulloch: A Study in Classical Economics*. London, George Allen and Unwin

PEARSON, K. (1900). On the Criterion that a Given System of Deviations from the Probable in the Case of a Correlated System of Variables is Such that it can reasonably be Supposed to have Arisen from Random Sampling. *Philosophical Magazine* **50**, 157–175

PEARSON, K. (1920). Notes on the History of Correlation. *Biometrika* **13**, 25–45

PEARSON, E.S. (1966). The Neyman–Pearson Story: 1926–34. Historical Sidelights on an Episode in Anglo–Polish Collaboration. In *Festschrift for J. Neyman* (ed. by F.N. David), pp. 1–24. London, John Wiley

PEARSON, E.S. (ed.) (1978). *The History of Statistics in the 17th and 18th Centuries. Lectures by Karl Pearson*. London, Griffin

PEARSON, E.S. and KENDALL, M.G. (1970). *Studies in the History of Probability and Statistics*, Vol. I. London, Griffin

RAWSON, R. (1885). Presidential Address. *Journal of the Statistical Society of London* Jubilee Volume, 2–12

REIERSØL, O. (1945). *Confluence Analysis by Means of Instrumental Sets of Variables*. Stockholm, Almqvist and Wiksell

SARGAN, J.D. (1958). The Estimation of Economic Relationships Using Instrumental Variables. *Econometrica* **26**, 393–415

SCHOLLS, C.M. (1875). Over de theorie der fouten in de ruimte en in het platte vlak. *Verhandlingen der Koninklyke Akademie van Wetenschapen* **15**, 1–75

SCHULTZ, H. (1925). The Statistical Law of Demand. *Journal of Political Economy* **33**, 481–504 and 577–637

SCHULTZ, H. (1928). *Statistical Laws of Demand and Supply with Special Application to Sugar*. Chicago, Chicago University Press

SCHULTZ, H. (1938). *The Theory and Measurement of Demand*. Chicago, Chicago University Press

SCHUMPETER, J.A. (1933). The Common Sense of Econometrics. *Econometrica* **1**, 5–12

SEAL, H.L. (1967). The Historical Development of the Gauss Linear Model. *Biometrika* **54**, 1–24

SIMPSON, T. (1756). A Letter to the Right Honourable George Earl of Macclesfield,

President of the Royal Society, on the Advantage of Taking the Mean of a Number of Observations, in Practical Astronomy. *Philosophical Transactions of the Royal Society of London* **49**, 82–93

SIMS, C.A. (1972). Money, Income and Causality. *American Economic Review* **62**, 540–552

SMITH, A. (1776). *An Inquiry into the Nature and Causes of the Wealth of Nations*. Ed. by E. Cannan and reprinted, 1976, by University of Chicago Press

STEWART, I.M.T. (1979). *Reasoning and Method in Economics*. London, McGraw-Hill

STIGLER, G.J. (1954). The Early History of Empirical Studies of Consumer Behaviour. *The Journal of Political Economy* **62**, 95–113

STIGLER, S.M. (1978). Francis Ysidro Edgeworth, Statistician (with discussion). *Journal of the Royal Statistical Society Series A* **141**, 287–322

STONE, R. (1980). Political Economy, Economics and Beyond. *Economic Journal* **90**, 719–36

STROTZ, R.H. (1968). Econometrics. *International Encyclopaedia of the Social Sciences* **4**, 350–359

SUITS, D.B. (1957). Use of Dummy Variables in Regression Equations. *Journal of the American Statistical Association* **52**, 548–551

THEIL, H. (1953a). *Repeated Least-Squares Applied to Complete Equation Systems*. The Hague, Central Planning Bureau (mimeographed)

THEIL, H. (1953b). *Estimation and Simultaneous Correlation in Complete Equation Systems*. The Hague, Central Planning Bureau (mimeographed)

THEIL, H. (1954). *Linear Aggregation of Economic Relations*. Amsterdam, North-Holland

THEIL, H. (1958). *Economic Forecasts and Policy*. Amsterdam, North-Holland

TINBERGEN, J. (1930). Bestimmung und Deutung von Angebotskurven. *Zeitschrift fur Nationalokonomie* **1**, 669–679

TINBERGEN, J. (1935). Quantitative fragen der konjunkturpolitik. *Weltwirtschaftliches Archiv* **42**, 316–399

TINBERGEN, J. (1939a). *Business Cycles in the United States of America, 1919–32*. Geneva, League of Nations

TINBERGEN, J. (1939b). *A Method and its Application to Investment Activity*. Geneva, League of Nations

TINBERGEN, J. (1951). *Business Cycles in the United Kingdom, 1870–1914*. Amsterdam, North-Holland

TOOKE, T. and NEWMARCH, W. (1838–1857). *A History of Prices and of the State of the Circulation during the Years 1793–1856*, 6 vols. London, Ingram

TORO-VIZCARRONDO, C. and WALLACE, T.D. (1968). A Test of the Mean Square Error Criterion for Restrictions in Linear Regression. *Journal of the American Statistical Association* **63**, 558–572

VINING, R. (1949a). Koopmans on the Choice of Variables to be Studied and of Methods of Measurement. *Review of Economics and Statistics* **31**, 77–86

VINING, R. (1949b). A Rejoinder. *Review of Economics and Statistics* **31**, 91–94

WALD, A. (1940). The Fitting of Straight Lines if Both Variables are Subject to Error. *Annals of Mathematical Statistics* **11**, 284–300

WESTERGAARD, H.L. (1932). *Contributions to the History of Statistics*. London, P.S. King

WOLD, H.O.A. (1959). Ends and Means in Econometric Model Building. In *Probability and Statistics* (ed. by U. Grenauder), pp. 355–434. New York, John Wiley

WOLD, H.O.A. (1960). A Generalisation of Causal Chain Models. *Econometrica* **28**, 443–463

WORKING, E.J. (1927). What do Statistical Demand Curves Show? *Quarterly Journal of Economics* **41**, 215–235

ZAREMBKA, P. (1968). Functional Form in the Demand for Money. *Journal of the American Statistical Association* **63**, 502–511

ZELLNER, A. and THEIL, H. (1962). Three-stage Least Squares: Simultaneous Estimation of Simultaneous Equations. *Econometrica* **30**, 54–78

Chapter Seven

Balance of payments theory

J.S. Chipman

7.1. Introduction

The emergence of economic science in Great Britain in the seventeenth to nineteenth centuries was to some extent an offshoot of the development of the theory of adjustment of the balance of payments. This chapter traces the evolution of this theory from Locke (1692) to Ricardo (1811b). The great figures in addition to these two are Hume (1752b), Smith (1776) and Thornton (1802), but minor figures such as Horner (1802, 1803) and Huskisson (1810) are also given their due.

Extensive surveys already exist of this topic, by Angell (1926), Haberler (1933), Viner (1937), Mason (1955, 1956, 1957) and Fetter (1965). The main object of this chapter is to give greater emphasis to the technical details of the arguments.

What emerges is a sophisticated theory involving exchange-rate fluctuations between gold points, substitutability between paper and metallic currency. Many of the theoretical differences among these early writers are based on different assumptions, often only implicit, as to whether, for example, the real exchange rate is at or above the gold-export point, or whether specie still co-exists with paper or has been driven out of circulation.

Contrary to an impression that has become widespread during the last decade, the classical theory was never an exclusively monetary one. From the very beginnings, the sorting out of the real and monetary aspects of balance of payments adjustment has been at the centre of concern; indeed, the problem of how best to do this was precisely what was at issue in the great bullionist controversy. One can recognize in this controversy virtually all of the arguments that have resurfaced in contemporary times: elasticity optimism versus pessimism; real versus monetary explanations of balance-of-payments deficits; the distinction between real and nominal exchange rates;

'seignorage' and involuntary foreign lending; the benefits of exchange depreciation over currency contraction under conditions of downward inflexibility of prices; all these and more appear in the writing of Locke, Hume, Smith, Thornton, Horner and Ricardo. For instance, Ricardo showed that an increase in paper money would, when specie is still circulating, lead to a fall in the *real* exchange rate and, once the gold-export point had been reached, to an export of gold; it would thus, within a well-defined interval, be non-inflationary. He also argued, against the 'elasticity pessimists' Thornton and Malthus, that the currency devaluation induced by a crop failure would normally call forth enough exports to pay for the required imports; but he admitted that, by creating a redundancy of currency, it could, if sufficiently severe, lead to an export of gold.

7.2 From Locke to Smith

7.2.1 LOCKE

It is useful to begin with Locke, who is the earliest writer referred to by both Thornton and Ricardo. First, Locke may be considered as the originator of the quantity theory of money; and second, he made a contribution to the theory of foreign exchanges which, while imperfect, at least served as a strong starting point for the subject. Regarding the demand for money, Locke (1692) had this to say:

Every man must have at least so much money, or so timely recruits, as may in hand, or in a short distance of time, satisfy his creditor who supplies him with the necessaries of life, or of his trade...

This shews the necessity of some proportion of money to trade: but what proportion that is, is hard to determine; because it depends not barely on the quantity of money, but the quickness of its circulation (p. 33).

This is followed by detailed illustrations of the unevenness of receipts and expenditures and the consequent transactions demand for money. One finds also quite a clear perception of the relation between prices and the money supply (pp. 69–70) and even a formulation of the very problem later taken up by Hume (1752b) of the effects of a sudden reduction in the quantity of money (pp. 77–78). He concluded that this would 'make our native commodities vent very cheap' and 'make all foreign commodities very dear', but he failed to reach Hume's conclusion that it would lead to a reflux of money from abroad—this despite the fact that later in his essay he provided the main idea behind Hume's doctrine in stating:

Nature has bestowed mines on several parts of the world; but their riches are only for the industrious and frugal. Whomsoever else they visit, it is with the diligent and sober only they stay (p. 117).

This suggests that Locke's incomplete treatment must have been a stimulus to Hume.

Locke did, however, continue with some interesting thoughts concerning the foreign exchanges. He remarked that silver (at that time the international money) 'is not of the same value, at the same time, in several parts of the world, but is of the most worth in that country, where there is the least money, in proportion to its trade' (pp. 80–81), noting that a silver price differential of a few per cent could be accounted for by 'the danger of leaving it there, or the difficulty of bringing it home in specie', i.e. risk and transport costs. Lest it be concluded, however, that Locke was an early proponent of an unqualified purchasing-power-parity doctrine, it must be added that he saw one other basis for variations in the exchange rate, namely capital movements.

Thus, while in a comparison with Hume, Locke's treatment comes out generally unfavourably, Locke did perceive an aspect of the situation that was missed by Hume: if there is a slight contraction of England's money supply, there will be no inflow of silver from abroad as long as the rise in the 'real exchange' is insufficient to cause it to exceed silver's transport costs, i.e. as long as fluctuations in exchange rates remain within the 'silver points'. Needless to say, Locke's example of a 50 per cent reduction in the domestic money supply—while not as drastic as Hume's four-fifths—cannot be regarded as a 'slight contraction'. Locke also made the interesting suggestion (pp. 81–82) that the law prohibiting the export of specie was advantageous, since it permitted wider fluctuations in the exchange rate[1].

Locke (1695) also provided interesting though not unobjectionable analyses of the causes of the melting down of specie into bullion. He recognized only two causes (pp. 34–39): unequal weights of coins of the same denomination and a deficit in the balance of trade. He regarded trade deficits as exogenous, and rejected the view that a debasing of the coinage and the consequent melting of heavier coins would lead to the export of the melted specie; this would be correct if the resulting supplies of bullion could find industrial uses and were still not depreciated to the export point. Here he was criticized by Thornton (1802; Hayek, 1939) as well as—obliquely—by Ricardo (Sraffa, 1951); Ricardo explicitly, but Thornton only implicitly, assumed that the real exchange was already unfavourable. Locke in a number of passages (1692, p. 191; 1695, 'short observations', pp. 1–2) sought to deny that a given weight of silver could be worth less as coin than as bullion. But, as Ricardo (1810; Sraffa, 1951) later explained, the penalties against melting coins (and against exporting coin or melted coin) were sufficient explanation for a discount in their value—even in a state of equilibrium (see also Tooke, 1824). Harris (1758; McCulloch, 1856) reproached Locke for not including the prevalence of a bimetallic standard as a cause of the melting of specie. And Steuart (1767) criticized Locke's error of admitting that creditors lost but denying that debtors gained from inflation.

7.2.2 GERVAISE

Gervaise (1720), more than thirty years before Hume (1752b), fully outlined the doctrine that the precious metals (which he called the 'denominator') would apportion themselves among countries in proportion to the 'produce of their labour'. Even more striking was his extension of this doctrine to encompass credit. In his words (1720, in 1954):

> If a nation adds to its denominator, such a portion of credit, as increases it beyond that proportion which by trade naturally belongs to it, that increase of credit will act on that nation, as if it had drawn an equal sum from a gold or silver mine, and will preserve but its proportion of that increase; so that the rest thereof will in time be drawn off by the labour of other nations, in gold and silver...And the contrary happens, when a nation retrenches from its denominator, such a portion of credit, as lessens it beyond its natural proportion; that diminution breaking the proportion, between that and other nations, will cause it in time, to draw gold and silver proportionally from other nations, until its denominator recovers its natural proportion (p. 9).

It may be noted that no mention is made of price differentials between the given country and the rest of the world—an omission that would meet with Samuelson's (1980) approval. The theory as stated is one of static equilibrium—a logical deduction from the quantity theory of money. It may be asked whether Gervaise had a convincing account of the dynamics.

Gervaise did proceed with an account of the adjustment process but it is rather disappointing. A subsequent summary is better:

> ...all the profit a nation gains, by unnaturally swelling its denominator, consists only in its inhabitants living for a time in proportion to that swelling, so as to make a greater figure than the rest of the world, but always at the cost of their coin, or of their store of real and exportable labour (p. 12).

7.2.3 CANTILLON

There is a problem as to where most appropriately to place Cantillon's work chronologically. The *Essai* (1755) was published only after his murder in 1734. As Higgs (1931) discovered, major portions of the English original showed up, totally plagiarized, in Postlethwayt (1749, 1951–1955, 1957), whose works might have been known to Hume and were certainly known to Thornton (1802). But there is no trace in Cantillon of Hume's idea of an equilibrium in the international distribution of the precious metals. However, Cantillon (1755; Higgs, 1931) offers an interesting idea quite at variance with Hume's approach.

> In England, it is always permitted to bring in corn from foreign countries, but not cattle. For this reason, however great the increase of hard money may be in England, the price of corn can only be raised above the price in other countries where money is scarce by the cost and risks of importing corn from these foreign countries.
>
> It is not the same with the price of cattle, which will necessarily be proportioned to the quantity of money offered for meat in proportion to the quantity of meat and the number of cattle bred there...
>
> Increase of money only increases the prices of products and merchandise by the difference of the cost of transport, when this transport is allowed (p. 179).

Not until Taussig (1917) did this idea appear again so forcefully in the literature on balance-of-payments adjustment. The idea was applied by Cantillon in an earlier chapter (Higgs, 1931) to a transfer problem between the capital city and the countryside within a nation, the point being that since the countryside pays taxes to the government to support the bureaucracy, as well as rents to the absentee landlords and tuition to the fashionable schools in the capital city, prices will be higher in the capital than in the country.

7.2.4 HUME

Hume's (1752b) contribution is well known, but for ease of comparison the main passage deserves to be cited:

> Suppose four fifths of all the money in Britain to be annihilated in one night, and the nation reduced to the same condition, in this particular, as in the reigns of the Harrys and Edwards; what would be the consequence? Must not the price of all labour and commodities sink in proportion, and every thing be sold as cheap as they were in those ages? What nation could then dispute with us in any foreign market...? In how little time, therefore, must this bring back the money, which we had lost, and raise us to the level of all the neighbouring nations? (pp. 82–83).

Samuelson (1980) has objected that prices were not needed in the argument; that it is enough that, with a reduced money supply, expenditure would be reduced—on both importables and exportables—leading to a surplus of exports over imports and an inflow of precious metals. Samuelson's main model assumed zero transport costs, and if these instead are considerable it may be argued that the only signal merchants will respond to is a price differential; this could be true even if there were no transport costs. In that case, Hume's approach seems not unreasonable, except in one respect: if a price differential is needed to ship merchandise, why is not the same true of gold? In fact, Ricardo (1810) was later to put much greater stress on the latter. There seems to be an implicit assumption in Hume that the relative prices of gold-in-Britain and gold-abroad remain undisturbed after the annihilation of gold in Britain, and that only the British merchandise prices fall; why the asymmetry? Presumably, if one starts from the hypothesis that trade patterns cannot be changed in the short run, all one is entitled to postulate on the basis of the quantity theory is that, after the four-fifths annihilation of gold in Britain, the *relative* prices of merchandise-in-Britain and gold-in-Britain must change; some other principle is needed to explain the relationships between these respective prices in Britain and abroad. Thornton (1802) was the first to understand the need to pose and solve this problem; to do so one needs a theory of foreign exchanges, but this was treated by Hume only incidentally, as a supplementary rather than integral part of the theory of the adjustment process:

> There is another cause, though more limited in its operation, which checks the wrong balance of trade, to every particular nation to which the kingdom trades. When we import more goods than we export, the exchange turns against us, and this becomes a new encouragement to export; as much as the charge of carriage and insurance of the money which becomes due would amount to. For the exchange can never rise but a little higher than that sum (p. 84n.).

Hume (1752b) also showed remarkable insight as to the role of paper credit in the adjustment process:

> Suppose there are 12 millions of paper, which circulate in the kingdom as money..., and suppose that the real cash of the kingdom is 18 millions: Here is a state which is found by experience able to hold a stock of 30 millions. I say, if it be able to hold it, it must of necessity have acquired it in gold and silver, had we not obstructed the entrance of these metals by this new invention of paper. ...Because, if you remove these 12 millions, money in this state is below its level, compared with our neighbours; and we must immediately draw from all of them, till we be full and saturate, so to speak, and hold no more (pp. 90–91).

This important principle—already recognized by Gervaise—was to become the foundation of Smith's (1776) theory of money and an essential part of Thornton's (1802) and Ricardo's (1810) doctrines.

Hume's other important contribution, which was destined to make a great impression on Thornton (1802), Malthus (1811a) and the antibullionists, was the doctrine of 'forced saving' (as Hayek (1932) later described it) developed in his essay on money (1752a), leading to the conclusion that the process of inflation had beneficial, if temporary, welfare effects, and the process of deflation harmful welfare effects, the latter outweighing the former.

7.2.5 HARRIS

Whether Harris (1757) really wrote his *Essay* before reading Hume (1752b), as intimated in the Preface, one cannot know. He was accused by Jevons (1881) of plagiarizing Cantillon. The same account, similar to that of Hume, of the effects of an increase in the money supply in stimulating the level of activity, is found in Harris (1757; McCulloch, 1856). There is the same failure as in Hume to explain why gold merchants should ship bullion, but by the same token, as was to be the case once again in Thornton's (1802) treatment, there is a hint of the principle of comparative advantage.

With respect to paper credit, Harris' treatment (1757; McCulloch, 1856) is somewhat less satisfactory, because of its equivocation, than Hume's:

...supposing the sum total of money, real and fictitious, now annually circulating in this country, to be 100 millions; 20 millions of which is in cash, and the rest in paper credit...: If this paper credit be increased,...suppose to the amount of ten millions; one of the following will necessarily be the consequence: Either all our commodities will rise ten per cent in their nominal value, which will render them too dear for foreign markets; or, this addition of paper bills will drain away ten millions of our cash, and so impoverish us in reality to that whole amount; or, the effect most likely will be, partly the one, and partly the other; but which ever it is, the nation will be equally endamaged (p. 409).

He remarked that debasing of the coinage would also lead to an outflow of bullion.

In the final section of his *Essay* he furnished a detailed description of the relationships required among prices of bullion in London and Paris, the exchange rate and transport costs, to make it profitable to ship bullion; but this was never related to his earlier more abstract account.

7.2.6 SMITH

Smith (1776) had a wide knowledge of economic facts and of the economic literature and had a keen grasp of general principles. He made at least five noteworthy contributions to balance-of-payments theory.

The first was a development of Hume's doctrine concerning paper money, though, because of the figurative terminology in which it was expressed, it might seem like a curious retrogression from Hume: his doctrine that there was in a country with given productive capacity a determinate 'channel of circulation', so that if paper money is 'poured into it' the channel must 'overflow', and since the paper cannot go abroad, gold and silver must (Vol. I, pp. 352–353). This appeared to substitute a metaphorical statement for an analytic explanation, and was incapable of being extended to the case in which gold and silver were entirely depleted. However, it contained a correct and valuable insight. Denoting paper money and specie by P and S respectively, the doctrine states that their sum, $P + S$, which is the supply of money, must be equal to the 'channel of circulation' or demand for money, M, which is proportional to 'the whole annual product of...land and capital', or national income, Y; i.e. $P + S = M = kY$. An increase in paper, ΔP, as long as it is less than the existing circulation of specie, S, simply dislodges an equal amount of specie, $\Delta S = -\Delta P$:

> Gold and silver...will be sent abroad, and the channel of home circulation will remain filled with a million of paper, instead of the million of those metals which filled it before.

These metals can be exchanged either for consumer goods or for capital goods, and in the latter case, 'the whole value of the great wheel of circulation and distribution is added to the goods which are circulated and distributed by means of it' (p. 356). Ignoring (as Smith did) the effect of the displaced gold and silver on the world money supply, an increase in paper money not only is not inflationary but constitutes a clear gain to the country (at the expense of the rest of the world, of course; but again, this is not mentioned by Smith). Because of its importance this may be described as the 'Hume–Smith principle'; it was understood and accepted by Thornton (1802) and Ricardo (1810), but by few of the other participants in the bullionist controversy. Smith himself muddied the waters by following his discussion by a statement involving an additional principle:

> The whole paper money of every kind which can easily circulate in any country never can exceed the value of the gold and silver, of which it supplies the place, or which (the commerce being supposed the same) would circulate there, if there was no paper money (Vol. I, p. 361).

The reason for this is that:

> Should the circulating paper exceed that sum, as the excess could neither be sent abroad nor be employed in the circulation of the country, it must immediately return upon the banks to be exchanged for gold and silver (pp. 361–362).

Convertibility of paper into specie, therefore, is what provides the upper limit to the amount of paper that can circulate; but this is not at all involved in the principle by which paper displaces specie, which is the convertibility (though illegal) of specie into bullion. It is not surprising, therefore, that many of Smith's successors (such as Boyd, 1801; King, 1803; Horner, 1802, 1803; Wheatley, 1803, 1807; and Blake, 1810) failed to understand the basic nature of the principle.

A second contribution made by Smith was the shedding of mercantilist beliefs about the value of the precious metals. While Gervaise, Hume and Harris had considered the outflow of precious metals resulting from the issue of paper to be most deplorable, Smith, on the contrary, considered it to be highly beneficial (p. 350). While this was an idea that was no doubt becoming fashionable among the business community, it was certainly a novel one in the serious economic literature.

A third contribution, which would hardly strike a contemporary reader as having any significance, but which marked an important change in habits of thought, was the treatment of the precious metals on a par with other commodities[2]. This arose, in connection with his famous refutation of mercantilist doctrines; but more important than this from the analytical view was the treatment of bullion—which he described as 'the money of the great mercantile republic' (Vol. II, p. 20), i.e. world money—as an article 'to be bought for a certain price like all other commodities' (p. 9). To think of gold being exported, not as a means of payment, but because it was profitable to do so on the basis of a calculation of prices at home and abroad and transport costs, was an important insight that greatly influenced Thornton (1802) and Ricardo (1810). Unfortunately, Smith never integrated this discussion with his discussion of how paper money would displace specie; this subject was left to be developed by Thornton and Ricardo.

The fourth contribution of note may be considered to be Smith's distinction, which again must have been fairly current in commercial circles, between the real and nominal ('computed') exchange rate (Vol. II, p. 60). This distinction greatly influenced Horner (1802), and underlay the basic analysis of the Bullion Report (1810).

The fifth contribution worth recording is Smith's treatment of what later came to be known as the 'transfer problem'. In some respects, this exceeded in its insights anything until Taussig (1917), Ohlin (1928) and Keynes (1930). While the last two treatments arose in connection with German reparations payments following the First World War, Smith's treatment arose in connection with the financing of war itself. He stated:

The commodities most proper for being transported to distant countries, in order to purchase there either the pay and provisions of an army, or some part of the money of the mercantile republic to be employed in purchasing them, seem to be the finer and more improved manufactures; such as contain a great value in small bulk, and can, therefore, be exported to a great distance at little expense. A country whose industry produces a great annual surplus of such manufactures, which are usually exported to foreign countries, may carry on for many years a very expensive foreign war without either exporting any considerable quantity of gold and silver, or even having any such quantity to export. ...In the midst of the most destructive foreign war, therefore, the greater part of manufactures may frequently flourish greatly; and on the contrary, they may decline on the return of the peace (Vol. II, p. 21).

While he did not actually state that the foreign expenditure was equal to the balance of trade (or export surplus), it was an obvious inference subsequently drawn by King (1803), and by Wheatley (1803). Smith went on to point out that only countries that produced such manufactures had the capability of making the kinds of adjustments necessary to finance wars.

7.3 From Thornton to Ricardo

7.3.1 BARING AND BOYD

In 1797 convertibility of notes into gold was suspended in England, and this led to discussion of the working of an inconvertible paper currency. Baring (1797) considered that

paper is as good a representative sign as gold, and in many instances it is better,—because it is more easy to manage and to transfer; ...such paper being the circulatory medium for the country where it issues; whilst gold or silver are the circulating mediums in every part of the world,—for both are no more than representative signs (pp. 3–4).

To avoid future panics he advocated that banknotes be made legal tender for a time, but limited in amount (p. 73), and argued that the Bank of England should be the lender of last resort (pp. 22, 47).

However, banknotes were not made legal tender, and their issue was left to the discretion of the (privately owned) Bank of England. Three years later Boyd (1801)[3] sounded the alarm concerning 'the increase in the prices of almost all articles of necessity, convenience, and luxury...which has been gradually taking place during the last two years', which he attributed to 'the issue of Bank-notes, uncontrouled by the obligation of paying them, in specie, on demand' (p. 3). His evidence for 'the great and general rise of prices' was impressionistic only, 'proved by the concurring testimony of a whole community' (p. 24). Subsequent researches of Tooke (1838) indicated that there had been a substantial rise in agricultural prices, resulting from 'the two very deficient harvests of 1799 and 1800', which was partially offset by declines in other prices. Boyd (1801) acknowledged that high agricultural prices could reflect crop failures, but believed the price rise to be much more general. His evidence for the increase in paper circulation was based on the figures £15 540 970 (for 6 December 1800) and £8 640 250 for 26 February 1797) as well as on the figure £11 975 573 for the average of the three years ending December 1795 (pp. iii–iv). It was later pointed out by Thornton (1802; Hayek, 1939) that the 1797 figure was the exceptionally low sum resulting from the run on the Bank; that the 1800 figure included £2 000 000 of one- and two-pound notes that had replaced guineas; and that by the spring of 1801 the circulation had fallen by £1 500 000, so that (excluding the £2 million) it was back to the average of 1793–1795.

Boyd (1801) had based himself on the following theoretical argument:

---

if a miracle had produced so much additional gold and silver, it would have required another to have kept amongst us whatever part of such additional quantity exceeded the natural digestive powers of the country. That surplus quantity would have found its way into other countries...But Bank Notes possess no such quantity. *They* cannot be exported... (p. 9)

This argument would be valid only if all specie had already been driven out of circulation. However, Boyd invoked the support of Smith without apparently being aware that Smith's theory, under Smith's (tacit) assumption that some specie remained in circulation, could not support his thesis.

Boyd was on stronger ground when he cited as evidence of excessive emission of banknotes the excess of the market price over the mint price of gold. This was later to be precisely Ricardo's (1810) criterion. He also was under the impression that guineas were still in, but passing out of, circulation. Finally he pointed to the (nominal) depreciation of the exchange with Hamburg. All the basic elements of the later bullionist position were present, but crudely and imperfectly put together.

7.3.2 THORNTON

Thornton's first intention had been 'to expose some popular errors which related chiefly to the suspension of cash payments of the Bank of England' but that in the process of developing it the work had 'assumed, in some degree, the character of a general treatise' (1802; Hayek, 1939). His main thesis was that:

> The immediate cause...of the exportation of our coin has been an
> unfavourable exchange, produced partly by our heavy [foreign] expenditure,
> though chiefly by the superadded circumstance of two successively bad
> harvests (p. 156).

It will also be helpful to distinguish carefully between the economic
content that lies behind this thesis, and the general question of what is
meant by attributing to any historical event a particular 'cause'.

Thornton (1802; Hayek, 1939) started out with the following
(rather dubious) proposition:

> It may be laid down as a general truth, that the commercial exports and
> imports of a state (that is to say, the exported and imported commodities, for
> which one country receives an equivalent from another) naturally proportion
> themselves in some degree to each other; and that the balance of trade,
> therefore (by which is meant the difference between these commercial exports
> and imports), cannot continue for a very long time to be either highly
> favourable or highly unfavourable to a country (p. 141).

To support this he added that 'a prosperous nation commonly
employs its growing wealth, not so much in augmenting the debts due
to it from abroad, as in the enlargement of its capital at home', and
then in an argument anticipating Alexander's (1952) treatment,
asserted that 'there is in the mass of the people, of all countries, a
disposition to adapt their individual expenditure to their income',
concluding that 'this equality between private expenditures and
private incomes tends ultimately to produce equality between
commercial exports and imports' (pp. 142–143).

With this background, Thornton went on to consider the effect of
remittances abroad, such as expenditures of the military and loans
and subsidies to allies, and came to the following remarkable
conclusion:

> Although exports and imports of this class form no part of the commercial
> exports and imports which we have spoken of, they affect the quantity of those
> commercial exports and imports, and they contribute, exactly like the
> circumstance of a bad harvest, to render the balance of trade unfavourable;
> they tend, that is to say, in the same manner, to bring Great Britain into debt to
> foreign countries, and to promote the exportation of our bullion (pp. 144–145).

Here, Thornton appears to have fallen into a double semantic trap. If
the loan is paid in bullion, the balance of *trade* (as opposed to the
balance of *payments*) cannot be rendered unfavourable; while if it is
paid in merchandise, the balance of trade must be rendered

'favourable' rather than 'unfavourable'. Loans to foreign countries do not 'bring Great Britain into debt to foreign countries'; they bring foreign countries into debt to Britain. In terms of the example used by Thornton in the ensuing long footnote, of a loan to the Emperor of Germany remitted through the draft of bills of exchange in Vienna on London[4], the immediate effect would be an excess supply of these bills in Vienna (which may be taken to be the definition of an 'unfavourable balance' of *payments*) and a consequent fall in their price (which was the measure of the pound–florin exchange rate), that is an 'unfavourable exchange'. Thornton concluded, on the basis of his previously enunciated principle, that in the long run, balanced trade would be restored. It was in this state that he left the transfer problem dangling, not to be taken up again. In the remainder of his discussion, the illustration he used of an 'unfavourable balance' was one resulting from a bad harvest.

However, he did proceed with a most interesting discussion of the causes and consequences of gold outflows, which clearly made a deep impression on Ricardo (1810). He noted that while gold had been treated in his analysis up to this point merely as a means of discharging payment, it could be thought of as a commodity, which is shipped abroad only if it fetches a higher price there. He then showed how an unfavourable exchange would raise its price in Hamburg relative to London, and cause it to be exported. In a development which Ricardo subsequently criticized, he assumed that gold would continue to flow out indefinitely, as though there were no self-correcting mechanism. Granted that assumption, however, he pointed out that once the supply of bullion was exhausted, its price would rise (above the mint price) and guineas would be melted down for exportation. He made an even more interesting remark, namely that, because of the interchangeableness of coin with paper, 'goods, in comparison with gold coin, are made dear. The goods which are dear remain, therefore, in England; and the gold coin, which is cheap..., goes abroad' (p. 150).

It is at this stage that Thornton reached the conclusion that 'an excess of the market price above the mint price of gold...if it arises on the occasion of an unfavourable balance of trade, and at a time when there has been no extraordinary emission of notes, may fairly be considered as an excess created by that unfavourable balance, though it is one which a reduction of notes tends to cure' (p. 151). Ricardo (1810) was later to reach the opposite conclusion: that failure to contract the note issue in the face of those circumstances was the cause of the excess. Which (if either) position is correct is obviously a question of logic rather than economics. However, much more than logical quibbling was involved in the differences between Thornton and Ricardo.

Thornton further elaborated his theory of the effect of an

'unfavourable balance' on the price of gold. It started with an explanation, in terms of what today would be called 'elasticity pessimism' (Machlup, 1950), of why a gold outflow would be required:

> In order…to induce the country having the favourable balance to take all its payments in goods, and no part of it in gold, it would be requisite not only to prevent goods from being very dear, but even to render them excessively cheap. It would be necessary, therefore, that the bank should not only not encrease its paper, but that it should, perhaps, very greatly diminish it, if it would endeavour to prevent gold from going in part of payment of the unfavourable balance (p. 151).

There followed an expression of his strong concern over the adverse consequences of a contraction of note issues required for the increased imports to be paid in merchandise rather than gold. Here, Thornton appeared to be strongly influenced by Hume (1752a) in his account of the depressing effect of a contraction of the money supply. But there was a curious inconsistency in his argument: why should the loss of gold, permitted in order to avoid a contraction of banknotes, not have equally adverse consequences? For Thornton's argument to make sense, one would have to assume, not that the Bank of England refrained from contracting its note issue, but that it actually increased it to compensate for the lost gold. Indeed, in further elaborating his argument, Thornton admitted precisely this; the Bank would have to draw down its own reserves:

> For this reason, it may be the true policy and duty of the bank to permit, for a time, and to a certain extent, the continuance of that unfavourable exchange, which causes gold to leave the country, and to be drawn out of its own coffers: and it must, in that case, necessarily encrease its loans to the same extent to which its gold is diminished (p. 152).

This admission that the note issue should be increased to compensate for the lost gold cannot but detract from the credibility of Thornton's thesis that the immediate cause of the export of coin (which could only take place if the market price of gold exceeds the mint price) was the 'unfavourable exchange' brought about by the bad harvest.

Thornton went on to say that the substitution of paper for gold involved in the above process was a net benefit to the country, since 'gold is an unproductive part of our capital: …the interest upon the sum exported is so much saved to the country' (p. 153). What he neglected to add was that in the case of a bad harvest (the example used in this discussion) this policy implied throwing the entire burden of the crop failure onto foreign countries.

For all its blemishes, the above theory—all packed into Chapter V of Thornton's work—was an extraordinary accomplishment. One can recognize in it nearly all the issues that have arisen in contemporary times in discussions of balance-of-payments adjustment.

Discussion of Thornton's work would not be complete without inclusion of his subsequent treatment, in Chapter VIII, of the way in which an increased issue of paper would produce an excess of the market over the mint price of gold. The passage in question (pp. 198–200) was quoted in its entirety by Horner (1802; Fetter, 1957), who also subjected it to a searching criticism. Ricardo, in turn (1810; Sraffa, 1951), criticized Horner's amended treatment of the subject in great detail. It will therefore be advantageous to discuss Thornton's theory in conjunction with these two important criticisms; for the technical points at issue lie at the heart of the classical theory.

In the first part of this passage, Thornton assumes a general rise in the price of commodities (following from the increased emission of paper), but does not state explicitly whether he means to include bullion among these commodities; however, in order to make sense out of the ensuing argument it is necessary to assume that he does not. He proceeds to the conclusion that 'as goods are rendered dear in Great Britain, the foreigner becomes unwilling to buy them' and likewise 'the high British price of goods will tempt foreign commodities to come in'. He then goes on to state that 'these two effects (that of a diminished export, and that of an encreased import) will follow, provided that we suppose, what is not supposable, namely, that, at the time when the price of goods is greatly raised in Great Britain, the course of exchange suffers no alteration'. Since the exchange rate must depreciate (because drawers of bills on Britain will outweigh remitters), this will 'prevent the high price of goods in Great Britain from producing that unfavourable balance of trade, which, for the sake of illustrating the subject was supposed to exist'.

Horner (1802; Fetter, 1957) criticized this argument on the ground that the original rise in prices would include bullion. Since the *bullion prices* of other commodities (i.e. their prices relative to the price of bullion) are then unchanged, these commodities 'are not rendered dearer to the foreign merchant, who pays for them ultimately in that bullion which is the common measure of his currency and ours'. Of course, this objection is not fully satisfactory either, even on its hypothesis, since it begs the question of what is meant by 'ultimately'. Nevertheless it certainly is fatal to Thornton's argument, if Horner's hypothesis is admitted; for what is involved is none other than the law of comparative advantage, as applied between gold and other commodities. One is thus left with the dilemma of whether to accept Horner's hypothesis and dismiss Thornton's argument as fallacious, or give Thornton the benefit of the doubt and reject Horner's hypothesis. In order to proceed it will be necessary to follow the latter course, but the issue will be taken up again presently.

Thornton then concludes that, owing to the depreciation of the British currency, both the paper and 'the coin which is interchanged with it' are devalued, and then:

> Now, when coin is thus rendered cheap, it by no means follows that bullion is rendered cheap also. Coin is rendered cheap through its constituting a part of our circulating medium; but bullion does not constitute a part of it. Bullion is a commodity, and nothing but a commodity, and it rises and falls in value on the same principle as all other commodities. It becomes, like them, dear in proportion as the circulating medium for which it is exchanged is rendered cheap, and cheap in proportion as the circulating medium is rendered dear (pp. 199–200).

This is the conclusion that was sought: The market price of gold (bullion) exceeds the mint price (the face value of the coin). But this very passage is what led Horner to conclude, with respect to its last sentence: 'No other account of the fact can be given; and no farther explanation will be required.' That is, if an increase in note issues leads to a rise in all commodity prices *including bullion*, relative to paper and coin, that is the end of the matter; an alternative reasoning can then be supplied (and was supplied by Horner) for the fall in the nominal (also called 'apparent' or 'computed') exchange rate.

Horner based himself on the above quotation from Thornton for his belief that a rise in paper issues would raise bullion prices as well as merchandise prices; he did not provide, nor see the need to provide, an independent argument. Presumably one would have to rest on the argument that gold bullion has alternative industrial uses and that the gold products into which it enters as inputs are articles of current consumption. Were it not for these alternative uses, or if in these uses gold enters only as a capital good, the price would presumably rise only if gold were at its export point, since it would then represent claims on foreign commodities. This suggests what is possibly the correct way to interpret Thornton's argument. A rise in paper issues raises merchandise (but not bullion) prices, and lowers the exchange rate in accordance with Thornton's argument (or indeed, by the still simpler argument suggested by Horner that bills on London, which are denominated in sterling, depreciate since they represent claims on fewer goods); the fall in the exchange rate then increases the export supply price of gold bullion; and, if gold was initially at its export point (which Thornton always seems tacitly to assume), this, then, is what raises the domestic price of bullion. Thornton's slogan 'bullion is a commodity, and nothing but a commodity' (later to become very popular among Torrens, McCulloch and others) could be interpreted to refer to its role in international trade, rather than in the operation in the quantity theory of prices. After all, commodities other than bullion were not minted into coin.

It remains to consider Ricardo's objection to Horner's argument. This was that it would be valid 'at a time when the currency consisted wholly of paper not convertible into specie, but not while specie formed any part of the circulation' (Sraffa, 1951). This would not essentially damage *Thornton's* argument, however. In the paragraph immediately following the one quoted above, Thornton went on to describe 'that temptation...to convert [coin] back into bullion and then to export...', showing that he clearly had in mind a situation in which specie still formed part of the circulation. What was lacking in Thornton, however, was an explanation of how the melting and export of coin, by lowering the money supply, would bring merchandise prices back down, hence the exchange rate back up, hence the market price of gold back down, until it was restored to equality with the mint price, consistently with the Hume–Smith doctrine. This—surprisingly, it might seem—was missing from Ricardo's account too, because he concerned himself largely with static equilibrium, rather than the dynamic process of adjustment.

7.3.3 KING

King (1808) made a valuable scientific contribution: probably the first correct formulation of the transfer problem[5]. It arose out of the contention that had been put forward in the debates of the House of Lords that the depreciation of the Irish pound was attributable to the increase in remittances to Irish absentee landlords since the Union in 1801. It was King's contention that, on the contrary, the cause of the depreciation was the excess issue of paper by the Bank of Ireland. To make his case, he had to show that the increased remittances would not produce this result. It went as follows:

> It must undoubtedly be admitted that very considerable payments arising from Irish property are annually made to residents in England...; but it by no means follows that these payments have been made by an actual transfer of bullion... Such continued remittances cannot possibly be made by a nation, like Ireland, which has no means of providing a constant supply of the precious metals. ...In the case of Ireland it is evident that the course of trade and the proportion of the exports and imports must adjust themselves to the nature of its connection with Great Britain. In proportion to the increased necessity of remittances to this country the exports of Irish produce and manufactures must be increased, and the imports of English produce and manufactures diminished, till the amount of foreign demands is paid by Irish exports, and the balance of trade restored. This operation of commerce is much assisted by the fact itself which creates the demand for remittances. The residence of Irish proprietors in England has the necessary effect of diminishing the Irish imports, because the expenditure of revenue is transferred to another country; and it also increases the export of that produce which is no longer consumed at home (pp. 83–86).

He went on to point out that the excess of Irish exports above imports could be confirmed from the Custom-house books; and in a footnote referring to Britain's 'foreign subsidies and demand for corn' he added that 'it is probable that the greater part of the remittances was paid by an increase of exports and diminution of imports'.

The above passage does contain a slight blemish: the confusion between balance of payments and balance of trade that pervades the literature of this period. Further, it overlooked the fact that, on good Humean principles, one would expect the shift in levels of expenditure to induce a once-for-all movement of specie. But it did, along with Foster's (1804) development, correctly formulate the process of adjustment of export and imports to the expenditure flow in a manner not to be matched until Bastable's (1889) contribution. By modern standards, the argument implicitly assumes identical homothetic preferences as between countries and absence of transport costs. Relaxing the first of these, as was later done by Pigou (1932) and Samuelson (1952), would have entailed some adjustments in relative prices (changes in either direction in the 'terms of trade'), but this would not have materially affected the argument. Relaxing the second, on the other hand, would have; for if the absentee landlords were to spend part of their remittances on rent payments (or other non-tradables) in Britain (with a corresponding opposite reduction in Ireland), there would be an excess demand for bills on London in the Dublin foreign-exchange market, leading to a depreciation of the Irish pound. But it remained for Taussig (1917) and his followers to introduce this type of formulation. Throughout the ensuing debate, therefore, the anti-bullionists, who were probably closer to the truth on this point than the bullionists, did not manage to answer King's argument. Even had they succeeded in doing so, however, with respect to the particular point at issue King was undoubtedly right, since, as he pointed out (p. 35) 'the balance of trade [read: payments] alone can never occasion any greater difference in the state of the exchange above par than what will be sufficient to pay the expenses and profit of the merchant who exports the precious metals to restore the balance'; and the Irish pound had depreciated far beyond that point.

7.3.4 FOSTER

Foster (1804) is one of the few writers of the period to show a clear understanding of the transfer problem. He introduced the distinction between the 'balance of debt' and 'balance of trade', thus avoiding the confusions Wheatley (1803) had fallen into. He also further developed (although without specific acknowledgement to him) King's formulation of the transfer problem, and rendered it even more detailed and explicit. Since the two most important passages have been quoted in Mason (1955), it will be unnecessary to do so here. Unfortunately, these contributions were overshadowed by two defects: (1) a theory that a monetary contraction would stimulate industrial output (p. 11), and (2) a dissertation that the British loan to Ireland, offsetting the remittances to absentee landlords, somehow only made things worse (pp. 34–35). It is these defects that mostly occupied Horner (1806) in his review, though he also expressed regret that Foster had not 'attempted to explain in what way that [British foreign] expenditure influences the exchange' (p. 115).

7.3.5 JAMES MILL

The elder Mill (1808) set forth his views in what was ostensibly a review of Thomas Smith (1807). In an implied criticism of both Thornton (1802) and Wheatley (1807) in addition to his subject, he remonstrated against the 'succession of authors [each of whom], while he naturally imagined that he himself had made important discoveries, uniformly found that no discoveries had been made by their predecessors' (p. 35), and proceeded forthwith to take the position that since the 1797 suspension of cash payments, 'the science has not, in fact, been enriched with a single idea', but that 'the doctrine of money...remains as it was left by the great Father of political economy'. The second part of the review consisted of an interesting development and elaboration of Adam Smith's principle of the 'channel of circulation', in which he explicitly introduced the 'small-country assumption' in the following terms:

> If...the currency of all nations be so immense a quantity, compared with ours, that any possible fluctuations which it can undergo, resemble the addition or subtraction of a drop in the waters of the ocean, then...Dr. Smith...was probably right in asserting, that when the channel of circulation is full, if anything more is thrown in, it overflows (p. 54).

He continued with an interesting defence and elaboration of the 'real-bills doctrine', which Thornton (1802; Hayek, 1939) had attacked—although apparently in the context of a situation in which the circulation consisted entirely of paper (pp. 227–228, 252–258). What truth there is in the real-bills doctrine rests largely on the Hume–Smith principle[6]. But instead of distinguishing between the cases in which specie remained part of, and was no longer in, circulation, Mill distinguished between the cases in which the paper money was issued by banks and held voluntarily, and issued by government and forced. The weak point of his argument was the contention (p. 59) that the former would not drive specie out of circulation and that the latter would. Mill in this review was found by Horner to be 'guilty of deplorable heresies' (Sraffa, 1951).

7.3.6 RICARDO (1810)

Ricardo's pamphlet, published in 1810, is not easy to interpret. Ricardo varied the assumptions somewhat as between different but related problems. He starts with an illustration in which a gold mine is discovered in one country, hence:

> the currency of that country would be lowered in value in consequence of the increased quantity of the precious metals brought into circulation, and would therefore no longer be of the same value as that of other countries. Gold and silver, whether in coin or in bullion, obeying the law which regulates all other commodities, would immediately become articles of exportation; they would leave the country where they were cheap, for those countries where they were dear (Sraffa, 1951, Vol. III, p. 4).

Already this involves two implicit assumptions: (1) that the currency depreciates somewhat—since otherwise the relative price of gold as between countries would remain unchanged; and (2) that gold was initially at its export point—since otherwise the reduction in its price at home relative to the price abroad may still not be enough to give rise to a positive price differential in excess of the transport cost. Ricardo continues: 'In return for the gold exported, commodities would be imported...'. Later 'If gold be dearer in France than in England, goods must be cheaper;' thus, a third implicit assumption is revealed: (3) that the currency does not depreciate by the full proportion of the increase in prices—since otherwise the relative prices of goods as between countries would remain unchanged. The assumed effect on the exchange rate is intermediate between those assumed by Hume (tacitly) and Wheatley (explicitly).

Ricardo goes on to consider, in place of a new gold mine, the establishment of a bank with the power of issuing notes. He then states:

> after a large amount had been issued..., the same effect would follow as in the case of the mine. The circulating medium would be lowered in value, and goods would experience a proportionate rise. The equilibrium would only be restored by the exportation of part of the coin (pp. 54–55).

Ricardo does not make clear here whether the price of bullion rises or maintains its parity with the circulating medium (paper and specie). Two distinct mechanisms of adjustment could be envisaged: (1) At one extreme, the price of bullion initially remains unchanged (apparently Thornton's case); since bills on London represent claims on fewer British goods, the exchange rate will depreciate, say, by the full proportion of the price increase (in accordance with 'purchasing-power parity'). Then gold in Hamburg rises in terms of sterling, creating an inducement to export bullion (provided the exchange depreciation has brought gold below its export point). Competition among bullion merchants now raises the price of bullion in Britain. Since the market price now exceeds the mint price, there will be an inducement to melt coins and sell them to the bullion merchants; as these are withdrawn from circulation, prices fall back again until equilibrium is restored. (2) At the other extreme, the price of bullion initially rises along with those of goods (Horner's case), and there is an immediate inducement to melt coins; at the same time the exchange rate depreciates, for the same reason as before. The excess supply of melted coins pushes down the price of bullion, and once again there is an incentive to export it under the same conditions as before. In both these mechanisms just described, at some point the market price of gold must exceed the mint price, to provide an inducement for the melting of specie. Ricardo's discussions are sometimes confusing, since at some points he appears to deny this, because he is usually concerned with the final equilibrium. For the same reason, the question of whether one could infer a 'depreciation of the currency' from an excess of the market price over the mint price of gold was not clear-cut, because it could not have been any easier then than it would be now to decide whether such an excess was a temporary phenomenon reflecting the necessary dynamic process of adjustment, or an equilibrium phenomenon reflecting a situation in which all specie had been finally driven out of circulation. Indeed (as Ricardo (1811a) was later to explicitly recognize), one would need corroborating evidence as to whether specie remained in circulation.

Ricardo continues with an analysis in which convertibility is explicitly assumed:

> The Bank might continue to issue their notes, and the specie exported with advantage to the country, while their notes were payable in specie on demand, because they could never issue more notes than the value of the coin which would have circulated had there been no bank.
>
> If they attempted to exceed this amount, the excess would be immediately returned to them for specie; because our currency, being thereby diminished in value, could be advantageously exported, and could not be retained in our circulation (p. 57).

At the end of the first paragraph he added a footnote with an important qualification to the 'small-country assumption': 'They might, strictly speaking, rather exceed that quantity, because as the Bank would add to the currency of the world, England would retain its share of the increase.' Ricardo went on to show that convertibility could not prevent depreciation of the currency, because excess issue would lead to Smith's 'web of Penelope'—the vicious circle described by Thornton between the coiners and melters; and equilibrium could only be restored by contraction of the note issue.

In an important footnote added in the third edition of *The High Price of Bullion*, Ricardo commented on Horner's (1802) contention that an increase in paper would raise the price of bullion along with other commodities, as follows:

> This would be true at a time when the currency consisted wholly of paper not convertible into specie, but not while specie formed any part of the circulation. In the latter case the effect of an increased issue of paper would be to throw out of circulation an equal amount of specie; but this could not be done without adding to the quantity of bullion in the market, and thereby lowering its value, or in other words, *increasing the bullion price of commodities*. It is only in consequence of this fall in the value of the metallic currency, and of bullion, that the temptation to export them arises; and the penalties on melting the coin is the sole cause of a small difference between the value of the coin and of bullion, or a small excess of the market above the mint price (p. 64).

The phrase 'lowering its value' suggests that Ricardo would have agreed that bullion initially rose in price. The passage does not recognize that, temporarily, the excess of the market above the mint price might need to exceed the risk premium, in order to call forth the specie. But the passage is significant in its recognition that convertibility in no way enters the argument underlying the Hume –Smith principle.

Of especial interest in Ricardo's pamphlet was his disagreement with Thornton over the effect of a bad harvest. Ricardo's position is summed up as follows:

> Mr. Thornton has not explained to us, why any unwillingness should exist in the foreign country to receive our goods in exchange for their corn; and it would be necessary for him to show, that if such an unwillingness were to exist, we should agree to indulge it so far as to consent to part with our coin (p. 61).

This (and the discussion leading up to it) expresses two hypotheses: (1) that foreign demand for Britain's exports is elastic ('elasticity optimism'); and (2) that the domestic demand for money is highly (income-) inelastic. At first, the proposition might seem puzzling, since Ricardo also affirms that 'specie will be sent abroad...only when it is the cheapest exportable commodity', and he makes quite clear his awareness that gold has the smallest transport cost in relation to its value of any commodity. If Ricardo's position is to make any sense, only one inference is possible: gold is above its export point. In modern terminology, *gold is the non-traded good*; only a strong perturbation will cause it to be traded. How does it happen that the good with the *smallest* transport cost in relation to value is precisely the good that is *not* traded? It is, of course, because in its use as currency it is held as an asset—a stock rather than a flow per unit of time; this creates a strong inelasticity in its supply. But Ricardo expressed himself so tersely that his argument was met with considerable scepticism—particularly on the part of Malthus (1811a).

On the subject of foreign expenditures Ricardo was even more terse:

> If, which is a much stronger case, we agreed to pay a subsidy to a foreign power, money would not be exported whilst there were any goods which could more cheaply discharge the payment. The interest of individuals would render the exportation of the money unnecessary (p. 63).

In what was a brilliant but surely unfair debating tactic (p. 83) Ricardo agreed with Thornton that exports and imports tended in the long run to equality, and thus, turning Thornton's own argument against him, used this as a basis for contending that the foreign expenditure could not have been the cause of the sustained unfavourable exchange. However, as the evidence of the Bullion Report (1810) subsequently showed, at the time Ricardo wrote, Britain was still undertaking foreign expenditures on a large scale, and there was thus still a sustained excess of exports above imports. Even if these expenditures were being financed by the export surplus, the theoretical presumption would still be that they would have a depressing effect on the exchange, and lead to a once-for-all export of bullion. But Ricardo never did fully analyse the transfer problem.

7.3.7 HORNER AND THE BULLION REPORT

Since Horner wrote anonymously, attribution to him of four reviews on international monetary questions (1802, 1803, 1806, 1807) is necessarily uncertain, although that of the first two is well documented (Fetter, 1953, 1957). Each of the four contains an apparently self-identifying reference to the preceding one, although to complicate matters the last one also refers in the same way to reviews that are attributable to Brougham (1803, 1806). But all four contain the same emphasis on Smith's distinction between the real and nominal exchange[7]. The main methodological contribution of the Bullion Report was the empirical computation of these exchange rates and their relationships, with the aim of ascertaining whether the computed exchange rate was depreciated to a greater extent than the real exchange rate, from which it could be concluded that paper currency had been issued to excess. The affirmative conclusion was the position of the bullionists. As chairman of the Bullion Committee, Horner was the guiding spirit of the Report, but Thornton (who had come around to the bullionist position) and Huskisson also wrote substantial portions of it (Fetter, 1965). It was Ricardo's (1810), and later also Tooke's (1824) position that the excess of the market over the mint price of gold was sufficient indication of excess of paper; but, as Tooke pointed out (pp. 11–13), if (as was often the case) no gold quotations were available in London, one would have to use the Hamburg price and the transport cost, provided the latter were known.

In 1810, Napoleon's armies had overrun Germany and Hamburg, and trade between England and Hamburg was prohibited. The transport cost necessarily included a sizable risk premium. It was one of the accomplishments of the Bullion Report to estimate this augmented transport cost at about 5 per cent of the value of the bullion, showing that there was considerable room for fluctuation in the real exchange rate.

7.3.8 HUSKISSON

Huskisson (1810) followed Blake in assuming, in a passage (pp. 27–28) subsequently criticized by Ricardo (1811a; Sraffa, 1951), that a rise in paper issues would lead to a rise in the price of bullion along with other commodities. He continued with the explanation that since it would be profitable to export gold 'as currency', 'the diminution which it effects in the total amount of the currency, has a tendency to support the value of the remainder'.

Perhaps the most interesting part of Huskisson's work was a digression on the gains from trade (pp. 56–67), which was clearly influenced by Brougham's (1803) criticism of Wheatley (1803). Adapting Wheatley's proposition that 'an exchange of equivalents is the foundation of all commerce' he gave it, however, a different meaning, namely that 'no nation...can permanently export to a greater extent than it imports...'. But he went on:

> It may, perhaps, be asked, if commerce is nothing more than an exchange of *equivalents*, and the *Balance of Trade*...only the measure of our foreign expenditure, in what way is a country enriched by trade? (p. 60).

While his ensuing explanation did not essentially go beyond Brougham (1803), it was so suggestive and full of detail that it must have been a great stimulus to both Torrens (1815) and Ricardo (1817). Torrens (1812), who started out as an unabashed anti-bullionist, devoted an entire chapter (pp. 194–237) to criticism of Huskisson's pamphlet; but in later years (1858), after criticizing Thornton (1802), he asserted that 'the erased foundations of monetary science were restored through the labours of Huskisson, Horner, and Ricardo' (p. 127). While Ricardo (1817) must himself have been influenced by Torrens (1815) in the formulation of the law of comparative advantage, it is likely that both of them (particularly Torrens) drew a good part of their inspiration from Huskisson.

7.3.9 RICARDO (1811a)

Among the several anti-bullionist pamphlets that followed the publication of the Bullion Report—most of which were quite weak in their theoretical analysis—that of Bosanquet (1810) was particularly provocative to Ricardo, being specifically directed at his work and charging him with espousing abstract theories that were at variance with the facts. Ricardo responded in (1811a). Of greatest interest was probably the detailed analysis of the balance of payments mechanism. He stated:

> gold would not, even if famine raged among us, be given to France in exchange for corn, unless the exportation of gold was attended with advantage to the exporter, unless he could sell corn in England for more gold than he was obliged to give for the purchase of it (Sraffa, 1951, III, p. 208).

Ricardo also criticized the Blake–Huskisson account of the adjustment mechanism, contending that 'no rise would take place in the price of bullion, in consequence of an addition of paper currency, whilst the currency was either wholly metallic, or consisted partly of gold and partly of paper'. This followed because of 'the convertibility of coin into bullion' (p. 211); Ricardo recognized that this type of convertibility, rather than the convertibility of paper into coin, was crucial. But, for the conversion to take place, the value of gold in bullion would have to exceed *temporarily* that in the coin, as appears to be recognized in the question: 'Does it not follow, therefore, that the value of gold in coin, and the value of gold in bullion, would speedily approach a perfect equality?'

Ricardo held that this would be so even in a closed economy:

> If such country were insulated, and had no commerce whatever with any other country, this diminution in the value of gold would continue till the demand for gold for its manufactures had withdrawn the whole of its coin from circulation, and not till then would there be any visible depreciation in the value of paper as compared with gold, whatever the amount of paper might be which was in circulation (p. 211).

He went on to consider the case of an open economy in which the exchange rate was initially at par, so that gold 'could be neither advantageously exported nor imported'. Then he supposed that inconvertible paper was issued in an amount equivalent to the existing circulation of specie, and concluded that 'the coin [would] be melted and sold as bullion at home, till the value of bullion had so much diminished in its relative value to the bullion of other countries, and therefore to the relative value of commodities here, as to pay the expenses of transportation'. This was a significant refinement of his previous theory, which appeared tacitly to assume that the real exchange rate was initially at the gold-export point. Ricardo concluded, more in agreement with Thornton than Horner:

> It appears, therefore, evident, first, that by the addition of paper to a currency consisting partly of good and partly of paper, gold bullion will not necessarily rise in the same degree as other commodities; and, secondly, that such addition will cause depression not in the nominal but in the real exchange, and therefore that gold will be exported (p. 213).

This is a very striking difference between Ricardo's theory and the theories of Horner, Blake and Huskisson.

7.3.10 MALTHUS

In a review of Mushet (1810), Ricardo (1810), Blake (1810), Huskisson (1810), Bosanquet (1810) and Ricardo (1811a), as well as of the Bullion Report itself, Malthus (1811a) praised Ricardo (1810) for formulating the theory of money in terms of the principles of supply and demand, and in particular for formulating 'the doctrine, that excess and deficiency of currency are only *relative* terms; that the circulation of a country can never be superabundant, except in relation to other countries' (p. 341). However, his review was mostly critical. 'The great fault of Mr Ricardo's performance,' he stated 'is the partial view which he takes of the causes which operate upon the course of Exchange' (p. 342). By this he meant that factors other than excessive issue of paper currency could lead to gold outflows, the reasoning being that a disturbance (such as a crop failure) could lead to an excess of imports over exports, requiring payment in bullion. He sided with Thornton in believing that there would be an 'unwillingness of the creditor nation to receive a great additional quantity of goods not wanted for immediate consumption, without being bribed to it by excessive cheapness', particularly because 'the prices of commodities are liable to great depressions from a glut in the market' (p. 345).

He criticized Blake (1810) for 'implying...that an alteration in the amount of the currency of a country...has no tendency to affect the real exchange', agreeing with Ricardo that 'as long as there is any quantity of coin to be displaced', excess paper issues would increase the bullion prices of commodities (p. 347).

Malthus made his own contribution to the theory by supposing 'a diminished supply from the mines' of the world's precious metals, which would lead to an excess of the market price of bullion 'for a time above the mint price'; coin would then be exported and 'the whole currency...would be diminished in quantity...; the market price of bullion would soon sink to the mint price...' (p. 355)[8]. This filled in an important gap in both Blake's and Huskisson's analyses. With respect to the latter's discussion of the gains from trade, Malthus expressed the opinion that 'in all commercial transactions, both parties gain what, in the estimation of each, is decidedly more than an equivalent for what it has given' (p. 357n.). Thus, except for the important concept of a production–transformation locus, all the ingredients were present in this review for a theory of comparative advantage. The inclusion in this paper also of an interesting extension of the Hume–Thornton doctrine of forced saving, though partially qualified in a subsequent review (Malthus, 1811b), make this one of the most interesting contributions of the period.

7.3.11 RICARDO (1811b)

The key to understanding Ricardo's basic position is to be found in the following passage:

> That the exchange is in a constant state of fluctuation with all countries I am not disposed to deny, but it does not generally vary to those limits at which remittances can be more advantageously made by means of bullion than by the purchase of bills (Sraffa, 1951, Vol. III, p. 109).

Thus, Ricardo's theory of balance-of-payments adjustment was, in the first instance, a theory of flexible exchange rates. Given that Britain did not have gold mines of its own, and was expanding in productive capacity relative to the rest of the world, the real exchange rate was, probably, normally much closer to the gold-import point than to the gold-export point. Given, further, the risk premium that had to be added to the transport cost during the Napoleonic Wars, Ricardo was undoubtedly on firm ground in supposing that the width of the band of possible fluctuations in the real exchange rate provided a substantial cushion to external shocks.

In answering Malthus, Ricardo reverted to the importance of treating bullion as a commodity, exported only when it was the private interest of merchants to do so. He conceded that a bad harvest might lead to an export of gold, but insisted that it would do so only by causing the currency to be redundant:

England, in consequence of a bad harvest, would come under the case...of a country having been deprived of a part of its commodities, and therefore requiring a diminished amount of circulating medium (p. 106).

If tne shock were not sufficient to bring the real exchange rate down to the gold-export point, it would be profitable for merchants to export previously exported commodities, but still not profitable to export gold.

7.4 Conclusion

This chapter has argued that Ricardo's theory built upon the theories of his predecessors, notably Locke, Hume, Smith and Thornton, and Ricardo came closest to providing a general synthesis. While there were very important points of difference between Ricardo and Thornton, still more important were the insights that Ricardo gained from Thornton and incorporated into his own theory. The main differences between them can be reduced to differences in assumptions.

The differences between Thornton and Ricardo arose mainly in connection, not with the analysis of excess paper issues, but with the analysis of 'real' disturbances such as a crop failure or a unilateral transfer. The source of these differences was exceedingly simple: Thornton assumed that the real exchange rate was initially at the gold-export point, and Ricardo assumed that it was initially above it.

Thornton's three principles, which Ricardo accepted, also assumed that gold was initially at its export point. Thus, there was an inconsistency in Ricardo's theory, which he came close to resolving in his *Reply* (1811a) to Bosanquet but did not completely work out. It is here that Wheatley (1807) made a contribution, by pointing out that an excess paper issue, when gold was initially above its export point, would lead to a depreciation of the paper and the coin, a rise in prices and a fall in the (real) exchange rate—the case considered by Locke (1692). But Wheatley erroneously turned this into a general principle, and mistakenly believed that the joint depreciation of paper and coin would take place only if the paper was convertible into coin.

Finally, there was an important difference in assumptions between Horner (1802), Blake (1810) and Huskisson (1810) on the one hand, and Ricardo (1810, 1811a) on the other. The first three assumed that an increased note issue would initially increase the price of bullion as well as other prices, whereas Ricardo held that the price of bullion would not rise as long as specie was still circulating. This difference is probably largely one of dynamics; Ricardo might have accepted the Horner–Blake–Huskisson view if these authors had carried their dynamics through to show that the melting of specie would bring the market price of gold back to the mint price.

ACKNOWLEDGEMENT

The author wishes to express his thanks for research support to the National Science Foundation (SES-80008047), the Stiftung Volkswagenwerk and the German Marshall Fund of the United States.

Notes

1. A similar suggestion was made much later by Torrens (1819, p. 35).
2. One finds this also in Steuart (1767, Book III, Part II, C. I; II, p. 2): 'Gold and silver are commodities merely like every other thing.'
3. On Boyd, see Fetter (1965, p. 31), Wheatley (1803, p. 79).
4. Francis II, who was also, as Francis I, Emperor of Austria. Given Boyd's role in this loan, Thornton's choice of example was probably not entirely accidental.
5. Unfortunately, this was overshadowed by his discussion of the reasons for Britain's export surplus with the Continent, which he ascribed to the need to obtain silver in order to pay for an import surplus with the East Indies. The weakness of his argument was exposed by Foster (1804, pp. 19–21); it was also criticized by Wheatley (1807, pp. 240–247).
6. For a comprehensive history of this doctrine, see Mints (1945).
7. Horner (1802, pp. 184–185; 1803, pp. 408–410, 413–414, 419–420; 1806, p. 124; 1807, pp. 288–289). This concern is a virtual signature of Horner's, since no other writer of the period kept harping so much on the distinction; and the reviews definitely attributable to Brougham make no reference to it.
8. Herries (1811, pp. 100–101), one of the ablest of the anti-bullionists, seized upon this illustration to demonstrate the illogic of describing the currency as depreciated (as opposed to gold being appreciated) in these circumstances, and appealed to Hume (1752a) in arguing against the depressing effects of a monetary contraction. Somewhat more sophisticated treatments of the question of whether one can distinguish between currency depreciation and gold appreciation are found in Torrens (1819, pp. 33–34) and Blake (1823, p. 87).

References

ALEXANDER, S.S. (1952). Effects of a Devaluation on a Trade Balance. *International Monetary Fund Staff Papers* **2**, 263–278

ANGELL, J.W. (1926). *The Theory of International Prices*. Cambridge, Mass., Harvard University Press

BARING, F., SIR (1797). *Observations of the Establishment of the Bank of England & on the Paper Circulation of the Country*. London, Sewell and Debrett

BASTABLE, C.F. (1889). On some Applications of the Theory of International Trade. *Quarterly Journal of Economics* **4**, 1–17

BLAKE, W. (1810). *Observations on the Principles which Regulate the Course of Exchange; and on the Present Depreciated State of the Currency*. London, Edmund Lloyd

BLAKE, W. (1923). *Observations on the Effects Produced by the Expenditure of Government during the Restriction of Cash Payments*. London, Murray

BOSANQUET, C. (1810). *Practical Observations on the Report of the Bullion-Committee*. London, J.M. Richardson

BOYD, W. (1801). *A Letter to the Right Honourable William Pitt on the Influence of the Stoppage of Specie at the Bank of England on the Prices of Provisions and Other Commodities*, 2nd edn, pp. 52, 62, 85. London, J. Wright

BROUGHAM, H.L. (1803). Wheatley's Remarks on Currency and Commerce. *Edinburgh Review* **3**, 231–252

BROUGHAM, H.L. (1806). Lord Liverpool on the Coin. *Edinburgh Review* **7**, 265–295

BULLION REPORT (1810). *Report of the Select Committee on the High Price of Gold Bullion*, pp. 95–108. London, J. Johnson. Repr. in *The Paper Pound of 1797–1821* (ed. with introduction by E. Cannan). London, P.S. King

CANTILLON, R. (1755). *Essai sur la nature du commerce en général. Traduit de l'anglois*. A Londres, Chez Fletcher Gyles

FETTER, F.W. (1953). The Authorship of Economic Articles in the *Edinburgh Review, 1802–47. Journal of Political Economy* **61**, 232–259

FETTER, F.W. (ed.) (1957). *The Economic Writings of Francis Horner in the Edinburgh Review 1802–6*. New York, Kelley and Millman

FETTER, F.W. (1965). *The Development of British Monetary Orthodoxy, 1779–1875*, pp. 36–39, 40. Cambridge, Mass., Harvard University Press

FOSTER, J.L. (1804). *An Essay on the Principle of Commercial Exchanges and More Particularly of Exchange between Great Britain and Ireland*. London, J. Hatchard

GERVAISE, I. (1720). *The System or Theory of the Trade of the World*. London; J. Roberts (Repr., with foreword by J. Viner and introduction by J.M. Letiche, Baltimore, The Johns Hopkins Press, 1954)

HABERLER, G. (1933). *The Theory of International Trade with Its Applications to Commercial Policy*, trans by A. Stonier and F. Benham. London, William Hodge, 1936

HARRIS, J. (1757). *An Essay upon Money and Coins. Part I. The Theories of Commerce, Money and Exchanges*. London, G. Hawkins. Repr. in McCulloch (1856), pp. 339–429

HARRIS, J. (1758). *An Essay upon Money and Coins. Part II. Wherein is shewed, that the established Standard of Money should not be violated or altered, under any pretence whatsoever*. London, G. Hawkins

HAYEK, F.A.v. (1932). A Note on the Development of the Doctrine of Forced Saving. *Quarterly Journal of Economics* **47**, 123–133

HAYEK, F.A. v. (1939). *An Enquiry into the Nature and Effects of the Paper Credit of Great Britain (1802)* by Henry Thornton, pp. 214, 216n., 246. London, George Allen and Unwin

HERRIES, J.C. (1811). *A Review of the Controversy Respecting the High Price of Bullion, and the State of Our Currency*. London, J. Budd

HIGGS, H. (ed.) (1931). *Essai sur la nature du commerce en général* by Richard Cantillon, English translation and other material, pp. 148–159, 383–385. London, Macmillan

HORNER, F. (1802). Thornton on the Paper Credit of Great Britain. *Edinburgh Review* **1**, 172–201

HORNER, F. (1803). Lord King on the Bank Restrictions. *Edinburgh Review* **2**, 402–421

HORNER, F. (1806). Foster on the Commercial Exchanges. *Edinburgh Review* **9**, 11–136

HORNER, F. (1807). Wheatley on Money and Commerce. *Edinburgh Review* **10**, 284–299

HUME, D. (1752a). Of Money. In *Political Discourses*, pp. 41–59. Edinburgh, A. Kincaid and A. Donaldson

HUME, D. (1752b). Of the Balance of Trade. *Political Discourses*, pp. 79–100. Edinburgh, A. Kincaid and A. Donaldson

HUSKISSON, W. (1810). *The Question of the Depreciation of our Currency Stated and Examined*. London, John Murray and J. Hatchard

JEVONS, W.S. (1881). Richard Cantillon and the Nationality of Political Economy. *Contemporary Review* **39**, 61–80

KEYNES, J.M. (1930). *A Treatise on Money*, 2 vols. London, Macmillan

KING, P. (1803). *Thoughts on the Restriction of Payments in Specie at the Banks of England and Ireland*. London, T. Cadell and W. Davies

KING, P. (1804). *Thoughts on the Effects of the Bank Restrictions*, 2nd edn. London, T. Cadell and W. Davies. Repr. in *A Selection from the Speeches and Writings of the Late Lord King*, 1844, pp. 47–61. London, Longman, Brown, Green and Longmans

LOCKE, J. (1692). *Some Considerations of the Consequences of the Lowering of Interest, and Raising the Value of Money*. London, Awnsham and John Churchil

LOCKE, J. (1695). *Further Considerations concerning Raising the Value of Money*. London, Awnsham and John Churchil

MCCULLOCH, J.R. (ed.) (1856). *A Select Collection of Scarce and Valuable Tracts on Money*, pp. 405, 406, 409, 427–429, 471. London, Political Economy Club

MACHLUP, F. (1950). Elasticity Pessimism in International Trade. *Economia Internazionale* **3**, 118–137

MALTHUS, T.R. (1811a). Depreciation of Paper Currency. *Edinburgh Review* **17**, 339–372

MALTHUS, T.R. (1811b). Pamphlets on the Bullion Question. *Edinburgh Review* **18**, 448–470

MASON, W.E. (1955). Some Neglected Contributions to the Theory of International Transfers. *Journal of Political Economy* **63**, 529–535

MASON, W.E. (1956). The Stereotypes of Classical Transfer Theory. *Journal of Political Economy* **64**, 492–506

MASON, W.E. (1957). Ricardo's Transfer-mechanism Theory. *Quarterly Journal of Economics* **71**, 107–115

MILL, J. (1808). Smith on Money and Exchange. *Edinburgh Review* **13**, 35–68

MINTS, L.W. (1945). *A History of Banking Theory in Great Britain and the United States*. Chicago, University of Chicago Press

MUSHET, R. (1810). *An Enquiry into the Effects Produced on the National Currency and Rates of Exchange, by the Bank Restriction Bill*, 2nd edn. London, C. and R. Baldwin

OHLIN, B. (1928). The Reparation Problem. *Index* **28**, 2–33

PIGOU, A.C. (1932). The Effect of Reparations on the Ratio of International Interchange. *Economic Journal* **42**, 532–543

POSTLETHWAYT, M. (1749). *A Dissertation on the Plan, Use and Importance of the Universal Dictionary of Trade and Commerce*. London, John and Paul Knapton

POSTLETHWAYT, M. (1751–1755). *The Universal Dictionary of Trade and Commerce*. London, John and Paul Knapton

POSTLETHWAYT, M. (1757). *Great Britain's True System*. London, A. Millar

RICARDO, D. (1810). *The High Price of Bullion, a Proof of the Depreciation of Bank Notes*. London, John Murray

RICARDO, D. (1811a). *Reply to Mr. Bosanquet's Practical Observations on the Report of the Bullion Committee*. London, John Murray

RICARDO, D. (1811b). *Observations on Some Passages in an Article in the Edinburgh Review, on the Depreciation of Paper Currency*. London, John Murray

RICARDO, D. (1817). *On the Principles of Political Economy, and Taxation*. London, Murray

SAMUELSON, P.A. (1952). The Transfer Problem and Transport Costs; the Terms of Trade when Impediments are Absent. *Economic Journal* **62**, 278–304

SAMUELSON, P.A. (1980). A Corrected Version of Hume's Equilibrating Mechanisms for International Trade. In *Flexible Exchange Rates and the Balance of Payments* (ed. by J.S. Chipman and C.P. Kindleberger), pp. 141–158. Amsterdam, North-Holland

SMITH, A. (1776). *An Inquiry into the Nature and Causes of the Wealth of Nations*, 2 vols. London, W. Strahan and T. Cadell

SMITH, T. (1807). *Essay on the Theory of Money and Exchange*. London, T. Cadell and W. Davies

SRAFFA, P. (ed.) (1951). *The Works and Correspondence of David Ricardo*, Vols I–IV, Vol III, pp. 9, 58, 64n., 189, 209–210. Cambridge, Cambridge University Press

SRAFFA, P. (1952). *The Works and Correspondence of David Ricardo*, Vols V–IX. Cambridge, Cambridge University Press

STEUART, J., SIR (1767). *An Inquiry into the Principles of Political Oeconomy: being an essay on the Science of Domestic Policy in Free Nations*, 2 vols, Vol. I, p. 556. London, A. Millar and T. Cadell

TAUSSIG, W. (1917). International Trade under Depreciated Paper. A Contribution to Theory. *Quarterly Journal of Economics* **31**, 380–403

THORNTON, H. (1802). *An Enquiry into the Nature and Effects of the Paper Credit of Great Britain*, p. 67. London, J. Hatchard and F. and C. Rivington

TOOKE, T. (1824). *Thoughts and Details on the High and Low Prices of the Thirty Years, from 1793 to 1822*, 2nd edn, pp. 9, 10. London, Murray

TOOKE, T. (1838). *A History of Prices, and of the State of the Circulation from 1793 to 1837*, Vols I and II, Vol. I, pp. 228, 254. London, Longman

TORRENS, R. (1812). *An Essay on Money and Paper Currency*, pp. 194–237. London, J. Johnson and Co.

TORRENS, R. (1815). *An Essay on the External Corn Trade*. London, J. Hatchard

TORRENS, R. (1819). *A Comparative Estimate of the Effects which a Continuance and a Removal of the Restriction upon Cash Payments are Respectively Calculated to Produce: with Strictures on Mr. Ricardo's Proposal for Obtaining a Secure and Economical Currency*. London, R. Hunter, Successor to Mr. Johnson

TORRENS, R. (1858). Lord Overstone on Metallic and Paper Currency. *Edinburgh Review* **108**, 126–149

VINER, J. (1937). *Studies in the Theory of International Trade*. New York, Harper and Brothers

WHEATLEY, J. (1803). *Remarks on Currency and Commerce*. London, T. Cadell and W. Davies

WHEATLEY, J. (1807). *An Essay on the Theory of Money and Principles of Commerce*. Volume I. London, T. Cadell and W. Davies

Index